Creativity and the Arts in Early Childhood

T0385252

of related interest

Create, Perform, Teach!
An Early Years Practitioner's Guide to Developing Your Creativity and Performance Skills
Nikky Smedley
Illustrated by Sam Greaves
ISBN 978 1 78592 431 6
eISBN 978 1 78450 799 2

Supporting Toddlers' Wellbeing in Early Years Settings
Strategies and Tools for Practitioners and Teachers
Edited by Helen Sutherland and Yasmin Mukadam
ISBN 978 1 78592 262 6
eISBN 978 1 78450 552 3

School Readiness and the Characteristics of Effective Learning
The Essential Guide for Early Years Practitioners
Tamsin Grimmer
ISBN 978 1 78592 175 9
eISBN 978 1 78450 446 5

Developing Empathy in the Early Years
A Guide for Practitioners
Helen Garnett
ISBN 978 1 78592 143 8
eISBN 978 1 78450 418 2

Nurturing Personal, Social and Emotional Development in Early Childhood
A Practical Guide to Understanding Brain Development and Young Children's Behaviour
Debbie Garvey
Foreword by Dr Suzanne Zeedyk
ISBN 978 1 78592 223 7
eISBN 978 1 78450 500 4

CREATIVITY and the ARTS in EARLY CHILDHOOD

Supporting Young Children's Development and Wellbeing

Ruth Churchill Dower

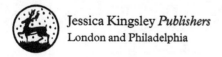
Jessica Kingsley *Publishers*
London and Philadelphia

List on p.42 is reproduced with kind permission from Tina Bruce

First published in 2020
by Jessica Kingsley Publishers
73 Collier Street
London N1 9BE, UK
and
400 Market Street, Suite 400
Philadelphia, PA 19106, USA

www.jkp.com

Library of Congress Cataloging in Publication Data
A CIP catalog record for this book is available from the Library of Congress

British Library Cataloguing in Publication Data
A CIP catalogue record for this book is available from the British Library

ISBN 978 1 78592 613 6
eISBN 978 1 78592 614 3

Printed and bound by CPI Group (UK) Ltd, Croydon CR0 4YY

Contents

Acknowledgements

The idea of writing a book always seems like a good idea until you actually sit down to begin! All I can say is that passion is a very wonderful thing in so many ways. However, passion still needs to be fuelled, and this book would never have been realised without the endless kindness and support of a few wonderful people.

I am ever grateful to my aunt, mentor, sub-editor and sit-down comedienne, Penny Thomas, whose insights, dedication and humour brought huge amounts of light to the long days.

Also to my lovely friend Rachel Brook, who first set my ship sailing on this course and without whom I would never have believed any of this was possible.

Also to the photographers, educators, artists, managers and parents who very kindly gave me access to images of their children deeply immersed in the joy and wonder of creative practice – something I am passionate to share.

Also to the many children whose refreshing curiosity, trust, challenges and sheer openness to all things creative have taken me on many adventures I never would have had otherwise. Every time we work together, their insights cut right through the nonsense of all things adult and pull me back to the real purposes of life.

I must also thank my lecturers and fellow researchers at Manchester Metropolitan University for walking, hopping and running with me on the masters' course in social science research methodologies, putting up with numerous questions, interruptions and suggestions and still being willing to support me through my doctorate. Their dedication to cracking open new ways of thinking about and sensing the world has been brilliantly energising. I feel privileged to be part of this movement of living knowing.

Finally, to my utterly realistic and very lovely husband, Pat Dower, and my wonderful children, Evan and Chia, for putting up with days, weeks and months of, 'I think I'm almost there!' As if.

Introduction

As an educator, artist in education or carer, you have no doubt supported a child who does not respond to activities in the way other children do. They may be shy, lacking in confidence or they may have some challenges with language. They may not be able to speak, they may not have English as a first language or they may have communication, social or physical difficulties. All children are different, and somehow we try to support their different needs, especially when they are not developing as we are told to expect according to social norms and child development theories.

Much of the focus in society is placed on verbal language as a measure of wellbeing in our children. We use this to judge their progress against certain learning outcomes, to measure their behavioural responses, to understand what they are trying to communicate, to mediate during upsets and to help them stay safe and happy.

However, for many children, verbal language just is not something they are able to fully embrace. Many children will be too young to be diagnosed with a particular 'condition', which is sometimes what adults look to for confirmation that something is 'wrong'. Failing that, children are singled out as having 'bad' behaviour or not responding 'properly', and even before starting school, they have taken on an identity that they are somehow not good, or worse, not normal.

In this book, I want to urge a shift in our thinking away from the idea of a universal norm, defined by statistics and housed in a language of conditions, deficiencies or disorders, and towards the idea that we are all neurodiverse in one way or another. We are all developing at different rates and yet, because of the dominant frameworks that govern how we view education against a particular set of standards which are considered the 'norm', many children (and adults) will struggle to keep up with the expectations that are placed on their language and literacy skills, their social and communication skills. If we were able to redesign our health, education and social care structures to be more inclusive and less standardised, we would not view the child who progresses differently as 'other' or in some way abnormal. We would see them – and they would see themselves – for who they are, as a unique and complete child, a complex and beautiful human being.

Over many decades of arts projects, case studies, research findings and cultural programmes, professionals have gathered a plethora of testimonials to the differences the arts can make to children in many situations, cultures and socio-economic backgrounds. These are differences that improve their skills and abilities such as in communicating or articulating complex concepts; differences that impact on their confidence and self-assurance to feel more positive and build stronger relationships; and differences that help them towards a clearer understanding and expression of their identities, to know who they are in relation to this world around them and how to express their agency and power (I will expand on this throughout the book).

For some children, in the context of our outcomes-driven education, health and social care systems, the arts are the only thing that do make a difference in the relentless and difficult struggle to navigate their way through life. For some, it is the key to unlocking a deeper reservoir of potential that springboards them into alternative ways of being and doing that would not otherwise have been available to them. For some, it provides the opportunity and skills base to articulate an innate desire to create, to release their aesthetic drive, to make art of one form or another. Very rarely have I ever come across a situation where the arts or creative thinking has *got in the way* of a child's natural trajectory, unless the facilitation of it has overly defined or closed down the possibilities for a child to explore their own creative drive.

This is the main point of this book. I argue that to properly facilitate children's amazing creativity and to stop us reducing who they are, and what they are capable of, to a set of one-size-fits-all standards dictated by an economic-driven agenda, we need a sea-change in the way we support the adults who support our children. Educators, artists, cultural leaders, parents and caregivers can all offer tremendous creative opportunities that, once stimulated, can afford benefits to both themselves and their children that have a lasting impact way beyond the period of formal education. But sometimes, as adults, we do get in the way. We can think of a hundred reasons why not to engage in the arts or creative experiences, not least because of concerns about funding, resources, time, lack of competence or confidence and, of course, the fear of judgement.

I will show not only why access to the arts and creative experiences is essential for body, soul, mind and brain development in all our children (and adults), but also how people have tried to nurture it, shape it and measure it over the centuries. I will examine how it has been the bedrock of our social, cultural and personal identities since time immemorial and continues to be increasingly important to who we are now. Above all, this book will express why creativity is the essence of who we are as people, the fundamental core of both spirit and soul, and ultimately helps us understand a sense of our own power and potential.

We may not be able to change the whole world overnight, or even the education assessment regimes in the next few years, so educators still need something by which to measure 'progress'. I consider whether a *creativity schema* is possible as a set of principles and starting points, guidelines for educators on how to spot, nurture and scaffold children's creativity – perhaps more of a schema for adults. It does require a more in-depth understanding of what creativity is, getting our heads around the purposes, techniques and possibilities offered by different art forms. It challenges us to rethink our pedagogies, whether and how our teaching and learning environments live and breathe creativity at their core, influencing our perspectives on all areas of learning and our role as educators. But most of all, it requires a shift in power to recognise the agency of the child so that their whole creative being and belonging has space to exist, to breathe and to grow. There is still a chasm between theory and practice, however, and our biggest challenge is knowing how to resist boiling down the essence of human nature into a set of pithy sentences and measurable behaviours.

Therefore, this book is written in two halves. The first half outlines the theoretical thinking behind creativity as a science, a theory, an educational tool, a cultural context and a core element of who we are as brains, bodies, socially connected people and unique personalities. The second half explores practical strategies for putting these personal, human and environmental contexts into play in generative and positive ways, to support educators, artists, parents and caregivers.

My original draft title for this book was a little controversial: 'Now we know the formula, can we bottle young children's creativity?' The intention was partly a play on words referencing the formula milk that we put in babies' bottles. This act in itself comes laden with judgement from parts of society about the quality of formula milk compared with breast milk for babies. In the same way, one of the biggest obstacles to our creativity is the sense of scrutiny that is perceived to come with it – is our creativity going to be good enough by another's standards? We have to feed our little ones one way or another, so we overcome that obstacle in one sense, although plenty of others come to take its place, many based on the perceived judgements from those around us. But sometimes it is easier to choose the less creative path and stick to what we know. And so, very often, the obstacle wins.

The draft title was also a reference to the fact that so many creativity 'formulas' exist that provide *everything you need* in a pack/box/tin. What none of those formulas can provide is the inner drive to be imaginative – in fact, ironically, ready-made kits sometimes create the biggest obstacle to imagination itself by the very nature of them being predefined by someone else's ideas. Other, more meaningful formulas are the type that provide a sense of structure – or conditions – to allow creativity to emerge, such as ensuring that the right resources, environment, skills and opportunities are in place for children to have the best chance to be creative. Others still provide no material structure but ask facilitative questions and offer provocations to help you choose a creative path for yourself. There are many different varieties and qualities of this kind of emergent formula.

So, to answer the question, can we bottle our children's creativity? The answer has to be no! Categorically, absolutely, not. The whole point of creativity is that it is the one thing that is owned and defined by children, not by us as adults. We can put boundaries around aspects of creative output that can be measured but essentially we cannot capture the unlimited potential of the imagination in the way we can capture learning outcomes. No, when a child's creativity is unleashed, we do not want to tie it down by applying our own interpretations that reinforce adult-oriented judgements of what is considered 'good'. We want to uncork the bottle and let the genie fly.

Who is this book for?

I have spent the majority of my professional life accumulating knowledge about the various ways in which the arts can support artistic, learning, communication, social, leadership, emotional and, of course, creative objectives. Some may consider these to be the instrumental purposes of a domain that should not need to justify itself through other agendas (Naughton, Biesta and Cole, 2017). However, I have also had the privilege of being able to share incredible artistic and creative experiences – ones that bring this knowledge to life – offered to me by children, educators, special needs professionals, therapists, leaders, parents and caregivers as well as artists around the world. And it is clear that, certainly with young children, the benefits and purposes of the arts and of creative experiences are multiplicitous and highly individual, no matter how they are framed.

However, throughout my training, I have always felt that there is something more to this creativity issue than meets the eye – something more than my carefully gathered, catalogued and analysed libraries of evidence were able to capture. So many facts have come to light in the last few decades about early brain development, early childhood psychology, children's spiritual and philosophical agency, emotional intelligence, attachment, attunement, social interaction, mental and physical health, and the many different roles played by creative interactions in these contexts. And yet, there is a dearth of interdisciplinary research available that unites the threads of thinking across these different fields of expertise.

This book does not set out to achieve the interdisciplinary fusion that is required to make sense of it all. It would take decades of research and much greater minds than mine to really get to grips with the place of creativity in and among so many areas of expertise. But I have set out to identify some of the key aspects of creativity in relation to early education, its uses across different disciplines, its challenges and concerns for us as artists and educators, researchers, policy makers and practitioners. The aim is to help us locate the concept of creativity more firmly within our own work and play, and, of course, to strengthen the political, social and cultural arguments for prioritising this, and the teaching of the arts, across all educational agendas.

Charles Darwin and his half-cousin Francis Galton were among the first scientists to really explore interdisciplinary perspectives in the natural and social sciences both in epistemological and methodological terms. Darwin (1872) summarised his scientific findings on the biology and psychology of emotion in *The Expression of the Emotions in Man and Animals*, closely followed by Freud (1895), whose experiments to create a hybrid 'natural science' of neurobiology and psychology were written up in *Project for a Scientific Psychology*. These findings were examined and developed by childhood psychoanalyst John Bowlby (1940), who made a significant proposal. He suggested that the integration of:

> a spectrum of sciences would yield the most powerful models of both the nature of the fundamental ontogenetic processes that mediate the infant's first attachment to another human being, and the essential psychobiological mechanisms by which these processes indelibly influence the development of the organism at later points of the life-cycle. (Schore, 2000, p.24)

Bowlby was asserting that, unless we consider all the different realms of science as inherently connected and interdependent, including our brains, bodies, minds and how the natural world works, we won't really understand what it is that creates a bond or relationship between an adult and child, and how the environment as well as the genetic heritage of that child will affect who she is for the rest of her life. He was essentially calling for an end to independent disciplinary thinking, where each scientific field thought it had the answer, and an end to the Cartesian language that separates brain and body, head and heart, as if one could exist without the other. This was the heralding of contemporary interdisciplinary research as we know it, and even Bowlby's own developmental thinking about attachment between parent and child has since been broadened and progressed.

Despite remarkable contemporary contributions to interdisciplinary understanding in relation to young children, these are mostly by polymaths, neuroscientists, paediatricians, psychologists and psychiatrists who bring a particular clinical or developmental perspective, and not by artists, social scientists or childcare professionals whose perspective can give us a very different springboard into joined-up thinking. Eminent scientists such as Allan Schore (UCLA – University of California, Los Angeles), Bessel Van der Kolk (Boston University, Massachusetts), Bruce Perry (Child Trauma Academy, Texas), Jaak Panksepp (Bowling Green State University and Washington State University) and Jack Shonkoff (Harvard University's Center on the Developing Child) have positively influenced policy, research and practice and brought an urgency to respecting the child as a whole being (not just a brain, a body or a passive recipient of adult wisdom). Their work has had far-reaching effects in changing grass-roots practice for the better, especially in relation to the impacts of adverse childhood experiences, and particularly in the United States, where interdisciplinary research receives more investment and support. However, despite their very brilliant minds, I think it is fair to say that these scientists will present research through a particular lens according to their culture, class, gender, privilege and socio-economic background, which perhaps does not represent the whole picture – especially the predominantly female contribution to early education and care. There is no doubt that a huge gap exists to explore and perhaps explain some of the more nuanced, integrated, interdisciplinary understandings of creativity across the natural, social, formal and applied sciences, and to discuss this in ways that include the diverse, intersectional identities of our children, families and the professionals who support them.

Essentially, I wanted to write this book to try to tease out some of what that deeper essence is that links all those disciplines together in the world of creativity and helps us understand the 'why' behind the 'what' that many of us in arts education intrinsically sense but cannot easily articulate.

This book is for all the educators, creatives, activists, pacifists and passionatos out there who care for our youngest children. Your work is so important on a scale you may never get to witness as our children grow up and make their own contributions to the world. Please do not stop believing in, and doing, what you do. Just strive for deeper understanding and many more opportunities to nourish your imagination!

As arts education scholar Elliot Eisner affirms:

> The way we assess most learning in schools is by asking students to perform at a certain time. Yet the effects of teaching may not show up until long after the student has left school and in ways the teacher never dreamed of. But what matters is that such occasions do matter, and continue to matter long after the child has left the classroom. (Eisner, 2005, p.50)

Overarching definitions

Wherever possible, I try to resist using homogenised groupings to describe people, as if anyone could ever fit into one 'category' of identity, and why would we want to reduce complex identities to simple labels anyway? However, when discussing a concept that is universally important such as creativity, it is almost impossible to find an alternative way of writing without collating job roles at least into professional or social groups. Therefore, to enable a shared starting point (and to save paper), in this book I include some generic terms, which incorporate most arts education professionals into specific groups, as below:

Educators means all types of trained early years professionals working with young children, including teachers, headteachers, teaching assistants, practitioners, childminders, nannies, setting managers, learning support assistants, nursery nurses, playgroup staff, play workers and anyone else caring for young children in a communal setting on a voluntary or professional basis.

Artists means trained, creative professionals (or company of professionals) in any art form such as music (all genres and including singing and music technology), visual arts (such as painting, collage, print making, drawing, design), crafts (such as book making, felting, textiles, mosaics, jewellery making, decorating), media arts (such as photography, video), dance and movement (but not covering sports or health-based movement such as yoga), theatre (including storytelling, role play, puppetry, drama), sculpture (including modelling and clay play), literature (such as poetry, writing, narrative), environmental arts (outdoors and in), and a few others!

Parents and caregivers recognises that families come in all shapes and sizes and means all the people who have direct familial responsibility for raising a child, including grandparents, siblings, aunts and uncles or other relatives, close family friends, foster carers and legal guardians.

Creativity (or creative practice) briefly means the processes of feeling or being creative and imaginative to explore or express ideas and bring them to life. It is not dependant on using arts skills or making a product, but can include these. A more detailed exploration of what this means will be discussed throughout the book.

Underlying values and philosophical assumptions

I should pin my colours to the mast right at the start and clarify a number of assumptions that ground the discussions in this book. Primarily, I believe in the following concepts:

- Children as purposeful, intelligent, multimodal, complex, resourceful and imaginative human beings in their own right, who are worth taking seriously and paying attention to (Keller, 1985; Rinaldi, 2001; Ackermann, 2001; Bruce, 2005a). They are in the process of:

  - *having been* (they have a cultural and genetic heritage which shapes who they are)

  - *being* (they have agency and presence which is valid and worth celebrating now – it is not a temporary stop on the journey to being 'better' in the future)

  - *becoming* (they have extraordinary, unknown potential and every cell in their brains and bodies is constantly in a state of flux towards this, ever-changing, growing or dying).

  I propose that a child's 'becoming' should not be defined as a preparation to meet reductionist educational targets based on what *type* of adult employers might want in order to be most productive in the future, but rather accepted as an 'otherness', an unknowable potential which adults do not own or control (Ackermann, 2001; Dewey, 1963; Bruner, 1990; Runco, 2003; MacLure, 2006), and should be respected in itself, as opposed to the notion of respect being an earned value (Davies, 2014).

- The importance of nurturing children's innate creativity from birth because of the multiplicities of impacts this can have on their identities and human nature (Runco *et al.*, 2014), their healthy brain and body development (Schore and Marks-Tarlow, 2018; David *et al.*, 2003), and the potential of creative and artistic actions and environments for transforming the growth, strengthening, expression, healing and connectivity of young children's psychology, physiology, biology and neurology (Runco *et al.*, 2014; Van der Kolk, 2015).

- The power of play for heterogeneous (diverse) social relationships and equitable collaborations between arts and early education professionals, parents, caregivers and children, and for stimulating creative agency, imagination, power and essence within these (Bruce, 2005a; Vygotsky, 2004).

- Humanitarian principles of equality, democracy, justice, forgiveness, connectivity, multiple perspectives and shared understandings. My research aims to authentically underpin the voices, identities and *knowing* of children who are competent yet vulnerable (Mukherji and Albon, 2018), revealing something generative in their multimodal stories which allows new ideas to be imagined. This means finding alternative narratives to the dominant *grand narrative* (the accepted meanings) around early childhood, ones that question who decides which knowledge is privileged and valuable, whether all children's voices are represented or some are excluded from the story or picture, and how this shapes our worldview of children (Dahlberg, Moss and NetLibrary, 2005).

For readers interested in the philosophical underpinnings of my research, I will set out my influences and standpoints below. For the sake of transparency, I will say that my ontology (what we believe about reality and how things exist), epistemology (what we believe about knowledge and how we know what we know) and axiology (our values, ethics, faiths and aesthetics) are in a continual cycle of informing/transforming and being informed/transformed by themselves.

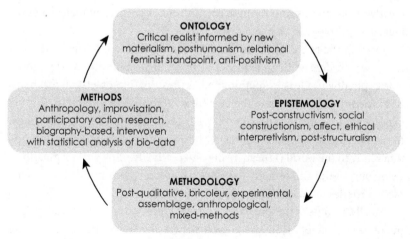

Figure I.1: Theoretical and methodological underpinnings of the concepts in this book

Therefore, what I believe is the basis for all life, knowledge and value today will, I hope, be informed by what I learn from yesterday and experience tomorrow. So the preceding figure is fluid, non-linear, open to debate and may change before this book is even published.

This book is not the place to go into too much philosophical detail but at the end is a brief glossary of the philosophical terms used in this chart. Some of these may describe your approach to life as well, but do not worry if not. My standpoints are not yours because we all have different identities, experiences and cultures, and it is this diversity that makes the world such an interesting place to live in. Our challenge (and adventure) is to arm ourselves with the knowledge, experience and relationships that help us to navigate life as imaginatively and generatively, and with as much insight, wisdom and discernment, as possible.

If you are interested in having an adventure of your own, please consider further training in social science or educational philosophy (many universities offer free online courses as well as fee-paying ones, and libraries offer a tonne of good training materials for free). It provides a superb bedrock from which to better understand ourselves, our children, our relationships and the world around us.

Given the breadth of professionals working across the arts, education, childcare, health, social care and social science sectors, the book aims to offer a comprehensive journey of both theoretical and practical perspectives to address many cross-cutting themes for these sectors. But it does not offer a toolkit of solutions. If the research undertaken for this book has taught me anything, it is that there are no single truths out there that explain a child's creativity, or can position it singularly within a cognitive, biological, neurological, psychological or social field.

In scientific terms, there probably isn't a single truth of the matter out there, which doesn't help us in our striving to simplify the world and be able to pin down at least something that is meaningful, something that helps us to identify what works in the current educational environment. But my experience tells me that being creative is about being fully present (body, mind and spirit), questioning what we know and why, taking risks, listening differently to the world (I mean, really differently), fuelling our imaginations, being purposeful and building curious, trustful relationships with the many other varieties of humanity.

Finally, if some of the language or concepts are new to you, please don't be put off. Any attempt to plumb the depths of creative thinking is bound to take us out of our comfort zone, as it has mine in writing this book. Please relish the challenge to explore deeper into your own minds and don't be afraid to use your search engine while reading. Otherwise, I hope you will find this book enlightening, worrying, uplifting, challenging and, dare I say it, useful. And, most importantly, I hope it inspires you to take the deep dive into your own, and your children's, creativity.

Ruth Churchill Dower
Earlyarts Director
Manchester Metropolitan University PhD Student
March 2019

Part 1

Chapter 1

What Is Creativity All About?

Imagination is more important than knowledge. For knowledge is limited.
Imagination encircles the world.

Albert Einstein (Viereck, 1929)

Definitions of creativity

Creativity is one of those words that is tricky to get our heads around. On the one hand, we know what it means when we feel creative or are inspired by someone else being creative. On the other hand, it's hard to pin down and put a satisfactory definition to it. One of the reasons for this is because creativity encompasses so many aspects of what it means to be human, from imaginative and conscious thought to more intuitive, less conscious sensations; from the physical to the emotional; from the brain to the body; from the spirit to the soul. In whatever way you describe it, creativity is possibly one of the most important aspects of growing up from birth, and affects so many elements of our lives for good, as we will discover in this book.

The feelings that come from seeing, or being told about, a work of art or performance of some description, such as wonder, satisfaction, intrigue, curiosity, excitement and so on, can become intensified when personally participating in it. This has a lot to do with the different responses happening in the brain and the body, which will be addressed later in this book. Each person's neurology, psychology, physiology and biology are informed by their own social (i.e. environmental) and cultural (i.e. genetics and heritage) contexts. Therefore, each person's response is subjective and different, making it even harder to pin down what is good about the arts and creativity, and how to stimulate and sustain these different elements.

Scholars around the world have defined creativity as being inventive, original or innovative; turning a new idea into something that has not been made before, creating a new product, or an idea that is both novel and useful in a particular social context (NACCCE, 1999; Schore and Marks-Tarlow, 2018). I do not disagree but, from the many hundreds of creative encounters I have experienced with young children, I think it is something even more fundamental than this. It is about being able to discover and express your emotions, your passions, your ideas, your resourcefulness, your identities and your unique view on life in a variety of ways regardless of social constraints such as time, money, academic standards, stress or peer pressure. Therefore, I might attempt to define creativity simply as an expression of humanity.

One of the most widely adopted definitions by both cultural and educational communities was created by the National Advisory Committee on Creative and Cultural Education (NACCCE):

> Our starting point is to recognise four characteristics of creative processes. First, they always involve thinking or behaving imaginatively. Second, overall this imaginative activity is purposeful: that is, it is directed to achieving an objective. Third, these processes must generate something original. Fourth, the outcome must be of value in relation to the objective. We therefore define creativity as: Imaginative activity fashioned so as to produce outcomes that are both original and of value. (NACCCE, 1999, p.30)

This presents a conundrum – the statement starts by focusing on the characteristics of creative processes, which is all well and good. But it ends by focusing on their outcomes, or products, creating a somewhat contradictory, and binary definition, i.e. if the imagination is not producing original outcomes of value (that can be measured), it is definitely not being creative. While this may describe an appropriate framework for thinking about the creativity of older children and adults, I'm not so sure it is relevant to the many different tangible and intangible ways in which younger children explore and express their creativity. However, this seminal text written by the NACCCE was exceptional in its time and created many in-roads into progressive thinking about the role of the arts and creative practices in education, as will be discussed in Chapter 5.

Since then, the eminent psychologists and neuroscientists (some of whom I mentioned in the introduction) have proposed a definition closer to my experience that is not so outcomes focused. It is based on the understanding that the right brain creates strategies to cope with, assimilate and process novel situations, and that the right prefrontal cortex is 'centrally involved in artistic creativity' including the removal of inhibitions and the increase of creative thinking (Schore, 2017). They propose that a child's creativity is intrinsically linked to her early experiences of affection, attachment, self-regulation and love. Essentially, the positive emotions and behaviours that arouse the curiosity, inspiration, novelty, joy and play in babies to be creative are largely triggered by loving interactions, which makes the argument for love to be a central tenet of early education even more pressing.

> The mutual exchange of love fuels a young child's desire to explore the environment, drink in novelty, and eventually to fire up imagination in service of creativity. As children grow and develop, this initial dose of love gets internalised into passionate engagements throughout life, including a love for life itself. (Schore and Marks-Tarlow, 2018, p.4)

The problem is that, when it comes to observing and 'measuring' children's creativity for the sake of identifying and supporting their learning progress, educators often do not feel creative themselves or know what their own creative faculties are. Therefore, how can they feel competent in mapping out this area successfully with their children? This is addressed more fully in Chapter 11.

As international adviser, author, speaker and Earlyarts Patron, Sir Ken Robinson highlighted:

> One of the myths of creativity is that very few people are really creative. The truth is that everyone has great capacities but not everyone develops them. One of the problems is that too often our educational systems don't enable students to develop their natural creative powers. Instead, they promote uniformity and standardisation. The result is that we're draining people of their creative possibilities and producing a workforce that's conditioned to prioritise conformity over creativity. (Robinson, 2006)

This is not the same with most core areas of learning and development in the Early Years Foundation Stage (EYFS), where educators will have had at least some basic training or experience, if not during their pre-service or professional training, then during their own time at school. We would be seriously concerned if early years teachers were not adequately trained to teach literacy and numeracy, for instance. But, it seems, the same urgency is not assigned to teaching creativity (or even teaching creatively) and many teacher training courses simply do not include more than a cursory mention, usually in relation to supporting children's basic arts skills, which are not the same as their creative thinking skills or their overall creative being.

Parents and caregivers are even more in the dark when it comes to identifying what creativity means to them and their children and, indeed, whether it is of any importance in the home at all. And yet experts in many fields including education, science, health, business and the public sector are telling us with increasing urgency how important creativity is for our children.

With a century of research into intelligence and creativity behind us, we have been provided with some valuable knowledge about what this phenomenon called creativity actually is, and how to measure its constituent parts. Most researchers involved in this journey have reached agreements that the core definitions revolve around a creative product, object or idea being so because it is novel and purposeful, i.e. it is original and has intent and meaning, even if only on a personal level for the creator themselves (Clapham, 2011; Runco *et al.*, 2014).

The elements of novelty, ideation and purpose sit well with young children, for whom most actions and creations in their play are full of surprising ideas and very purposeful, i.e. made with intention (NACCCE, 1999). Many thoughts and ideas are original to them as they construct or experience or create knowledge, even if they seem to be quite random at the time. If, taking into account their social and cultural context and their age, children are expressing new thoughts and ideas, or constructing objects, materials, tools, products or processes of thinking that are imaginative and adventurous to them, then, according to the accepted research definitions, this is an expression of their creativity.

One of the biggest challenges for educators and caregivers alike is in simply understanding the concept of creativity and how to cultivate it in practice. We will unpack the various approaches to both theory and practice in later chapters but first, let's consider the difference between creativity and the arts.

Creativity and the arts – what's the difference?

Being creative is not the same as learning how to use an art form for exploration or expression, as will become clear. But, while this is an important question to ask, it is somewhat of a red herring, a distraction if you will, from the underlying issues that stop us from being creative, such as the perceptions of 'not being creative' or having to be 'good enough' to be an artist. This has been partly driven by the cultural perception of the arts being 'owned' by competent, prominent, high-achieving artists in the various domains – often referred to as 'Big C' creatives (Runco *et al.*, 2014).

Clearly, creativity does not reside exclusively in the domain of the arts – in fact, some artistic processes are highly technical and not at all imaginative or creative. People can enjoy and express their creativity in a number of ways throughout everyday life, whether it is while cooking, gardening, project managing, going for a walk, tidying up or, yes, even budgeting. If these activities involve expressing passion, resourcefulness, joyfulness, playfulness, spontaneity, evaluation and new ideas, then they may be involving creativity to differing degrees, even if it is not obvious that this is what is happening.

Alternatively, creativity can be expressed perhaps more readily through the arts, as a mode that both draws in, and gives out, inspiration. This is because the arts explore and reflect 'the qualities of human experiences' where we:

> try to give form to the feelings and perceptions that move us most as human beings: our experiences of love, grief, belonging, and isolation, and all the currents of feeling that constitute our experience of ourselves and of others. It is through the arts in all their forms that young people experiment with and try to articulate their deepest feelings and their own sense of cultural identity and belonging. (NACCCE, 1999, p.79)

As Sir Ken Robinson acknowledged in his keynote address to the 2012 Earlyarts UnConference, 'Only through the arts and by being creative can children explore *the inner world* of their imagination and feeling...the world that is uniquely them' (Robinson, 2012).

Whereas we can learn arts techniques, some more easily than others, I believe that creativity is programmed into our blueprint – part of our inherent nature – that enables us to experience a powerful sense of possibility and purpose, of messiness and mastery from birth. As socio-cultural psychologist Vygotsky believed, creativity is not just the province of a few gifted people; it is within the power of everyone who has ideas to harness.

> If we understand creativity in its true psychological sense as the creation of something new, then this implies that creation is the province of everyone to one degree or another; that it is a normal and constant companion in childhood. (Vygotsky, 2004, p.33)

Not many early educators would say that they were not playful. It comes with the job description. And there are plenty of excellent studies to help us understand the strength of connections between creativity and playfulness, which are explored later in this book. So it might not be such a difficult step to take to reposition our role as a 'player' to a role as a 'creative thinker'. This can help enormously in early education roles to explore play in more imaginative ways as well as transforming some of the less exciting aspects of early education.

Diving off to the right or left to learn a new art form is slightly less easy as it requires time, attention and an investment in training. But coming at this with an open mind to bring new techniques, resources, skills and ideas into the classroom from a position of creativity makes a huge difference to how the arts can become more embedded in daily practice, by making them relevant to children's ideas.

There is no doubt that a discipline and mastery of tools, materials, skills and ideas can lead to a high quality of creative or artistic output. We have all heard of people – historical and contemporary figures – with exceptional creative talent who have ploughed new furrows of understanding and achieved breakthroughs in science, maths, technology, medicine, the arts and literature. Of course, it is good to nurture the strengths of our youngest children, any one of whom may turn out to be the next pioneer to push back the frontiers of human knowledge and potential. But these super-talented individuals are rare and that level of skill and discipline is not the most appropriate benchmark by which to measure most people's creative potential. Even though we may feel inspired by their achievements, this level of mastery is neither a prerequisite nor the only starting point for being able to tune into, and release, our own creativity.

Bamford (2006) charts the influences over the centuries of many theorists who promoted creative or arts education from an early age. American philosopher John Dewey dedicated much of his life to educational reform through art, as described in his book, *Art as Experience* (1934). Prolific artist, researcher, educator and psychologist Viktor Lowenfeld was hugely influential and best known for his theory of stages in artistic development, as explored in his book with W. Lambert Brittain, *Creative and Mental Growth* (1987). Influential childhood psychologist Jerome Bruner acknowledged the important effects of culture in a broad and balanced education in his book, *The Culture of Education* (1996).

Eminent educator and psychologist Barbara Rogoff asserts the prioritising of multicultural approaches to enhance children's innate human and creative aptitudes in her book, *The Cultural Nature of Human Development* (2003).

And artist, teacher and educator reformer Franz Cizek, best known for starting the Child Art movement in Vienna in 1897, believed that every child had a natural tendency towards creative and artistic expression, which should be fostered through imaginative learning environments. According to Cizek (1921), 'Art is a natural aspect of human development from birth, the absence of which impairs mental growth and social fitness' (in Bamford, 2006, p.32).

Throughout this book, we will take a more in-depth look at what we mean by creativity from different perspectives and ask some key questions such as: Where does creativity come from? What are its benefits for learning and life? Can we, and should we, be measuring the educational impacts of creativity? Can creative teaching make a significant difference to learning? Does creativity have an impact on the development of the brain? And is it actually possible to measure – or test – for individual creative traits anyway?

For now, we will focus on the sources of creativity, how babies and young children develop it and how we can understand it in relation to children's play.

REFLECTIVE QUESTIONS

* What does creativity mean for you?

* Do you feel happy to measure creativity based on a product or an outcome?

* Can you think of examples of how creativity involves both the brain and the body or reflects the social and cultural elements of who we are?

* Do you agree that it is an essence of our humanity or do you think it is something we learn (or both)?

* Do you think it is possible to measure the quality or depth of someone's imagination?

* Have you experienced situations where imagination is fired up through an inspiring relationship?

* If the arts can express our inner worlds, can you think of something you have done that expressed your inner world – would you have considered this artistic or creative?

* What's the difference for you, in playing or being creative with your children?

* Are you happier considering yourself more in one role than the other? If so, why is this?

Chapter 2

The Origins of Creativity

Are children born creative?

One could argue that children are born aesthetically aware, in terms of being aware of the beauty of sound or the richness of touch, and engage in creative expression long before they can speak, read or write independently. According to child psychologist Colwyn Trevarthen (2002), a sense of musicality (sound, rhythm, tone, pitch, pulse) is developed while in the womb and, from birth onwards, becomes a natural form of communication for babies wanting to gain the attention of their parents or primary carer. This happens not just to fulfil their needs but to develop forms of social interaction that nurture the emotional, social and physical bond between them. This does not necessarily mean that all babies are born with the potential to develop abilities in different art forms. Rather that they have the potential to express their feelings from a very early age for a specific purpose, and later on for the sheer enjoyment and fulfilment of self-expression and sharing languages.

Early childhood psychoanalyst John Bowlby (1969) asserted that social interaction, including creative forms of communication, takes place from birth not only to build an attachment with a significant caregiver but also to prepare the young child for survival skills for the unforeseeable future.

In his analysis of Bowlby's work, neuropsychologist Allan Schore describes Bowlby's understanding of attachment as being 'instinctive social behaviour with a biological function' where the young child is 'seeking not just proximity but access to an attachment figure who is emotionally available and responsive', i.e. co-constructing and co-regulating the child's emotional states (Schore, 2000, p.26).

Bowlby builds on Freud's call for an understanding of instinctive behaviours, how these form and are formed by the 'cognitive mapping' that goes on in building a sense of self through relationship with others. Many researchers of creativity theories have since tried to ascertain what this unconscious, instinctive or intuitive nature is, and how it shapes a child's creativity. Miller (in Runco *et al.*, 2014, p.27) concluded that 'aesthetics and intuition are notions that can be discussed in a well-defined manner and are essential to scientific research as are mental imagery in descriptive and depictive modes', which suggests a fundamental relationship between instinct and creativity.

The instinctive desire of babies to express their feelings, to co-construct communication, to be playful and to feel fulfilled, attached, validated and connected (Schore and Marks-Tarlow, 2018) reveals a natural and purposeful element of creativity. This biological and psychological drive for shared expression and relationship building alone shows how essential creativity is as a form of human connection.

In fact, anthropological scholar Ellen Dissanayake (2017) reveals the origins of different art forms in ethology (behavioural biology) emphasising that being artistic is about *who people are*, their ways of life and creative behaviours, rather than *what art is* in terms of identifying an object or skill of quality. It is no accident that this closely mirrors psychologist Stuart Brown's hypothesis that play is not something we do (i.e. an activity or product separate from the person), but something we are (Brown and Vaughan, 2009). Dissanayake hypothesises a behaviour of 'artification', which is a child's desire for lifelong engagement with play and the arts stimulated by a mother's love, which fuels a passion for curiosity, joy and exploration of both positive and negative emotions, or what is referred to as their 'interpersonal neurobiology' (Dissanayake, 2017, p.144).

Evidence dates back to prehistoric times of young children and adults communicating via drawing, dance, story and song, passing on cultural traditions, drumming, chanting, body decoration, expressions of love, security and protection, engaging in religious or ceremonial rituals and warning of danger and risk. It seems that being creative has been an intrinsic part of our human make-up, personality and behaviours for a very long time – it's an integral part of who we are and our evolution over many, many generations.

Indeed, neurobiologist Jaak Panksepp has shown through his research on rough-housing play in mammals that 'the sources of [creative] play in the brain are instinctual and sub-cortical' (Panksepp, 2005, p.63). Dissanayake's research shows that there is something that goes deeper when using creativity to communicate the languages of expression and attachment than just the purposes of basic survival, safety and protection, as Bowlby and Panksepp have asserted.

More recent research with younger infants has shown 'quite remarkable and unexpected early abilities and proclivities for interaction and intimacy' which suggest that attachment 'should be viewed as a late-appearing consequence of a prior, equally innate, and universal adaptive predisposition to engage in relationship and emotional communion, over and above the need for protection' (Dissanayake, 2017, p.146). Therefore, very young babies and their caregivers are able to create synchronous patterns of meaning between them from using sounds, gestures, touch, rhythmic movements, eye tracking and song. These are sensations that begin in the womb through tone and pulse, alongside the growth of primitive reflexes, and can be continued and sustained post-birth as babies learn the languages of musicality long before they learn to talk (Fritz *et al.*, 2014; Winkler *et al.*, 2009; Trevarthen, 2002). These interactive modes demonstrate the significance of multimodal, sensory communication for younger children (before language development), the modalities of which are processed holistically in the infants' brain (Schore, 2000).

This 'mutually improvised interaction' (Dissanayake, 2017, p.146) is what caregivers and babies are constantly and creatively working together to achieve – the coordination of a biological, emotional, psychological and neural synergy that creates a strong attachment bond, or what Dissanayake refers to as 'building and refining their mental algorithms' (Dissanayake, 2017, p.153). This can be seen clearly when a caregiver cuddling a baby breaks eye contact and acts even for just a few moments out of synchrony, leading to the baby showing distress signals such as muscle tension or crying. In these cases, the infant increases their efforts to regain a coordinated, reciprocal interaction, sometimes spontaneously initiating highly creative methods of communication, showing a complex set of social cognition skills from a very young age. Psychologist Ed Tronick highlights this superbly through his famous *Still Face* experiment from 1975,[1] which still constitutes a reliable experiment for childhood psychology research programmes today.

One might suggest that these remarkably complex, coordinated interactions are simply a natural, biological response. Many studies show that

---

1   See www.youtube.com/watch?v=apzXGEbZht0

the synchronised movements and sounds between caregiver and child produce chemical reactions, including the release of endorphins (leading to a feeling of joy or a euphoric state), oxytocin (leading to feelings of affiliation, trust and receptivity) and the suppression of the stress hormone cortisol (promoting openness to risk-taking, adaptability, collaboration and innovation – all elements of a creative disposition) (Gerhardt, 2004; Levitin, 2012; Van der Kolk, 2015). However, in isolation, this does not explain the many developments of social as well as biological behaviours that creative interactions stimulate in children.

For instance, we see intrinsic creative behaviours becoming more developed in the actions of older children who, often quite subconsciously, reconstruct everyday events or storylines in play, despite not understanding the context or purpose of the event. Swiss psychologist Jean Piaget referred to this assimilation – taking in and fully understanding information and ideas – as the 'key to creative thinking', unlocking the imagination and re-organising cognitive structures and conceptual schema 'in order to take new information into account' (Runco, 2003, p.320).

This creative act of story-building and role play, often carried out in collaboration with other players, is a way of helping children to see themselves in that context, work out things about relationships, emotions, differences to others, cause and effect, how to make things change and generally who they are in relation to the world around them (Bruce, 2005a). In fact, when the subject matter is something they care about, children are more likely to take a greater interest or be intrinsically motivated to explore it creatively.

This comes close to describing the definition of imagination I am using throughout this book. By imagination, or imagining, I am referring to the capacity of a child to *create hypotheses or theories about the world*, the process of which might include some make-believe or pretend, some ideation (formation of ideas), or consideration of other perspectives (such as what would the world look like if I became a monster, or a bird, for instance). They may use their imagination to *go beyond the conventional reality* in front of them, to see the unusual or surprising aspects in something. This might remain contained within the mind, as in imaginary thinking, or it might be expressed externally in the form of role/narrative play, object/material play, dance/movement play, or other types of play. Being imaginative is purposeful and intentional, which is not the same as having predetermined outcomes, and, it seems to me, is very similar to divergent thinking, which is accepted by many psychology theorists as one of the core prerequisites of creativity.

Extending the idea of new perspectives on things, Craft (2002) discusses imagination within the concept of 'possibility thinking', i.e. imagining 'what if...' as an intentional desire to explore ideas, problems and possible solutions – a way of framing 'potential' before it exists. Craft holds that, by acting 'as if' you were someone or something else, you can begin to take on that identity until the mannerisms and beliefs associated with it become familiar, such as acting as if you were a teacher on starting a new job in education. In taking on these roles, children and adults alike learn how to assimilate their new identities and, it could be argued, the same is true for creative behaviours.

El'konin (1994, in Brėdikytė, 2011) talks about imagination regarding the concept of the 'creative act' as having special potential in terms of creating milestones in children's cognitive development. Influenced by the environment, experiences, relationships and communications around each child, each creative act has irreversible implications because the understanding gained from it then transforms and changes the original subject of that role play. Children's constructions of reality become a *new reality* that reflects their worldview (Vygotsky, 2004). They are not inventing something new or unique for the world, in the way we often understand adults' creativity, but constructing a new image (or sense) of the world for themselves.

> One of the most important areas of child and educational psychology is the issue of creativity in children, the development of this creativity and its significance to the child's general development and maturation. We can identify creative process in children at the very earliest ages, especially in their play...children at play represent examples of the most authentic, truest creativity. (Vygotsky, 2004, p.11)

Indeed, Runco (2003) highlights the importance of assigning value and desirability to children's original creativity in its own right, not set against adult creativity which has its own measures of performativity and achievement that are not appropriate for children. He urges educators to recognise children's creative actions as a process that is original to themselves, in order to recognise their potential since, 'if we are unable to recognise their potentials, we certainly will not be able to help fulfil them' (2003, p.320).

More discussion as to how we observe children's creative acts can be explored in Chapter 7, together with an understanding of the conditions for stimulating creativity. With a commitment to seek out inspiring conditions for creativity, children's innate need for creative acts can be better realised and their fundamental human capacity for imagination nurtured and nourished.

To understand this further, we need to examine the different classifications of creativity that enable empowerment or oppression, the range of conditions of possibility for these to exist and the implications for early years practice as a result.

Challenging a developmental theory of creativity

Most contemporary theories of creativity agree that divergent thinking (having imaginative ideas and seeing a range of possibilities) is a major feature of this complex concept and that this is distinct from the other core features or aptitudes measured in other intelligence tests (Clapham, 2011).

Divergent thinking is quite a different concept from that of convergent thinking, i.e. finding a single right answer, which is often associated with logic-based domains such as maths, natural sciences and technology. However, that implies that these subjects are essentially uncreative, which is simply not true as can be seen from the myriad achievements and progressive projects that have catapulted such domains in many different, unusual and creative directions, such as the internet for a start. All domains need both creativity and logic at different times and should resist being defined in such binary ways. As Craft explains, 'What the two types of thinking, convergent and divergent, have in common, it seems to me, is the foundation of possibility thinking' (Craft, 2002, p.112), which we will explore further in Chapter 11.

However, the current educational landscape is designed around developmental theories of child psychology from the 19th century where children are expected to develop sequentially through the ages and stages of universal developmental milestones (Piaget, 1973), as if these are the child's *natural* way of being, rather than their non-linear, socio-cultural timelines. Education is preparing children for young adulthood or reaching a level of logical, cognitive, convergent and rational maturity, based on a middle-class, able-bodied, western-cultured view of 'normal' childhood. This bias, which has grown up through the ages of scientific research, assesses (and attempts to fill) the gaps in a child's knowledge (*know-what*) and skills (*know-how*) but doesn't assess – or value – *who* they are as a competent, divergent, complex person now, whatever their ability or culture.

So, as a homogenous, universal standard towards which children are expected to *progress*, this leaves little room for any child who does not meet the 'norm' and, worse still, categorises them as deviant, alien, other, incapable of choice or moral agency, unnatural or a problem (Murris, 2016). The non-conforming child is dehumanised and cast as the villain before they have even had chance to explore and express their own views on the world. To understand more about the problems of the developmental view of the child, I would recommend a short video made by Professor Karin Murris of the University of Cape Town which articulates these ideas in more depth.[2]

This is partly why creativity has been left out of education over the centuries, as it is to do with *who we are* rather than *what we know* – it is the most *natural* way of a child's being. Recent moves to include the arts or creativity have still been based on measuring standardised outcomes as far as they can be seen through ideas or products. However, this does not necessarily capture that more elusive, but essential, human essence or instinct – the transcendental nature of creativity. This is an essence that goes beyond the boundaries of biology and psychology in developmental theory, an essence with its own agency, not in relation to reasoning or critique against someone's set of normative values.

Despite the plethora of research attempting to define creativity as a 'powerful capacity of human intelligence' (Prentice, 2000, p.156) or as inventive, original or innovative acts, based in the imagination, creating ideas or products that are both useful and novel (NACCCE, 1999; Schore and Marks-Tarlow, 2018), none of these traditional definitions seems to take into account the non-verbal, transcendental, instinctive elements of creativity that are embodied in children's passion, spirit, emotions, senses, empathies, bodies, gestures and unique viewpoints. These emerge while striving to express creativity and make 'imaginative connections between present experience and future possibilities; between who they are and who they might become' (Prentice, 2000, p.156), and are important to nurture if we are to support the whole child.

Eighteenth-century philosopher Kant believed in a *transcendental* idealism which determined that we can only ever carry a perception of a thing in our minds (Crotty, 1998), but never the essence of the thing itself, the *noumena*. For instance, we might have a perception of what a particular chair is like, but we can't know the intricate details of every molecule, atom,

---

2   See www.youtube.com/watch?v=ikN-LGhBawQ

displacement of air, relation to its surroundings, impact on its sitters or the very core essence – a single truth – that describes exactly what that chair is. However, I would like to suggest that humans can access, or sense, a creative essence or *noumena* beyond articulation, identification or measurement within the human sphere, and that young children seem to have little problem with this 'more-than-human' concept (see 'New materialism' in the Philosophy Glossary for more details on this concept).

This may be because their youthfulness and limited experience in the world mean they are less influenced by social norms, less governed by preconceptions, less constrained by the boundaries of language, more open to possibility thinking, and therefore can direct their intentionality in a more holistic and purposeful way towards objects and ideas, gaining a fuller meaning of them. It could also be to do with the exponential growth of synaptogenesis within the first three years of brain development, rendering young brains more open to experiencing non-materialistic phenomena (and *noumena*) than at any other stage in their lives (David *et al.*, 2003). In fact, in one cross-cultural study in Hong Kong and Brisbane, children were asked 'What is art?', to which a number of children responded in all seriousness that 'art was a mystery' (McArdle, 2016, p.11).

It seems to me that the arts cannot be contained within the Cartesian dualisms of mind and body that traditionally perpetuate the developmental view of children. The famous words of French philosopher Descartes, 'I think, therefore I am' (1637), underlined his belief that an absolute truth in what exists is demonstrated in the very fact that, because he can think, therefore he must exist. He attempted to prove that, while the mind was categorically real and thinking could be scientifically verified, the body was made up of many senses that constantly changed and, therefore, could not be trusted. So mental cognition took on a status as an important scientific instrument above embodied cognition, and the two were considered entirely separate.

You may be wondering if the chap had a bit too much time on his hands, but his investment in abstract thinking in fact influenced the majority of the western world's views in most major fields.

This kind of thinking pervades education where children are seen as vessels to be filled with our infinitely superior adult knowledge, and tested in the success of this by measures of language and other cognition-based methods.

Yet there are so many ways in which the arts value body, gesture, song, image, line, texture, shape, form, fantasy, ideas and imagination as valid forms of communication above sequential sentences and developmental milestones. In applying a more holistic, creative approach, we have the most wonderful opportunities to adapt how we communicate with, support, teach and listen to young children.

Despite our natural desire for clear starting points and yardsticks by which to measure progress, we might need, for the purposes of this book at least, to accept that the complex, multidimensional nature of creativity will ultimately resist the acceptance of a single, universal definition (Treffinger *et al.*, 2002). But that doesn't mean to say there aren't measurable impacts associated with generative creative practice.

REFLECTIVE QUESTIONS

* Can you identify and extend some of the different musical sounds babies make in trying to express themselves or find synergy with you, their carer?

* Does the attention you give them fuel their desire for further expression, curiosity and exploration (your interpersonal biology) in a way that doesn't happen when they are alone?

* What sorts of gestures, sounds, movements, touch or sensations create a positive interaction with your child? Try to notice them and extend them to see what happens.

* Can you identify examples of your children being creative or expressive with different 'roles' as they try to make sense of everyday events?

* What surprises you when you see children are in these roles?

* Most educational curricula are based on a normative view of the 'ideal' child (which is a myth). Does your educational framework or practice reinforce this view in ways that might be reductive for your children (make them feel 'less than' who they 'should' be or unhappy with who they are)?

* Can you identify practices that help nurture your children's uniqueness and strengths, even where they might not meet developmental milestones?

* How can you adapt observations and assessments to spot, appreciate and celebrate children's creative essence (or *noumena*) as a natural part of their human growth?

Chapter 3

The Benefits of Creativity

An overview of arts and creativity across the domains

To understand who our children are as humans, in relation to the world around them, it is important to see their creativity in context. This is the broader context of how creativity works in society, how its potential to motivate and inspire, improve and heal, strengthen and support offers a myriad of different perspectives that give us new, surprising and sometimes disturbing insights on life.

There is a strong body of evidence pointing to the importance and value of early childhood arts and creative practice, for children's learning and development, for family and community, for aesthetic and innovative purpose, and for society in general. High-quality creative experiences in early childhood appear to have a significant impact on learning and development, with, in many cases, lifelong impact. In fact, creativity researcher Russ claims that 'the rewarding feelings experienced when a child plays are responsible for the lifelong desire to behave creatively' (in Runco, 2016, p.99).

One large cohort, longitudinal study of 25,000 young people over 11 years of age showed that the ones who had participated in the arts from an early age achieved significantly higher levels than those who had less arts involvement in both academic skills and positive social engagement, with particularly striking results for students from low-income families (Catterall, 2012).

The following summary highlights key research findings in the last decade on the main benefits of creativity in young children's physical, social, emotional, cultural, educational, psychological and relational development:

- Creative or cultural experiences that involve children experimenting with new ideas, techniques and materials can help children develop subsequent abilities in the arts which will be useful throughout life (Russ, 2016; Cultural Learning Alliance, 2012).

- Conversely, training in specific art forms can impact the brain's development in other areas of cognition. For instance, music has been found to activate the same areas of the brain that are active during reading (in tasks relating to decoding, tone and phonological awareness) and in mathematical processing, especially in tasks common to both such as counting, ratios or intervals, creating patterns and sequences, tone groupings and spatial reasoning skills (Sousa, 2006; Lonie, 2010).

- Arts-based teaching approaches can lead to an improvement in numeracy and literacy skills (Cultural Learning Alliance, 2012; Duffy, 2010; Sousa, 2006), retention of subject content knowledge and working memory in science (Hardiman et al., 2019), language development, observation and concentration (Heath and Wolf, 2005).

- Early childhood arts and cultural activities can significantly strengthen parent–child bonds and engage families in their children's learning, providing a positive focus for shared experience and communication (Schore and Marks-Tarlow, 2018).

- Creative, play-based experiences in early childhood can help children communicate authentically and effectively, expressing their feelings, emotions, thoughts and ideas in non-verbal ways (Duffy, 2010). They can help them develop curiosity, critical awareness, ability to make choices and apply scientific reasoning, leading to a better understanding of themselves and others, and helping to build respectful and positive relationships (Bruce, 2005a).

- Art forms with a strong social element, such as theatre, dance, story and music, can help develop intrinsic human qualities like love, self-expression, independence, self-awareness and empathy, self-esteem, awareness of difference and connection with others (NACCCE, 1999; Bamford, 2006; Schore and Marks-Tarlow, 2018; Witkin, 1974; Page, 2018).

- As well as helping to preserve our cultural heritage, the arts create a safe space for young children to bring lived realities into view, helping children develop their own languages, foster a sense of belonging and pride, and shape their sense of identity and individuality as well as their identities within local and global communities and cultures (Duffy, 2006; Bamford, 2006; Rinaldi, 2001; Brown and Sax, 2013).

- Creativity strengthens human connection by building trust and connecting children across cultural, religious, generational and socio-economic divides. It breaks down language barriers, cultural prejudices and societal differences, and acts as a powerful force to tackle social problems such as inequality and injustice (Runco *et al.*, 2014; NACCCE, 1999).

- Stimulating and compelling experiences at museums, galleries, theatres, libraries, dance, arts or music venues will offer many parents and caregivers the ideas, confidence and resources to play with their children as a natural part of everyday life (Piscitelli, Everett and Weier, 2003).

- Collaborations between arts and early years professionals, children and caregivers can result in multiple perspectives, deeper understandings of, and attention to, a child's interests (Churchill Dower and Sandbrook, 2013; Clark, Griffiths and Taylor, 2003). Creating with co-learners can also stimulate greater ideas-generation, more sustainable learning progression, improved richness of learning and a sense of fulfilment for educators and children (NACCCE, 1999; Duffy, 2010).

- Creative and arts-based methods also promote strong physical growth, such as dance which supports gross motor, coordination, proprioceptor, vestibular (motion and balance) and sensory development, a properly functioning nervous system and vitality. Mark-making, drawing, crafting and singing help with fine motor coordination, muscle memory and proprioception (body position awareness) systems required for sensory learning. The strength and quality of a child's physical development has a direct impact on their emotional wellbeing and learning potential (Daly and O'Connor, 2016; Grace, 2017).

- Creative activities can support positive mental and psychological health through immersion, expression, inspiration, spontaneity and joy. They can help to make positive neural connections, reduce anxiety, build self-esteem and self-confidence, increase a sense of agency and power, develop strong self-regulatory processes, increase the immune function and decrease a reliance on health care (Boyatzis and Hazy, 2015; Catterall, 2012; Cultural Learning Alliance, 2012; Brown and Sax, 2013; Schore and Marks-Tarlow, 2018; Witkin, 1974).

Each of the above statements draws on both quantitative and qualitative research from researchers around the world whose experience adds up to a powerful picture. The individual elements of that picture are explored in more detail throughout this book.

The links between creativity, imagination, play and emotion

In her analysis of the 12 characteristics of effective play, early childhood play expert Tina Bruce concluded that, across the world, make-believe play is a universal phenomenon characterising a child's active participation in her own worlds (as opposed to being a passive participant of an adult-constructed world) (2005b). Her work demonstrates the innate desire and need in all young humans for creative fantasy play. Children naturally seek opportunities to have their creative curiosity satisfied by nurturing their imagination, which psychologists such as Panksepp (2005) and El'konin (1989, in Brėdikytė, 2011) believe happens in order to support the development of vital mental, physical and spiritual capacities, i.e. that creativity is a life-giving and vital part of children's lives.

Bruce (2005a), identifies 12 key elements that capture the nature of play and could arguably also describe the nature of creativity:

1. It is an active process without a product.

2. It is intrinsically motivated.

3. It exerts no external pressure to conform to rules, pressures, goals, tasks or definite direction. It gives the player control.

4. It is about possible, alternative worlds, which lift players to their highest levels of functioning. This involves being imaginative, creative, original and innovative.

5. It is about participants wallowing in ideas, feelings and relationships. It involves reflecting on and becoming aware of what we know – 'metacognition'.

6. It actively uses previous first-hand experiences, including struggle, manipulation, exploration, discovery and practice.

7. It is sustained and, when in full flow, helps us to function in advance of what we can actually do in our real lives.

8. During free-flow play, we use technical prowess, mastery and competence we have previously developed, and so can be in control.

9. It can be initiated by a child or an adult.

10. Play can be solitary.

11. It can be in partnership or groups, with adults and/or children, who will be sensitive to each other.

12. It is an integrating mechanism, which brings together everything we learn, know, feel and understand.

(Bruce, 2005a, pp.261–262)

Bruce maintains that one of the key enablers for authentic, deep-level, free-flow play is simply the opportunity to 'wallow' in play, which is akin to Csikszentmihalyi's concept of flow (1997), discussed in Chapter 7. Sometimes this is a solitary activity, and at other times a social one, both of which are important. Through solitary play, children have the space and freedom to build ideas and test out their own theories, to experience a level of autonomy, mastery and self-regulation in a space that is not challenged by the authority of another's expertise. Through social play, children build relationships, negotiation strategies and a breadth of perspectives from different social contexts and languages (verbal and embodied) to help them find many more ways to explore problems and escape the limitations of conventional thinking (Sternberg, 1999).

In his clinical role as Chief of Psychiatry at a large San Diego hospital, eminent child psychiatrist Dr Stuart Brown recognised the devastating effects of play deprivation on his clients, so much so that he decided that both his psychology students and clients should undertake a series of assessments on their 'play history', i.e. the amount, types and quality of play that had taken place in their own lives. Believing play to be an evolutionarily designed state that is integral to competency and essential for survival, he wanted to find out 'what *is* play and why is it so important to health and emotional harmony?' (Brown and Vaughan, 2009). Six thousand assessments of people's play histories later, Brown was able to develop a clinical framework to help professionals assess serious play deprivation and its consequences throughout life.

Imagine our educators, children, parents and caregivers also doing this exercise and discovering links between their own play histories and the person they are now. On the surface this might appear an enlightening exercise to undertake, but it raises concerns about the nature of identifying clear, causal links from the complex mix of influences from genetic, cultural and biographical histories. How would such an exercise ensure that participants did not develop a sense of personal deprivation or abnormality rather than an appreciation of difference, unique attributes and potential? It seems to me that, like creativity, the effects of play (or lack of it) on people's lives would be hard to pin down and describe succinctly or accurately against a set of universal measures. However, Brown, Panksepp and other scholars all maintain that, despite our different cultures and starting points, the biological and neurochemical responses in our bodies and brains are similar and the outcomes of different 'play states' are common across all cultures, in the same way that Csikszentmihalyi (1997) describes the common features of 'flow states' in highly creative people.

The idea that creative play is an important 'state of being' (Brown and Vaughan, 2009) is further corroborated by affective neuroscientist Jaak Panksepp (2005, 2018) based on his research into the emotional states shared by all mammals. Through extensive functional magnetic resonance imaging (fMRI) scanning, Panksepp illustrates how all living mammals possess seven basic emotional states which are deeply embedded into neural circuitry at a subconscious level. As such, these states operate more like primitive reflexes than cognitive functions, because they emanate from deep within the core brain regions. The seven states he identifies are: seeking, fear, rage, lust, caretaking, grief and *play*. Panksepp's research shows that unique neurons are fired in direct response to these states quite apart from any other.

It seems that play is so deeply rooted in the central brain system that 'it has been shown to be a fundamental drive as are the drives for food, sleep and sex,' and has 'evolved long before other [human] cortical processes. The urge to play is basic to survival and to living in a changing and demanding world' (Brown and Vaughan, 2009, p.31). Yet, the common prioritisation of work over sleep and play has often led to 'exhaustion, implosion or boredom as we suffer a deficit of energy and creativity', suggesting that play is actually the true source of our creativity.

The common element that connects both play and creativity is the engagement of the imagination – both for aesthetic purposes and for the thousands of discovery, ideation and meaning-making routines that a person accomplishes each day. According to Lev Vygotsky (2004), this is especially true for babies and very young children who compensate for their limited life experiences by imagining what the world is all about, and why things happen in the way they do. The richer their environment and early experiences, the richer their imagination and their ability to construct worlds that make sense of the unknown to them.

Theatre director and actor Stanislavski (1988, in Brèdikytè, 2011) felt strongly that imagination could and should be developed as a matter of daily practice, noting the three types of imagination in people having different experiences:

- Active – triggered through one's own initiative.

- Passive – triggered by others' suggestions (but lacking own initiative).

- Poor – not triggered by others' suggestions but reliant on implementing others' ideas.

These observations were based on adult imaginative capabilities but still serve to illustrate the need to develop and nurture imagination on a regular basis in order to remain in the 'active' arena. For children, the image-making that takes place in their minds and bodies to fill the gap between experience and understanding is especially well exercised through the arts. Whether they play with crafting, painting, drawing, singing, modelling, sculpting, photography, movement or whatever expression it takes, these different forms provide limitless, unusual possibilities for image-making to happen.

It is like trying several different cuisines of food, all of which encourage experimentation and lead to taste satisfaction in one form or another. The arts strengthen children's imaginative skills, broaden their repertoire and help them make new images of the world based on existing knowledge (memory) and imagination (new ideas) (Vygotsky, 2004). One could see the arts as a gift to educators.

Imaginative activity enables children to process their thinking, ideas and knowledge through verbal (language or sound), non-verbal (embodied) or representational (image-based) behaviours. Creative thoughts may be more easily embodied for some young children in their movement than in their language – where they move to generate possibilities and ideas to aid their understanding. In fact, creative ideas can occur more easily when the body is in fluid movement and the mind is deep in thought (Daly and O'Connor, 2016). It is a form of mental play where, again, the world can be recreated in new and exciting ways. This idea of embodied creativity is important to embrace in order to support children's multimodal languages.

Wright explains this in relation to the act of drawing, which 'integrates sensorimotor and other forms of thinking, reasoning, feeling and learning, which emerge through the "thinking body". This is known as somatic meaning-making [and] involves exchanges between the psyche (mind), the soma (body) and the soul' (Wright, 2010, p.80).

As multimodal beings, children translate their imagination into expression, whether this is an image, sculpture, gesture, sound, body or verbal language, in order to communicate their ideas, thoughts and feelings, or to ask questions of the world around them. It is often a means of social interaction that, if recognised by another, will reveal significant elements of a child's inner world – their ideas about, and understanding of, who they are. This is particularly true for children with disabilities and different learning needs, for whom conventional teaching methods and content may create obstacles to learning. The NACCCE says that for children who learn in non-conventional ways (which is arguably every child):

> the opportunity to communicate through other forms of expression, including music, movement or art, can provide essential channels of communication to express ideas which are inhibited by conventional forms of speaking and writing. The point is not that the arts compensate for disability: it is that present conceptions of ability are too narrow. (NACCCE, 1999, p.67)

According to McArdle (2016), this is where brain-based theories break down. More often than not, they are focused to such a high degree of specificity on what happens in the brain when an artistic event happens that it only explains the neurobiological activity, but not the experience itself, nor its effect on the body, the emotions or the senses. Nor does it take into account previous influences of others who have shaped our lives and how we interact with art. Epigenetics is starting to address some of these issues by exploring what makes our genes change beyond the normal DNA sequence, with a focus on heritage, developmental biology and psychology, pollution, diet, disease, clinical and mental health issues and other socio-cultural influences.

However, French philosopher Gilles Deleuze takes a different perspective of the influences on neurological growth, which is a more encouraging proposition. He resists causal or instrumental explanations but instead maintains that 'the arts produce and generate an intensity which directly impacts the nervous system and intensifies sensation' (in Grosz, 2008, p.3). This seems to be the thread that connects the theories of Vygotsky and Dewey with the cognitive role of the imagination, extends the arguments of Panksepp, Levitin, Schore and Dissanayake in terms of the biological and neurological role of play and the arts, continues the thinking of Bruce and Brown as to the centrality of imagination in play, reinforces the insights of Rinaldi as to the embodiment of aesthetics within the senses and materials, and furthers the discussions of Eisner, Trevarthen, Csikszentmihalyi and Biesta in relating artistic and creative drivers to an essence of humanity, or 'more-than-humanity'.

Play is considered by most educators to be an important process that is not required to have a particular outcome or ending in mind for it to be worthwhile. We do not expect children to play at having a tea party just so that they can learn the correct way to set the table, not do we expect them to play at superheroes just to learn that these characters and their superhuman powers are not 'real'. These are more culturally and socially refined, perhaps limited, ways of seeing the world through adult eyes.

Rather, we know that children use role play, fantasy play and make-believe to construct the inner worlds of their imaginations, to try out different roles and see what happens, to better understand their emotions, to learn about relationships and how to communicate. All the time they are practising and rehearsing their creativity and imagination, to test their hypotheses and find out if the world works as they thought it would, or how to react to it if it does not (Rinaldi, 2001). It is such an important part of learning and growing that it is hard to understand how anyone could consider that creativity and play could be separated from 'serious' learning. In the same way, it is important to value and practise the processes of creativity without having an outcome in mind, to playfully explore creative constructs, and how the world of the imagination can work more effectively to support, and drive, pedagogy.

Psychologist Hutt (1981) revealed that children often move from an 'epistemic' mode of play (a serious attitude of concentration where they are finding out *how something works*, mastering a technique or investigating the properties of materials) to a 'ludic' mode of play (where, once their investigation is complete, they can move into a playful enjoyment of the resource or practising of their role play/creativity). This is a useful premise to bear in mind when considering the creative process. Once the epistemic period has been accomplished, children (and adults) can happily transfer into the ludic period 'to apply the knowledge gained through investigation in their play' (in Kolb and Kolb, 2010, p.4).

This transference between serious and joyful play is examined further by neuroscientist Hannaford (1995), whose research shows how this process in play connects the limbic system and frontal lobe of the neo-cortex by 'transforming and integrating the sensory stimuli into meaningful thoughts and behaviours'.

As many of the scholars mentioned here have examined, there seems to be an interesting symbiosis between play, creativity, imagination and emotion. Children's imaginative ideas often include emotional responses to their experiences since this is the basis of much of their learning in the early stages. Emotions can be aroused by the creative act, and indeed, the creative act can be stimulated by deep emotions, due to a number of considerations:

- Since young children have not yet fully mastered the skills of verbal or written forms of communication that are our dominant forms of expression, making themselves understood can be a frustrating exercise. Expressing themselves creatively can be a preferred way to ensure successful communications and fulfilling interactions.

- During this process, the images being created in their imagination are often big images, formed of big ideas, which arouse big emotions. Their ideas have deep significance because they represent a part of everything they know about the world at this time, and expressing emotions is a way of showing how they feel about their worldview.

- Imagination is a complex form of thinking that gains depth and traction the more it is utilised. According to Vygotsky (2004), there is hardly any boundary between abstract thinking (including imagination) and rational thinking (including knowledge) until reasoned thinking starts to develop any time between the ages of four to six (in developmental theory terms). Abstract and rational thinking appear to be dependent on each other as imagination becomes a necessary, integral aspect of realistic thinking. Therefore, imagination embraces the emotions as both abstract and rational, as the child attempts to express themselves or respond to the environment and situation they are in. As Brėdikytė confirms, 'imagination is an activity rich with *deep* and *real emotional experiences*' (2011, p.52).

Research by Kudriavtsev and Nesterova (2006, in Brėdikytė, 2011, p.52) reveals the 'interdependence of imagination and thinking' based on a study of relationships between creative imagination and logical thinking in preschool children. I support their conclusion that the development of the imagination should be considered the most important *school readiness* strategy, enabling every young child to create 'a bridge' between knowledge and understanding, thinking and expression, emotional awareness and possibility. Creativity and imagination are a child's most fundamental assets in their knowing and being, and an inherent strength of each individual.

REFLECTIVE QUESTIONS

* Which of these benefits strike you as being particularly important for your children?

* Are there any other benefits you have experienced which are not mentioned here?

* Where can you use this evidence to help promote arts and creative practices in your setting?

* Do you agree that creative play is an important 'state of being'?

* Can you cite examples of children's creative play being like a 'thinking body', linking the mind, body and soul?

* Is there adequate time and opportunity for your children to move from an 'epistemic' mode of play (finding out how something works) to a 'ludic' mode of play (a playful enjoyment of the resource) and back and forth several times in each creative play session?

* How can you help your children to better express their emotions through creative acts?

Chapter 4

Measuring the Impact of Creativity

The issue of measuring the impact of creativity is a historical problem of two halves. One revolves around the definitions, classifications and meanings attached to the concept and actions of creativity, as discussed in Chapter 1. The other is a set of social, cultural and political boundaries/values that simultaneously enable and constrain the understanding and growth of creative potential.

These boundaries and values determine whether creativity should be considered the preserve of the talented few or accessible to the masses – obviously, this is a political question as much as a social and cultural one but it is not as straightforward as it may initially seem. First, it is important to look at the scientific ways of measuring impact and whether it is, in fact, possible to demonstrate links between the cause and effect of arts or creative interventions and, if so, how.

Demonstrating cause and effect

One of the doctrines of traditional, positivist empiricism (see the Philosophy Glossary) that has caused ongoing problems for the arts and education sectors is that anything that cannot be seen or measured cannot be known or considered real (Benton and Craib, 2011). So, in a bid to ascertain cause and effect or, at the very least, correlation between tangible variables, positivists maintain that we cannot make sense of anything unless we can measure it using scientific methods.

Of course, no one would deny the sense in underpinning fundamental claims about knowledge and truth with comparable, data-based reasoning. Such rigour indicates reliability, validity and reduction of bias in any research, leading to greater respect in other sciences (Runco, 2003). But the tendency towards causal claims, such as musical talent causing statistically significant improvements in maths, language or literacy skills (Sousa, 2006; Nan *et al.*, 2018) can be over-simplified and somewhat misleading.

We can certainly say we have evidence of a visible behaviour such as increased concentration happening during an intervention such as a new musical activity, but we cannot say that this proves a strong correlation or causation (i.e. that playing a musical instrument alone caused increased levels of concentration) between the two without first identifying what other influences were also in play at the time.

For instance, perhaps the child had never experienced this type of musical activity before, so the high novelty factor may have triggered a reaction in the reward centre of the brain leading to higher concentration during the activity. Perhaps the child had experienced the pattern of this music before in another environment such as a football match and so their interest was immediately piqued because it was building on existing knowledge and experience. This might have enabled them to develop higher levels of thinking and concentration that may not have happened if the prior knowledge was not also in play. In both examples, factors other than the musical event are significant and are not easily identifiable (e.g. cultural, social and biological influences).

On this basis, one might question how the findings of Nan *et al.*, for instance, from the above research could be generalised to a broader population due to the small sample group from the same school with similar environmental influences. The controlled trial did not appear to be blind, i.e. children in the 'piano lessons' group would have known they were expected to 'perform' better and some may have had musical training; plus causal links between music and phonetic discernment were isolated from any other influence that might have improved the children's listening skills.

It is not that doing complex research like this is not a valid use of resources. It absolutely is and there are many similar research programmes doing a great job trying to identify correlations between music (or other art forms) and areas of cognitive development. The point I am making is that an *empirical* approach in isolation might not provide the best methodology for such research as it does not capture the whole story, and so it would be almost impossible to replicate these experiments and expect the same patterns to emerge every time. This is especially the case if we consider creativity to be based on a complex combination of psychological traits which may be developed over a long period, as well as 'biologically based capacities, specialised knowledge and technical expertise' (Kaufmann, 2003, p.237).

It does highlight the difficulty of collating rigorous research in the arts sector, although a number of longitudinal studies do exist using empirical methods to explain, for instance, musical impacts on learning (Lonie, 2010).

As Runco elaborates:

> Rigour, in the scientific sense specifically refers to objectivity, and this in turn, indicates that there is more quality control, more agreement about techniques to ensure that empirical work is reliable and valid, and less opportunity for bias and unjustified speculation. One presupposition of the objective view is that we need to be very certain about creativity. (Runco, 2003, p.317)

However, Runco admits, this is problematic as creative expression is often original, 'sometimes personal and not easily compared with normative standards' (Runco 2003, p.319).

The complexities of validating creativity research

As it is, most respected studies can identify relationships between art-form skills training, for instance, and improved cognitive skills, but wisely resist isolating this from other noted improvements in concentration, language processing, emotional regulation, creative expression and mathematical concepts such as sequencing and patterning, among others.

In addition, the quantitative methodology that is the calling card of positivist/empiricist studies claims a superiority in terms of validity and reliability which is surely to be questioned. As Denzin suggests, 'the assertion that connects accountability and improved performance with objectivity is dangerous. It focuses attention on the performance indicator and not on performance itself'. The statistical measures tend to ignore social contexts and 'relegate diversity, variation, difference and other indicators of cultural richness to non-normality or pathology, which 'gives research a dirty name' (Denzin, Lincoln and Giardina, 2006, p.772).

Therefore, I tend to reject the positivist position as a reliable methodology for arts education or creativity research, especially in early years, on the basis that creativity engages complex, metaphysical concepts from which we cannot:

- state emphatically that data exists in a fixed format that can be comparatively measured

- ignore the many (social, environmental, economic, political, cultural) influences on sense data, rendering identification of direct, replicable cause and effect impossible

- ascertain the direction of causation bearing in mind the point above, the cultural heritage and genetic predispositions a child brings into the world and that their development is not linear but a 'complex, dynamic, feedback mechanism' (Williams, 2016, p.15)

- restrict knowledge to only what we know with our senses or is beneath the metaphysical parapet

- sanitise our methods of observation from perceptions and value judgements. Who is to say that one group of sense data, collected and analysed in a certain way (ethical and quality principles all being equal), is any more valid than another?

In fact, it would be almost impossible for positivists to locate the concepts of creativity and multimodal learning within scientific empiricism since, for them, knowledge is anchored in a framework of objectivism where 'objects in the world have meaning prior to, and independently of, any consciousness of them' (Crotty, 1998, p.27).

Ironically, musicians skilled in the art of improvisation, where the attuned ear can compose original, harmonious playing in the moment in response to various stimuli (musical, emotional, imaginative, physical or cognitive), might agree with this statement insofar as 'objects' referred to 'music'. They might argue that music has a truth, an essence, in and of itself that springs from a well of natural, creative languages that exists independently of human control or consciousness.

However, since the empiricist doctrines that were formed in the 1800s revolved around the laws of nature as opposed to social science, it can be assumed that they did not account for a science of creativity within nature nor for any kind of transcendental causation influencing decisions over nature, humankind and animals.

Nevertheless, the biological and neurological aspects of a child's early development, and the fact that biodata and neurodata can be appropriately captured and analysed in response to a child's observable creative behaviours (Fink *et al.*, 2007), means there may be an argument for a naturalistic theory of creativity (Kronfeldner, 2009). For instance, sympathetic nervous system arousal, electro-chemical signal transmission, cerebral blood flow, temperature, blood volume pulse and heart rate variability can be captured through wearable microsensors (Porges, 2007) (such as are in some sports watches) that engage with the body in more discreet ways than fMRI scanners and are much more appropriate and less invasive for younger children. However, it is doubtful that such an evidence base consisting of captured biological responses to a creative event could stand alone as valid evidence of impact, ignoring the interdependent relationships between external forces, objects, histories and cultures and internal states, emotions, memories, thoughts, sensations, dreams, reflections and beliefs, as much as are accessible to us.

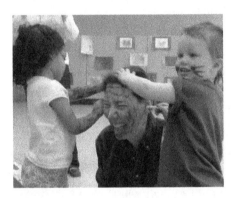

The theory of phenomenology can provide a helpful research framework here – it is one of several interpretive approaches to research, focused on the development of conceptual thought, examining how experience and consciousness transform our perceptions of the world. It includes perceptions from our imagination, not just from our senses, and traces how we come to have those perceptions, i.e. the processes involved in developing our understanding before we apply preconceived, inherited ideas or common sense (Benton and Craib, 2011). Phenomena 'calls into question what is taken for granted; it is about seeing things for what they really are, opening ourselves up to raw phenomena 'to see what emerges for us' (Crotty, 1998, p.82).

Even idealist philosopher Kant admitted that, while phenomenology can only be acknowledged within the constraints of time and space, there are 'things that are beyond mind' (Williams, 2016, p.96). But, as busy educators will attest, we tend towards the rationalisation of any kind of creative essence in order to understand it as a conscious reality, either in the imagination (ideas) or in material form (things) rather than any kind of *noumena* (see Chapter 2).

Phenomenologists might have supported the idea that creativity largely exists in everyday sense perceptions involving the imagination, extending the concept of interpretivism as 'culturally derived and historically situated interpretations of the social life-world' (Crotty, 1998, p.67). In one sense, they would be right as very young children (all basic needs for security being met) are *masters of momentariness*, unconcerned with historical or future existences, nor having embedded preconceptions, but making meaning through the immediacy of the world by intentionally constructing new knowledge, classification and synthesis in every moment of consciousness. This multimodal sense-making using their senses could be described as a creative phenomenon.

However, one of the biggest drawbacks of traditional (natural) scientific methodologies was highlighted by philosopher (and former nursery teacher) Karl Popper (1902–94), who developed what he called the 'falsification theory', which provided an alternative approach to (and, in fact, confronted head on) empirical positivism. He invited scientists to make a guess – any guess or hypothesis they wanted – and then try to prove it wrong. The theory was that, no matter how many scientists you throw at a hypothesis, they can try to prove something true all they like, but they may never be able to examine all the different variables in heaven and on earth that might impact on the matter. And so it may never be proven an absolute truth, it can only ever be a tentative truth. Only one example would need to be found which was at odds with the rule to prove something false. Hence the falsification theory – trying to prove a theory wrong instead of right.

In Popper's mind, anything that has so far been 'proven' is simply some-thing that, so far, scientists have been unable to prove false – merely a provisional statement (Crotty, 1998). This is a very challenging and humbling position indeed for people who are dedicated to verifying their work, rather than disproving it!

This is not to say that an entire methodology should be refuted due to the methods or conditions of research being problematic, just that we need to recognise the challenges of measuring something as unpredictable as creativity and make sure we acknowledge the relative contexts surrounding it. This is particularly the case with young children for whom a personal creative work might not be verbalised, or it might be expressed in a myriad of ways that are not interpretable by an observer. This challenges the very heart of empirical research, which relies on the outward expression and objective (as far as is possible) evaluation against certain cultural or social standards. This precludes the personal creativity of most children (Runco, 2003). That is not to say, however, that children's creative activity cannot be valued without public expression and recognition, just that we need alternative methods to do so.

We need to find research methods that consider the layering of knowledge, built up to make sense over time, which 'cannot be reduced to its constituent parts' (O'Gorman and MacIntosh, 2015, p.62). We should bear in mind the complex relationships between mind, brain and body that embody creativity through empirical experiences (what actually happens), causal events (relationships and connections) and complex underlying mechanisms (conditions of possibility) (Williams, 2016), all of which are in a dynamic state of change through time (being and becoming), which makes generalised comparisons of data almost meaningless.

Even Popper (1996), hinted towards a higher order thinking of abstract concepts – almost a spirituality of creativity – in his theory of Third World Knowledge where 'exosomatic knowledge' could be stored, transmitted to and transformed by many other brains through creative media such as music, books, imagery and video. Through this, he challenged the 'authority of the expert', who is a 'prisoner of his specialisation' (Popper and Notturno, 1996, p.ix) and argued that transcendental, creative thinking is accessible to anyone regardless of their intellectual background.

Therefore, we can perhaps acknowledge at least two ways of classifying creativity by the materialism of what we can see and/or measure and by the idealism (or transcendentalism) of what we cannot, which is no less real (Kaufmann, 2003). And we should recognise that an epistemology of uncertainty (i.e. not having absolute truths to hold on to about creativity), based on the theory of change over time and space, is highly relevant to the way young children develop, disrupt and express their own ideas, doing so to differing degrees at different ages, and in many different modes.

If scientific equipment becomes sophisticated enough to verify the properties of the predicted Higgs Boson particle, despite currently remaining 'elusive' (Williams, 2016, p.64), then we may also consider the possibility of creativity, and other metaphysical concepts, to become more measurable with the improvement of our own sophisticated equipment – our understanding. It seems obvious to say it but, the *more* we know, the more we *know*.

Methodological challenges for creativity research

The reason why different research methodologies are so important in obtaining greater validity is explained by Siegel (2006). He discusses *epistemological diversity* as multiple ways of knowing which enable us to better understand each other's worldviews and realities. This pluralism of epistemologies (theories on how we know what we know) and methodologies enables a progression in understanding that goes beyond tolerance and enables life-changing progress for societies and civilisations across the globe. We achieve this by questioning how we determine quality, who (or which overarching meta-perspective) determines the values behind the quality benchmarks that are accepted and how those are critiqued. This itself depends on 'who or which' (societies'/ cultures') epistemologies and ontologies we choose – and so we move in this cyclical way towards some kind of enlightenment. But it raises questions about how we circumnavigate the hierarchy of epistemologies based on the dominant 'hegemonic imposition' (Siegel, 2006, p.7) at any one time.

The hegemonic imposition refers to whose, or what type of, science is considered the most valid, reliable and useful, and usually falls back on to more traditional hierarchies, despite contemporary understanding that these do not enable us to gather the whole picture of what is going on. So, a typically traditional hierarchy of scientific disciplines might order the main sciences as follows (with some – but by no means all – disciplinary branches in brackets).

Table 4.1: A traditional hierarchy of scientific disciplines

Platinum standard	Pure/ Formal sciences	Mathematics (algebra/statistics/computer science/logic/systems theory)
Gold standard	Natural sciences	Astronomy (planetary/cosmology)
		Physics (particle/nuclear/atomic/quantum/relativistic)
		Chemistry (organic/biochemistry/materials)
		Biology (cell/ecology/neurobiology/plant & animal/evolutionary/ clinical medicine/physiology/anatomy/ethnography)
		Earth (ecology/geology/geography/climatology/meteorology/ oceanography/forestry/environmental/urban planning)
		Neuroscience (neurology/neuropsychology/genetics/epigenetics/ cognitive/educational/computational)
Silver standard	Social sciences	Psychology (behavioural/cognitive/developmental/ neuropsychology/clinical)
		Psychiatry (clinical application of psychology)
		Education (pedagogy/special educational needs)
		Sociology (law/ethics/economics/politics/economics/ anthropology/archaeology/criminology/forensics)
		Arts (art forms/creativity/arts education/cultural studies/library studies)
		Humanities (philosophy/ancient & modern languages/literature/ history/human geography)
Bronze standard	Applied sciences	Engineering (agricultural/biomedical/computer science/ electrical/civil/mechanical/robotics/software)
		Healthcare (medicine/veterinary/dentistry/midwifery/pharmacy/ epidemiology)
		Social care (social work/youth work/occupational therapy/play work/community care/special needs & disability care)

However, what is eminently clear is that any such hierarchy of scientific value or validity is neither truthful nor useful in our complex society and is what we might refer to as a 'reductionist' categorisation of reality. Social sciences, especially humanities, play a crucial role: first, in 'broadening and deepening young people's understanding of the world around them, its diversity, complexity and traditions; second, by enlarging their knowledge of what they share with other human beings, including those removed in time and culture from themselves; third, by developing a critical awareness of the society and times in which they live' (NACCCE, 1999, p.78).

What is required to explain the complexities of life on earth (and beyond) is more interdisciplinary research that blurs disciplinary boundaries, challenges the academic definitions of scientific validation, recognises unknown spaces and spotlights the subtle correlations between multiple and incomplete causes, effects and conditions. The social sciences are well positioned to overcome the illusion that co-constructing knowledge with the pure, natural and applied sciences will enable examination of the full lifecycle and possibilities of an idea, i.e. where it comes from and what it looks like in practice. However, the remaining danger is that scholarly cartographers, in 'learning how to dismantle, deconstruct and decolonize traditional ways of doing science, learning that research is always already both moral and political, learning how to let go' (Denzin *et al.*, 2006, p.770) with all good intentions, will end up designing 'new "gold standards"' for reliability and validity based on mixed methods (Denzin *et al.*, 2006, p.770). Hence the glossary at the end of this book, which outlines some of the emerging ideas around what these more equitable, post-foundational sciences might look like.

In the meantime, there are some basic principles that can be applied to ensure any kind of evaluation of creative or artistic intervention can be done well and remain accountable to ethical practices. Siegel (2006, p.8) offers a pragmatic set of benchmarks for pinning down methodological quality, asking researchers to ensure that:

- the research methods related to their epistemology are rigorous enough to produce reliable evidence.

- the evidence is sufficiently high in terms of quantity (with an adequate sample size), quality and variety to support the findings.

- subject and experimenter bias has been accounted for and counter-evidence considered.

- any explanations of the phenomena are true to the epistemology.

These benchmarks might encourage us to choose a mode of inductive reasoning that looks at the specific observations we have made, and then generalise these through an interpretivist lens.

However, this raises a dichotomy. Take the phenomenon of young children with a rare anxiety-based condition such as selective mutism, which affects around 1 per cent of the population. In these situations, a child is consistently unable to speak in unfamiliar settings due to excessive fear. This can lead to speech-avoidance behaviours and the reinforcement of non-speaking identities. And the problem is that symptoms are often not detected until a child starts school, when an acute fear of speaking and a 'fight, flight or freeze' response is triggered by the new environment, shutting down the Broca's area of the brain containing the language processing centre (Van der Kolk, 2015).

By this time, many of their beliefs about themselves as being a 'non-speaking' or 'mute' child have become embedded, often unwittingly reinforced by adults who speak for the child to save them from extreme discomfort. In arts interventions, children who cannot speak might gradually begin to talk after relatively few sessions with a trained artist focused on building their creative rather than verbal languages, looking at what they love to do and what opens up their imaginations rather than what causes them to shut down.[1]

Recent research into causes of post-traumatic stress disorder (PTSD) in children (Van der Kolk, 2015) shows that this phenomenon may have as much to do with their biological, physiological and neurological blueprint as their cultural, social and educational influences. A deductive, empirical method, therefore, would enable identification of the correlation between bio-data and this phenomenon, but would need to be combined with qualitative methods in order to seek new perspectives on the more complex, intangible influences on these children's languages of silence.

Ethical assessment methods for children's creativity

An important element of ethical research with young children rests in collapsing any *epistemic privilege* (taking on the role of expert authority) in order to achieve unity or equivalence between researcher and researched (Williams, 2016). The implications of getting this wrong are immense, as exemplified in the case of my daughter's dragon drawing. On presenting her artwork anonymously (Figure 4.1) to a multidisciplinary conference on early childhood creativity, I asked various experts to observe carefully and tell me what they could surmise about the drawer.

---

1   More information at: https://earlyarts.co.uk/blog/how-can-the-arts-help-children-who-cant-speak

Figure 4.1: Dragon drawing by Chia Dower, aged five

- The scientist talked about the naturalistic representation of three-dimensional scales on the dragon's tail.

- The engineer noticed the design symmetry of the three-toed, three-legged dragon, perfectly balanced to hold the weight of a large animal.

- The teacher commented on the consistent, bold, red strokes within the dragon's body and how well the drawer had kept within the lines.

- The dancer marvelled at the sense of movement from the fine strokes in the wings.

- The psychologist noted the anger in the dragon's eye and the passion with which it blew fire.

- The parent asked whether it was a dragon at all, perhaps a horse or a Christmas reindeer?

Just from observation, each expert generated a thesis on their view of this child's knowledge and prowess, noting precision, mastery, persistence, concentration, energy, complex ideas, movement, imagination, artistic skill and independent thinking. But not one of them had observed the child in context and could not tell how *creative* the child was, except in relation to their own perception of creativity. Most settled on an analysis of the child being a boy, aged six or above, with fascinations for flying, freedom and power, and probably with some emotional or attachment issues.

I then played a video of my five-year-old daughter drawing the animal (with her permission), talking as she drew, and revealing its (and her) story of creation. The truth of the matter surprised them, and revealed some shared understandings and marginalising prejudices about children's (and adults') creativity, as well as the glaringly obvious that all of their combined expertise could not elicit the truth about this child's creativity or potential without knowing her thoughts, her context and her human story. Even the video was not able to capture the nuances of relationship and interaction that sprang from spending time together and revealing the non-verbal, intuitive aspects of her creativity.

Yet these authorities, all working with children in some way, confirmed that much of their children's progress was measured on material products and externalised expression – mostly via written or verbal language – raising serious questions about the ethics of this institutionalised educational practice.

Feminist standpoint theorist and pragmatist Helen Longino (1990) maintained that, in order to truly recognise both the constitutive (internal) and contextual (social) values that shape it, science should be seen as a community activity, i.e. where conflicting theories and methods exist, the one with the most benefit for the community of interest should be chosen. According to Longino, a more accurate understanding can be established in two ways: the first where it reflects everyday 'issues of scientific realism', and the second in regards to 'modes of inquiry' (Longino, 1990, pp.62–63) that lead to socially valued knowledge. This is what I would call a *communitarian alternative* where 'power is relational, characterised by mutuality rather than sovereignty' (Denzin and Lincoln, 2013, p.153). This is the basis for my standpoint on relational feminism (see the Philosophy Glossary).

In practice, this means our research design needs to be grounded in a purpose that befits and benefits the children being studied, revealing something about their story that is generative and enables them to be seen, felt and heard beyond the traditional, reductive frameworks of assigned meaning. The challenge is that this is often a messy, unclear practice, welcoming both the known and unknown, resisting the need to clarify or contain, and sacrificing closure and certainty for unmeasurable, changeable, sense-based ways of knowing and being (Finlay, 2002; MacLure, 2006). It requires a level of reflexivity that questions epistemological and ideological authority and acknowledges one's own subjectivity in the processes and products of research.

While assessment methods can help to identify progress and improve the quality of teaching and learning, including in arts and cultural areas, how this is done is critical to the validity of the results which then inform any improvements made. Unfortunately, educational assessment is often reduced to limited criteria that favour factual knowledge, short-term measurable outcomes that cannot differentiate types and degrees of creativity, and observation methods that are open to teacher bias (or performative pressure). These are methods 'which at best, take little account of creative teaching and learning, and which, at worst, militate directly against them' resulting in teachers being 'unclear about the criterion to apply to children's creative work and lacking confidence in their own judgement' (NACCCE, 1999, p.122). Both teachers and children should be encouraged to take risks and trust the richness of their ideas and intuition, but the current system all but inhibits that process, resisting experimentation with new ideas or processes and resorting to conformity over creativity.

Ultimately, it seems clear that there is no one way to evaluate a child's creativity since it is always dynamic and transforming, but that a more ethical way is to acknowledge and respond to the external influences on the child that can either facilitate or obstruct such valid experiential knowledge.

The grand challenge of valuing creativity

Notwithstanding the immense work already done to classify creativity in the adult world (Runco, 2016), the attempts to define, nurture and value young children's creativity are important – shortcomings aside – because of their positive contributions to:

- neuroscience and the understanding of relationships between genetic patterns, consciousness and environmental influences

- mental health issues affecting chemical and psychological balance, anxiety, multiple identities and trauma

- child-empowering education strategies such as experiential learning, non-verbal communications, co-constructed learning, teaching-for-creativity, developmental movement play, arts education and so on

- the ongoing search for creative transcendence and aesthetic expression

- validating meaning-making within children's multiplicitous stories that 'produce and shape the meanings that circulate in everyday life' (Denzin, 1992, p.96)

- recognising young children as purposeful beings with the power to participate fully in life.

The challenge remains how to pay attention to the individual complexities and non-linear features of children's heterogeneous creative languages within a homogeneous system – one that denies the validity of such subjective expressions and requires educators to teach to the test, against the plethora of evidence on how young children learn best. This approach will inevitably reduce the experience to the least ambiguous outcomes, leaving a child's creative potential unfulfilled at best and denigrated at worst. In addition, we have to acknowledge that we cannot accurately observe and assess a young child's specific moment of experience when their sense is made over longer periods of time, as new knowledge is constructed and built on existing knowledge to create context and meaning (Craft, 2013; Duffy, 2006; Ackermann, 2001).

Then we face the seemingly almost insurmountable challenge (for educators, curriculum designers, policy makers and regulators) of embedding a constructivist, new-materialist, feminist standpoint through a generative, creative schema into a generalist, standardised 'broad and balanced' curriculum and a positivist culture of teaching and learning in such a way that the 'quality of evidence and argument can be considered independently of power and status hierarchies' (Benton and Craib, 2011, p.157).

If science is a 'rigorous attempt to represent the world as it is' (Benton and Craib, 2011, p.44), where does the identifying and valuing of creativity fit and how do we achieve this without breakdown or revolution?

Is the answer to accept the divisive conflict of political-institutional demands versus ethical, emancipatory philosophies but respond with intentional teaching that aims for an affective turn towards creative potentiality through love, embodiment and discernment? After all, not all educational systems or processes are 'bad' when designed to meet children's needs.

Is it possible to embrace a more democratic, integrated, anti-disciplinary approach that reflects the unpredictable, stratified, multi-faceted, intra-relational nature of life and our part within and outside it? One that moves away from the politically engineered, economically driven view of creativity as *the* desirable mode of everyday intelligence, towards a view of creative potential as a vital organ that is fundamental to *all* life, be it natural, social, human or non-human.

> Unlike learning theories, each epistemology attempts to describe every version of knowledge – that is, each attempts to be a complete lens – but in reality, none of them are. I believe there is an aspect of knowledge that is unknowable. In that way, I am a knowledge agnostic – I don't believe we can all know or define knowledge in any given way that will cover every corner of the box that is knowledge. There will always be room for the unknown or unknowable (Hogue, 2015).

REFLECTIVE QUESTIONS

* How often do we accept a curriculum framework or practice without question because it is 'evidence based'? Do we question if it is the whole story or just partial statistics?

* How do we create evidence bases that tell a more rounded story of who our children are and the contexts that influence their learning, not just what they are learning? What additional or alternative data-gathering methods might be useful?

* Data can never be truly objective but are we at least aware of what types of bias we bring to our own observation and assessments of children?

* Are we gathering data about children's creativity that shows the causal events (relationships and connections) and complex underlying mechanisms (conditions of possibility) as well as the actual experiences and events (what has happened)?

* Can we try to articulate the knowledge about our children or our creative practice that is held in what we can't see (but perhaps can sense or feel) as much as in what we can?

* Are we applying transparent, ethical principles to our research methodologies?

* How can we challenge ourselves to build up a more democratic, shared communal knowledge rather than reinforce the 'authority of the expert'?

Chapter 5

The Social, Educational and Political Context for Creativity

How important is creativity to society?

> Creativity is important because it enables us to respond to a rapidly changing world and to deal with the unexpected by extending our current knowledge to new situations and using information in new ways. (Duffy, 2010)

Creativity has a vital role to play in helping to transform economies. Creative skills such as innovation, imagination, ingenuity and problem-solving are the key characteristics of successful companies that gain the advantage over their competitors by recognising, investing in and celebrating these skills in their staff (NACCCE, 1999). As companies, small and large, continue to meet the relentless challenges of a global recession, the expectations for staff to work more creatively and become more effective in storytelling, relationship building, team working, diverse communications and product design and marketing are increasing.

A global benchmark study by Adobe (2012) on the state of creativity in five world countries shows that eight in ten people felt that unlocking their creativity was critical to economic growth and nearly two-thirds of respondents felt that creativity was valuable to society, yet a striking minority – only one in four people – believed they were living up to their own creative potential.

Seventy-five per cent of respondents said they were under growing pressure to be productive rather than creative, despite the fact that they were increasingly expected to think creatively on the job. More than half of those surveyed felt that creativity was being stifled by their education systems, and many believed that creativity was taken for granted (52% globally, 70% in the United States).

Many studies, including the one above and the 2010 *Future of Play* study from the LEGO Foundation (Ackermann *et al.*, 2010) also show how important spontaneity is to stimulate creativity and play, and to build deep relationships between children and adults through sharing a highly creative experience together. Yet many educators, parents and caregivers feel strongly that the education and economic systems they live and work in are increasingly stifling the opportunities for spontaneous learning and play. Early years educators report that they have to spend more and more time on assessing and averting possible risk, and on observing and assessing children's progress rather than playing with them and using their professional judgement to support progress (Bradbury *et al.*, 2018).

Yet, while necessary to help us spot the gaps in learning, assessments appear to be becoming increasingly reductive, with a disproportionate focus on literacy and numeracy at a younger and younger age, despite the plethora of expert knowledge about how young children develop in different ways during this period (Dahlberg *et al.*, 2005; Mukherji and Albon, 2018). A long-running recession, coupled with ill-fitting government policies on childcare, is forcing parents and caregivers to work longer hours and spend less time being present and spontaneous with their children.

We could mistakenly believe that the economy can only be changed for better or worse by the choices made by adults. Therefore, how will creative learning in nurseries or schools make a difference in the grand scheme of things? Well, experience shows that children have an increasingly important role to play in changing the world for the better, including the economy and the awareness of climate change. As well as developing a plethora of essential creative dispositions for life, through a wide network of school partnerships around the world, children are also connecting ideas, resources and people to develop a sense of community purpose, social coherence and economic regeneration. Using the arts, technology sciences and humanities, they are instigating projects that build creative and cultural resources in communities many thousands of miles away which 'can mitigate the economic problems of changing patterns of work while, and by, restoring confidence and community spirit through shared creative projects' (NACCCE, 1999, p.63).

Creativity as a movement for social and economic development

Research into the global relevance of creativity developed in earnest at the beginning of the 21st century across not just the arts but also education and business communities. Great pains were taken to produce research that demonstrated the 'universality' of creativity as a domain accessible to the many, not just the few (Hesmondhalgh *et al.*, 2015; Kaufmann, 2003; Runco *et al.*, 2014). The socialist arm of the New Labour government at the time was keen to eschew its democratic principles through the arts and education sectors in a bid to support the burgeoning contemporary capitalism of the creative industries and redress the claims of elitism that had been levelled at publicly funded cultural institutions over the years (Buckingham and Jones, 2001).

A seminal research project led by Sir Ken Robinson and the NACCCE heralded a renaissance in thinking which repositioned creativity at the heart of teaching and learning across the whole curriculum, as fundamental to 'the sciences…politics, business and in all areas of everyday life' as to the arts (NACCCE, 1999, p.27). Despite never being officially published by the government that had commissioned it, the NACCCE report had far-reaching effects due to its thorough analysis of the complex and changing market conditions. It demonstrated the need for a reorientation of cultural and educational practice that corporately implicated policy makers, funders, business leaders, researchers and practitioners.

The report strengthened the findings of global benchmark studies with regards to the vital role of creativity in transforming economies and societies (Adobe, 2012; World Economic Forum, 2017), unlocking personal potential (Adobe, 2012), dealing with the unexpected and adapting to a rapidly changing world (Duffy, 2006), gaining competitive advantage (Robinson, 2001) and enabling more productivity, empathy and purposefulness (Csikszentmihalyi, 1997).

The rhetoric of creativity as the linchpin for diversity, multiculturalism, democracy and emancipation in this radical rethink of education mirrored many of the progressivist ideas of Dewey (1963) and Bruner (1990) but with one vital difference – Robinson and his team broadened horizons to view the purpose of education through an economic as well as a socio-cultural lens, attempting to futureproof the interdependency of creativity to society and the economy as a whole. The report clearly identified the many creative tools available to children and educators that would lead to new forms of communication, emancipation, empowerment and economic surety.

Reminiscent of Marxism, this consciousness-raising around the oppression of cultural elitism helped to demystify the ideologies of capitalist structures. It challenged arts and education employers and funders to shake up the status quo and re-examine the material conditions that, up until now, had firmly placed creative practices within a (high-brow) *cultural entitlement* rather than a (universal) *human rights* paradigm.

However, this fuelled a more polemic, sometimes less nuanced, discourse between policy marketeers and arts education practitioners over the hierarchy of the instrumental versus intrinsic or aesthetic values of the arts and creativity (Prentice, 2000). On the one hand, the argument from the arts or cultural education standpoint focused on the major benefit of the arts in opening up what the world has to offer to children, and they to the world. Through this lens, arts and cultural opportunities are seen as a conduit to experiencing increases in confidence and wellbeing, tackling health issues, improving social interaction, cultural integration and community voice, and developing specific skills and understanding in areas such as language, literacy, maths and science. Much evidence has been gathered to show the social, cultural and economic benefits of the arts employed towards these objectives although, as discussed earlier, it is almost impossible to establish direct cause and effect.

On the other hand, practising artists and arts professionals might argue that these social intentions are 'instrumental', i.e. using the arts to achieve a 'side effect' that is not fulfilling the fundamentals of who a child is, or could be, as an artist. This reflects the position of often highly proficient artists who can appreciate the innate values and benefits of doing, making, creating and thinking artistically, developing skills, aptitudes and traits that are sometimes hard to define in terms of economic, social or cultural value, but can have deep impacts in all of these areas. This belief in our inherent artistic ability requires dedication and opportunities to experience and explore different art forms in depth before finding a niche – something not many educational settings can offer. It requires environments and relationships with living artists that can offer inspiration, opportunities to be connected to inner aesthetic traits or potential, and to be supported in developing specific technical skills that enable artistic flair to flourish.

In the 19th century, many artists and cultural thinkers advocated for *l'art pour l'art* (art for art's sake), meaning that the purpose and value of art should not come from fulfilling moral, utilitarian or instrumentalist intentions to serve other agendas, but that it should have a value-neutral position, serving an internal purpose or being externally subversive. While there is a clear justification to preserve the artistic or aesthetic integrity in any creative work (not just an artistic work), there were nevertheless several critics of this movement. Sand (1886) and Nietzsche (1990) were just two key thinkers who pointed out the dichotomy of trying to divorce art from moral or social purpose when, in fact, everyone's own purpose, or search for meaning, is inevitably etched into their own creative expression.

Various critics offered the insightful perspective that it is virtually impossible for an artist to exist outside any socio-political context, and any artistic activity that is experienced in the public sphere (including educational settings) will always have impacts and values far beyond what might have been intended by the artist. But that is not to deny the important, innate aesthetic purpose of the arts whether experienced by one or by many.

As with many arguments about the values of arts and culture, it is never a binary discussion and a more nuanced perspective is helpful when considering what works for both personal and community gain, considering a range, or continuum, of purposes and processes which may or may not be defined by personal, social or economic values. The problem comes when funding for the arts determines whose or what those values might be and limits the potential impacts for the very people it is designed to serve. And, while there is arguably a greater divide now between what is perceived as the *cultural elite* and those who do not have the opportunities to access the arts for whatever reason, I don't believe that there is such a clear ideological divide in defining the social and aesthetic values of the arts. In fact, many would agree on the urgency of their interdependence now more than ever before.

This is underlined by the numerous arts, education, health, social care and parenting networks and movements that exist to champion the work and intentions of artists in various different art forms, of all ages, across the professional and voluntary sectors and in many different settings, which serve to benefit rather than deny creative expression.

A right to arts and culture?

Policy (and regulation) can enshrine human rights in a way that makes them more likely to be applied in everyday practice. One such right is that of children (and adults) to participate in creative and cultural experiences throughout their lives. While we cannot refute the overwhelming evidence of the positive impacts of many arts and cultural activities on health, innovation, advancement and perhaps even survival, it is worth critiquing the underlying intention that this should, or even could, be implemented as a right in today's context.

Under Article 31 of the *UN Convention on the Rights of the Child*,[1] all adults and professionals have a legal responsibility for protecting and upholding the rights to cultural and creative experiences for all vulnerable people, especially those who are oppressed or prohibited from experiencing them. I wholeheartedly endorse this concept from the perspectives of care, respect, responsibility for, and stewardship of children's humanity. I also acknowledge an enormous debt to those who have fought on the battlefields of science, law, education, health, economics and politics to secure measures of justice and equality in order to shift the balance of power towards people who have been unheard and unseen.

However, the issue of people's rights has become problematic for a number of reasons. For a start, there is no way of measuring how, or how well, this responsibility is carried out, partly because there is no clear definition of creative and cultural participation, or shared understanding of quality, and partly because there is no accountability in place through which to uphold such opportunities or understanding.

Second, the rhetoric of the rights agenda has often become skewed so that 'it is my (child's) right' becomes a stick with which to beat others who may hold different views on what this entails. The rights landscape then becomes a battleground of subjective judgements, and one that encourages adults to demand fulfilment of their own child's rights to the exclusion or oppression of other children (Lawson, 2007).

---

1   See www.unicef.org/crc/files/Rights_overview.pdf

A third problem is the fact that these children's rights have to be provided or 'enforced' by another person, legally an adult, who then holds a privileged position of power to decide whether and how much access to these rights is provided, based on a whole raft of factors. Even with the very best of intentions and all the resources in the world, it is not possible to be completely objective and fair in making provision for children's rights – there are too many subjective variables involved, especially when it comes to non-tangibles such as culture and creativity. And so what started out as a set of principles on which we could build a fairer world for children becomes a tense debate around whose justice should be served, which might look very different from different cultural perspectives.

On a very practical level, the concept of rights also becomes problematic when the idea of creativity as an innate source of humanity (as I have argued here) requires experiences and opportunities for which there are inadequate (or no) resources to supply. So how do professionals and caregivers make decisions on what to fund? It is not that creative activity has to be expensive – it does not – but to champion, embed and facilitate it well in early education settings does require some longer-term investment. For example, we still need significant changes to the training and preparation of educators, environments and curricular frameworks in order for creativity to be valued and practised as a fundamental human right. In that sense, all of the rights expressed in the UN Convention are fundamental to being human, and it would be extremely difficult, and somewhat immoral, to rank the right to participate in arts and cultural activities over any another right to basic life-giving provision such as food, clean water, warmth and protection from harm when choices have to be made. As Lawson expresses so well:

> Attention to care ethics, rather than simply continuing our focus on justice, prompts us to extend our work beyond the theoretically and politically important notions of justice as a universal right… Care ethics is concerned with structuring relationships in ways that enhance mutuality and wellbeing. Care ethics also demands attention to emotions and affective relations (of love, concern, and connection) because of the complex ways in which power is embedded within them. (Lawson, 2007, p.3)

Access to arts and cultural opportunities has been significantly influenced by how the wheels of the agricultural, then industrial, then knowledge-based economies have turned. Perhaps, in future, this will be influenced by an emergence of networked creative economies, and I envisage that we may see a re-emergence of aesthetic valuing in society and a different sort of framework of cooperation, care, stewardship and responsibility that recognises creativity as part of our intrinsic human nature.

The politics of the early years and arts landscapes

The early years sector is a complex landscape and one that is extremely challenging for external agencies such as arts and cultural organisations to navigate. The reasons for this lie in some of the political and economic challenges and realities affecting the workforces in both sectors, which are broadly represented by two governing paradigms based on whether they are supply-/funder-driven or demand-/market-led (or, in the case of social enterprises such as the London Early Years Foundation (LEYF), a combination of the two[2]).

This shapes their entire existence from the type of business model and pricing structures employed, the scope of their relationships with customers (parents and caregivers) and partner agencies (such as speech and language professionals or local authority advisers) and the quality and content of their provision for young children, to their funding infrastructure, marketing, recruitment, training, professional development, outward vision and staff culture.

In the arts and cultural sector (focusing on organisations with an early years offer), there is a predominance of supply-driven, small-scale organisations that are largely dependent on grant funding to create and provide their supply of products and services, both to early years settings and also to families. According to the Department for Digital, Culture, Media & Sport (2018), approximately 88 per cent are micro-businesses with a turnover of less than £250,000 a year. These include theatres, art galleries, music companies, dance organisations, libraries, museums, arts centres and art-form national networks. Some are venue based, mostly delivering early years programmes for families as part of a broader arts education or outreach programme and some training events for professionals. Others are venues dedicated to children and young people with a specific arts remit. Others still are non-venue-based companies or artists who create and tour productions of dance, theatre, music, visual arts or mixed art forms to schools, nurseries, arts or cultural centres and even village halls.

However, whatever the shape or size of organisation, the best-fit business model is often not a straightforward one. Many organisations are increasingly reliant on mixed-economy models in order to subsidise the less economically viable, but no less effective, programmes. Grant aid is designed to bridge the gap between the actual cost of an entry ticket to a theatre performance, art

---

2   See www.leyf.org.uk/life-can-be-perfect-so-raise-a-glass-of-bollinger-to-a-world-of-social-enterprises

gallery, music event or museum open day and what the public is prepared to pay (which is often very little, especially in museums and libraries). However, grant aid rarely covers this gap so most organisations have to diversify their income streams to offer a combination of more profitable products. So, as well as providing the core programme or cultural offer plus an education and families programme (required to fulfil their public funding obligations), their other income streams might include training, consultancy, renting out useful spaces or resources, selling advertising in their own publications, events, festivals, webinars, publishing, merchandise and so on. A simplified version of their business models can look something like this (see Figure 5.1).

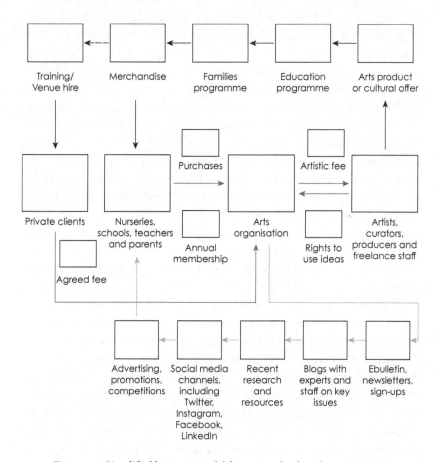

Figure 5.1: Simplified business model for arts and cultural organisations

It is not hard to appreciate the diversity of skills and connections arts and cultural organisations need to have in place in order simply to be able to provide a valuable core offer or product due to the fact that it usually costs much more than the public can pay. It often requires some expert tightrope walking by staff in order to stay focused on the values of the main offer and make that work financially without being too distracted by alternative income streams that may only be sugarcoated but actually require more investment than the organisation can offer.

The main exception to this is in more autonomous sub-sectors such as music and movement where a plethora of independent trainers, instructors and small, commercial franchises exist to provide regular classes, mainly to families, primarily without grant aid. Independent providers are often not venue based, but hire suitable premises for their classes. Although these providers may be considered more in the demand-led category, it does not always follow that their intentions are entirely focused on profitability. Indeed, the core driver for many independent arts providers is not just to make a living but also to build relationships with their clients for the purposes of offering purposeful, life-enhancing opportunities through their art form.

There is, nevertheless, a distinction between supply-driven or demand-led organisations and it often comes down to whether or not organisations anchor their provision within a pedagogical paradigm, influenced largely by early childhood development theories (aka social providers), or not (aka commercial providers). Social providers choose what and how to deliver more bespoke services or products on the basis of what they believe will support children's interests, often prioritising this above rapid business growth, sometimes at a personal cost. Commercial providers are more likely to be driven or influenced by market expectations, providing a typical programme or class within a certain price range that the market will pay.

There is, of course, space for both sorts of providers – and a whole range in between – and many will enjoy a freedom from the regulatory control, pedagogical assessments, audit procedures and staff or brand management that formal early years providers are subject to. While traditionally the arts and cultural sector has relied on its subject specialism training for validation of professional qualifications and status, recently more early years specific professional qualifications have been launched, such as the postgraduate courses in creativity and the arts in early childhood and early years music education at the Centre for Research in Early Childhood in Birmingham. There are also a number of creative learning or arts education postgraduate courses available, such as the Creative Arts in Education MA at Exeter University, which can incorporate early years interests.

In addition to venue-based organisations or producing artists and companies in existence, it is also worth highlighting the many excellent art-form projects, events, conferences, festivals and webinars that explore the development of early years creative practice in more depth, and enable both caregivers and professionals to experience creative play and pedagogical opportunities for themselves. These include children's theatre festivals, music festivals, national umbrella and campaigning organisations, libraries and museums networks, dance networks and visual arts programmes, alongside various practical resources.[3]

In a national survey undertaken for Arts Council England (Churchill Dower and Sandbrook, 2018), participants were asked to indicate the significance to their setting of various priorities. Top priorities included 'speech and language development', 'outdoor learning' and 'play-based learning', with 'nurturing creativity, arts and culture' coming behind these, alongside 'mental health and wellbeing' and 'family engagement' as a medium priority for around 70 per cent of group settings and 60 per cent childminders (the authors note that these survey respondents are likely to be more interested in arts and culture than the national average, plus there was a strong correlation between settings who rated 'nurturing creativity, arts and culture' as a higher priority and were rated 'outstanding' by Ofsted). The findings from these settings are boosted by the provision in the thousands of Froebelian, Montessori and Waldorf Steiner settings, all of which have a strong commitment to an integrated curriculum of arts, science and humanities, as do many independent settings.

In the early years sector, one of the complexities of the industry stems from the plethora of different business models, organisations and structures that

3   Many of these resources can be found at https://earlyarts.co.uk/index-resources

have grown up in response to demand for early childcare or education. These can be broadly categorised in four groups:

1. Group-based providers (identified from the Ofsted register): childcare providers including full day and sessional care for children below school age in non-domestic settings (mostly private or independent), and wraparound care for children under the age of 8.

2. School-based providers (identified from the School Census): reception provision, nursery provision in schools (including maintained and independent nursery schools), children's centres and wraparound care for children under the age of 8.

3. Childminders (identified from the Ofsted register): single or small-group childminders providing early years care and operating in domestic settings, not including those registered with an agency.

4. Voluntary, non-profit preschools, playgroups, stay-and-plays and toddler groups in halls, community centres, churches and other buildings.

The Department for Education's latest biennial Survey of Childcare and Early Years Providers, England (Department for Education, 2018) estimates there are:

- 23,600 group-based providers (down by 7.5% on 2016 – see Department for Education, 2016)

- 16,900 school-based providers (down by 6% on 2016)

- 40,900 practising childminders (significantly down by 12.5% on 2016)

- a total of 430,500 employed in the early education and childcare workforce (down by 5% overall on 2016).

Due to the historical lack of state investment in early education (International Development Committee, 2017)[4] the majority of children are in private care until they are four, unlike schooling in the UK for 5–18-year-olds. In fact, 70 per cent of early education and care operates within a commercial infrastructure driven by the privately owned nursery industry (LaingBuisson, 2017). One could argue that this infrastructure perpetuates

---

4   Also see www.theguardian.com/global-development/2018/apr/11/aid-early-years-education-opportunity-sarah-brown and www.cam.ac.uk/news/uk-should-invest-in-global-education-to-improve-lives-says-report-citing-cambridge-research

the exploitation of the early education workforce with poor pay and conditions and reduces the possibilities for staff to build a creative culture for themselves. The Department for Education reported that 'just over one-tenth (11%) of group-based nursery staff aged 25 and over received hourly pay below the National Living Wage, compared with 5% of school-based nursery staff aged 25 and over and 5% of reception staff' (Department for Education, 2018, 2016, p.9).

When we consider that there are 4.9 million 0–5-year-olds, which is 7.3 per cent of all UK citizens, of whom 17 per cent are in formal nursery education (equating to 833,000 children), it becomes clear that private nurseries not only contribute significantly to local economies, but also make a significant social and educational contribution in many children's and families' lives. They are a vital part of the jigsaw which complements state run nurseries, preschools, children's centres, portage and community health or social care services (see the Appendix for a map of provision in both public and private sectors).

Whereas historically children under five might stay at home with their parents (the large majority being mothers), the Labour government during its most recent term in office (1997–2010) increasingly focused on supporting mothers to go back to work by offering families more opportunities for flexible working arrangements around childcare. This satisfied their two-fold desire to boost the economy and secure more votes from a previously under-represented group (mothers). The party seized the opportunity to 'tackle the division and inequality in society'[5] by responding to the growing calls for parity of esteem, choice and income with working fathers, although this complex issue was never very comprehensively addressed.

The increase in returns-to-work triggered an increase in demand for childcare and so Labour invested in significant early years reform. Their burgeoning portfolio included:

- free part-time nursery places for every four-year-old (1997)

- the first National Childcare Strategy to provide good quality, affordable childcare (1998)

- Working Families Tax Credit (WFTC) and Childcare Tax Credit (CTC) (1999)

---

5   More details on Labour's decade of reform in relation to the early years can be found at www.nurseryworld.co.uk/nursery-world/news/1078531/labours-decade-reform-1997-2007

- introduction of the Foundation Stage Curriculum (2000)

- £300m for Neighbourhood Nurseries and Early Excellence Centres (2000–2004, re-branded Sure Start in 2003)

- expansion of Ofsted to include childcare (2001)

- replacement of baseline assessment with the Foundation Stage Profile and the introduction of a Birth to Three Matters framework (2002)

- establishment of the first ever Minister for Children and the Foundation Stage Unit (2003)

- free part-time nursery places for every three-year-old (2004)

- unveiling of a ten-year childcare strategy, promising 3500 children's centres by 2010 (2004)

- a new Ofsted inspection regime for nurseries and pre-schools (2005)

- a Children's Workforce Strategy, including early years professionals designed to lead all children's centres and day care settings by 2015 (2006)

- the passing into law of the Childcare Act, requiring local authorities to improve the five Every Child Matters outcomes for all preschool children and reduce inequalities (2006)

- launch of the Early Years Foundation Stage and one million children able to access one of the 1250 children's centres now open (2007)

Demand continued to be driven by the increase in numbers of working mothers (70% of whom had children under 4 in 2017), but the motivations for childcare became more complex than simply the opportunity for mothers to earn an income. In fact, LaingBuisson's report (2017) suggests that parents and caregivers have increasingly recognised the positive role that receiving high-quality education during early years has on child development.

However, where state provision does not exist, it is not independent (commercial) childcare provision that many families are turning to now. The Office for National Statistics (ONS) shows that, in fact, it is grandparents who provide the bulk of childcare for under 4s (Table 5.1) representing 65 per cent of the 1.9 million informal carers according to the Department for Education (2018), which is testament to the unfeasible financial burden of private childcare for many families today.

Table 5.1: National estimates of use of childcare
(percentage increase or decrease on 2017 figures)

Use of childcare	Number of families	Number of children
Any childcare	4,197,000 (-4.4%)	5,985,000 (-5.1% decrease)
Formal providers	**3,457,000 (-5.9%)**	**4,755,000 (-6.0% decrease)**
Nursery school	450,000 (+56.8%)	488,000 (+55.9% increase)
Nursery class in primary or infant school	239,000 (-6.6%)	248,000 (-11.7%)
Day nursery	475,000 (-15.8%)	520,000 (-15.9%)
Playgroup or preschool	160,000 (-38.2%)	167,000 (-41%)
Breakfast club or activity	492,000 (+2.4%)	559,000 (+6.3%)
After-school club or activity	1,808,000 (-13.5%)	2,387,000 (-12.1%)
Childminder	292,000 (-6.5%)	386,000 (-0.5%)
Informal providers	**1,924,000 (-4.1%)**	**2,545,000 (-2.1%)**
Ex-partner	241,000 (-4.7%)	328,000 (-2.1%)
Grandparent	1,244,000 (-5.0%)	1,646,000 (-6.2%)
Older sibling	236,000 (-6.3%)	245,000 (+5.2%)
Another relative	258,000 (-3.3%)	300,000 (-0.7%)
Friend or neighbour	297,000 (+10%)	347,000 (-9.8%)

(Department for Education, 2018)
Note: all figures are rounded to the nearest 1000.

Ironically, despite this, the private sector is currently growing faster than the economy at 2.7 per cent, mainly due to the consolidation of nursery provision among larger corporate providers. The top two 'super groups', Busy Bees and Bright Horizons, provide 54,000 of the 1.1 million available childcare places in England alone, and the next 23 mid- to small-sized groups provide 105,000 places between them (LaingBuisson, 2017). In fact, the growth of the sector has attracted investors from North America, Asia and Europe, with the number two group in France (Les Petits Chaperons Rouges) now ranked number seven in the UK.

A side effect of this is that smaller providers are struggling to maintain occupancy rates at 71 per cent, which is considered the standard level for a childcare business to remain sustainable. Operational and utilities costs are rising, the level of subsidy offered through the government's two-, three- and four-year-old funding schemes does not always cover actual costs, and local authority training and business support continues to decline due to cuts in public services. In addition, the recession has inevitably taken its toll – 39 per cent of nurseries said levels of parental debt had increased or increased significantly since 2015 and the 5 per cent overall decrease in numbers of providers (childminders being the hardest hit) since 2016 shows how unsustainable the current government policies on early years funding are for small businesses (LaingBuisson, 2017).

Early years businesses require a complex, mixed-economy model and many private nursery owners would quote the government's free entitlement funding and voucher schemes as the source of their financial oppression, which are lower than market value and do not cover the actual cost of providing places for children (An and Bonetti, 2017). This is set within an increasingly austere climate encouraging a more pragmatist poverty of aspiration within families, where economic survival takes precedent over any cultural ambition.

The result? A tick-box culture driven by economics and politics which simply does not recognise the relevance of personal or social identities to economic development (Benton and Craib, 2011). A child's value is represented only by numbers in terms of income, places, funding attracted, educational outcomes and so on. The extrinsic motivators to work in this environment are impersonal, anti-social and often not all that attractive, and the pressure on staff to meet these outcomes leaves little room for intuition, joy in the unexpected and creativity. Of course, many settings work hard to create sociable cultures and enjoyable working environments as with any industry, but the pressures on staff in early childhood care mean that the professional judgement of educators is rendered virtually powerless to support children's creative potential.

Educators will recognise that how their children are *naturally* often does not match the dominant targets of the *ideal* child that somehow they are expected to achieve to keep their setting's ratings high. Once there might have been more long-term professional development, capacity building and support from the various authorities to meet expectations of regulatory conformity, educational complexity and profitable businesses. But in times of austerity, early years educators are left with little air in their armbands with which to swim across this ever-widening channel. This creates a dichotomy. As McArdle asserts:

> One of the consequences of the transference of this 'time means money' business model to education and young children is that, seeing children just 'playing' or still doing paintings has come to be read as a 'waste of time', when they presumably could be more productively engaged. (McArdle, 2016, p.9)

How do you go about trying to post the round peg of subjective, multimodal, ambiguous, emergent creative practice (i.e. how children are naturally) into the square hole of state-controlled, target driven, reductionist, language-based assessment regimes? Uniformity, standardisation, best fit and maximising profit have become the sector's guiding lights and, with major financial cuts over the last decade closing many arts organisations which previously supported early educators, the divide between the professional arts and education sectors is wider now than ever before. So, when national expectations to perform far outweigh the pay, conditions and the professional support on offer, not to mention the misfit of outcomes-based education with the ways in which young children learn, and the early years educator is not required to think outside the box, then why would they?

Yet, despite the obstacles in this environment, many educators are hugely committed to providing the best start for their children, meeting their needs and supporting their interests as much as is within their gift to do so, for the simple reason of having an ethics of care for the child and their development (Lawson, 2007). The loving relationships that grow between children and adults cannot be valued economically, and yet relationships are often the key factor that provides the intrinsic motivation for many early educators. This is why it is so important to position the nurturing of creativity within those relationships, articulating mutual affection, care, connection and expression. Early childhood scholar Jools Page explains that this drives more effective practice since:

> babies and young children need caregivers who will 'listen' and who are able to 'tune into' them in a multitude of ways. This is not because these adults are paid to caregive but because they are compelled to respond with care and eventually with love that is formed over time within the context of closely attached relationships. (Page, 2018, p.131)

Arts and cultural organisations working in the early years sector

Underpinning the private early childhood industry is a heavily commercialised structure that does not provide an easy fit for public-funded, non-commercial organisations providing their educational products or services. When essentially social services such as childcare are privatised, this shift 'places control over crucial resources in private hands, with sobering implications for social justice and gender divisions of labour while bolstering market fundamentalism. These sorts of extensions of market relations have made it harder to raise care questions in many settings' (Lawson, 2007, p.2) and also creates huge barriers for other socially based organisations to provide integrated or targeted services.

Unfortunately, many creative and cultural organisations trying to build and sustain economic success in the early education market have been forced away from creating bespoke products or services where they are in control of the price points, quality and aesthetic values. Instead, many are driven towards scalable, mass-marketable products that can be sold through a third-party contractor with direct market access and general business skills but little specialist content knowledge or understanding of why an arts product or service is beneficial. In this situation, cultural organisations are dependent on the contractor's production values, marketing channels and reputation within the sector.

Many are small-scale arts organisations or freelances who often have to make their products attractive to a broader market by reducing customisability and creativity, while giving a significant percentage of profits to the contractor and having to navigate the wide variations in contracting systems. These might include local authorities, private nursery groups, clinical commissioning groups (formerly primary care trusts), schools, training agencies or educational publishers. Of course, some arts and cultural suppliers would rightly argue that this level of compromise is acceptable in order to sustain their business. It is justifiable on the basis of not having to build extensive market access themselves (Benton and Craib, 2011), nor having to operate in direct competition with the larger contractors who will always be able to find greater economies of scale. And with an unprecedented shortage of any public funding available for small-scale cultural business development, few organisations are still able to retain their independence, achieve targeted purposing and a high quality of their products at the cost of losing market and economic positioning (see the Appendix for a map of provision in both public and private sectors). It is currently one of the most complex and challenging economic landscapes for values-based arts and cultural businesses to survive within.

Arts, culture and creativity in the Early Years Foundation Stage curriculum

It is mandatory for every early education provider in England to implement the statutory Early Years Foundation Stage (EYFS) framework (Department for Education, 2012) to enhance the learning and development of 0–5-year-olds. Many other education departments in governments around the world (especially in the Middle East and Far East) are also now working to this framework. In England, settings are also obliged to receive inspections from the regulatory body, Ofsted, to ensure that the EYFS is being implemented correctly and that the highest quality of leadership and management, education, behavioural attitudes and personal welfare outcomes are being achieved. However, as we have seen, quality can be interpreted in many different ways when it comes to arts skills and creative capabilities.

Taking the previous definitions on board, it is fairly clear that creativity is present in the descriptions of all the three *characteristics of effective learning* for young children and this can be extended through practice in all areas of learning, and in all areas of the setting:

- play and exploring – engagement

- active learning – motivation

- creating and thinking critically – thinking.

It is worth noting the subtle semantic shift from process to product – in the first edition of the Early Years Foundation Stage curriculum in 2008, the overarching *Themes for Learning and Development* included *'creativity and critical thinking'*, with creativity expressed as a process-oriented adjective. This was revised in 2012, now under *Characteristics of Effective Learning*, to a product-oriented verb, *'creating and thinking critically'*, giving educators the subtle message that being creative should be understood (and assessed) as making and doing 'things'.

The revised EYFS also appears to endorse creative practice across the three *prime* and four *specific* Areas of Learning, of which one is Expressive Arts and Design (EAD), although this is limited to the following two areas of exploration:

Exploring and using media and materials

Optimum Early Learning Goal for a four-year-old: Children sing songs, make music and dance, and experiment with ways of changing them. They safely use and explore a variety of materials, tools and techniques, experimenting with colour, design, texture, form and function.

Being imaginative

Optimum Early Learning Goal for a four-year-old: Children use what they have learnt about media and materials in original ways, thinking about uses and purposes. They represent their own ideas, thoughts and feelings through design and technology, art, music, dance, role play and stories.

The EYFS is purposefully designed not to include detailed instructions for practitioners on what to do to achieve these goals, just on what an ideal child's behaviour might look like once the goal is achieved (based on developmental theory, deconstructed in Chapter 2). This is laudable in terms of trusting in educators' professional judgement to respond to a child's interests. But, even so, there is a distinct lack of support for educators to understand why these areas are important and therefore how they can support and develop further beyond these initial expectations of each child to perform to a certain target. It reflects a political move towards more structured, formalised teaching that imparts a set of basic skills (know-how) and knowledge (know-what) that are considered crucial for young children to attain, but without the know-why to grow a 'life-wide resourcefulness that enables the individual to successfully chart a course of action by seeing opportunities as well as overcoming obstacles' (Craft, 2002, p.44).

It seems clear that Ofsted intends for creative processes to help children achieve many of the Early Learning Goal descriptors. In a recent edition of *Nursery World* (21.01.19),[6] Ofsted Early Education Deputy Director Gill Jones emphasised that the quality of education would be judged on processes that reflect many of the ideas within this book in supporting children's creativity, including how well staff:

- watch, listen and respond to children

- read aloud and tell stories to children

6   See www.nurseryworld.co.uk/nursery-world/opinion/1166696/ofsted-we-want-to-hear-from-you

- support children to recognise and respond to their own physical needs

- enable children to explore and solve problems

- support children to express their thoughts and use new words.

What's missing is the detail of those creative processes, aptitudes, environments and principles (*not* activities) that might help advance practice. Early educators are encouraged to use the non-statutory guidance, *Development Matters* (Early Education, 2012), to inform their knowledge and understanding of what progress looks like in each area of learning and development. The guidance offered in the area of Expressive Arts and Design is specific to the technical skills children might acquire in this area rather than how to nurture and apply their broader creative faculties across all areas of learning, or how to observe children's creativity or creative potential.

Research suggests that, where creative approaches to teaching and learning are being used extensively, there is often a passionate leader or teacher in the setting who already subscribes to the benefits of creative practice for themselves, their staff and their children. Often, they already have experienced the agency or power of a child's creativity in helping them develop ideas and achievements, and are keen for these approaches to be available and practised more holistically throughout the setting.

Author and former director of the Thomas Coram Children's Centre Bernadette Duffy explains how they focus on the embedding of creative teaching and learning 'right across the curriculum' as 'all areas of learning have the potential to be creative experiences' (Duffy, 2010, p.21). As a result, 90 per cent of the cohort of children who left in 2009 reached or exceeded expectations for their age, although 'only 56 per cent reached expectations for their age at entry to the centre' (Duffy, 2010, p.26).

Similarly, American anthropologist Shirley Brice Heath highlights the impacts of employing an artist at the Hythe Community School during a year-long drawing intervention. The headteacher reported, 'Our maths scores are quite good but we don't teach it in a way that is that different from most other schools. Then it hit me that perhaps the reason our children did so well in the SATs was that they had, through this creative curriculum, had lots of experience of real-life problem-solving' (Heath and Wolf, 2005, p.44). Brice Heath continues:

> What the children did in their art brought them into contact with underlying concepts in mathematics and science and enabled them to have the confidence to know how to work their way through calculations...comparing sizes, measuring, and figuring differences. In addition, through their increased attention to drawing, they had garnered the stamina necessary to stay the testing course. (Heath and Wolf, 2005, p.45)

Surprisingly, the word 'creative' is not mentioned at all in the entire statutory EYFS curriculum (2012) and is only mentioned four times in the EYFS guidance material, *Development Matters* (Early Education, 2012) – two referring to the creative process and two referring to creative thinking and problem-solving. So it is perhaps less surprising that the terminology around creativity is not used a great deal in early years settings due to the lack of familiarity in practice or clarity around its meaning.

This is further exacerbated by the dearth of arts-based teaching materials (compared with other subjects), reflecting the general lack of arts and design expertise in early education and the fact that it has never been fully prioritised and included in teacher or practitioner training. With notable exceptions,[7] EAD materials that are available tend to be oriented around practical activities with little attention to the deeper pedagogical underpinning or how the arts can create opportunities for deeper-level learning across the whole curriculum.

This idea of the transferability of arts skills across other areas of learning is picked up again in Chapters 10 and 11 on creative approaches and creative pedagogies, but there is no doubt this is not easy to implement without significant investment in arts training for educators. From the original Curriculum Guidance for Foundation Stage (2000) and the Birth to Three Matters framework (2004), both of which informed the design of the first EYFS (2008), up to the change in government in 2010, there were a number of opportunities for arts and creative training courses

7   See https://earlyarts.co.uk/creative-toolkits

through the regional Pathfinder Hubs (which ran from 2003 to 2012) of the national network Earlyarts, through local authority and childminder network meetings, through individual arts and cultural organisations providing training for educators and through the small number of early years programmes run under the government funded Creative Partnerships scheme (2002–2010).

Since this time, mass funding cuts to arts and early years programmes have meant that training opportunities are few and far between. They are mainly provided by individual arts and cultural organisations which have secured funding under their early years remit, and have strong relationships with their local community to secure take-up, but this happens on a very localised, sporadic basis. In addition, a small number of arts authors and trainers provide courses through national networks such as Early Education, but very few settings can afford to buy in longer-term training or support to develop the skills and expertise required in this area.

As I said in the introduction, I firmly believe that making a significant impact on raising confident and competent children requires a sea-change in the way we support the professionals who teach or care for them. It is not just about running activities or modelling behaviours that might lead to imaginative outcomes (although this can help), as children already have the capacity for these in their minds and bodies. It is about professionals developing an understanding of, and confidence in, their own creative potential, being able to confidently find the starting points for the processes and environments for a positive, engaging and limitless creativity which comes from the core of who children are and grows through their reciprocal relationships with caregivers.

Creative play in childhood has been shown to be a strong determiner of adult creativity as it provides children with opportunities to practise using fantasy and symbolism (Runco, 2016) among others. But even if professionals do not believe in the power of creativity in their own life, research and experience shows that creative learning environments enable parents and professionals to build a better sense of purpose and motivation, as well as aspirations to raise their own levels of economic and educational standing (Cultural Learning Alliance, 2012).

> In our view a prerequisite for effective lifelong learning is sustained motivation towards self-improvement. This motivation is at its most powerful when it involves both love of learning and the desire for personal growth, realising the potential of the individual in some form of creative activity. (NACCCE, 1999, p.108)

I would go so far as to echo eminent social anthropologist and ethno-musicologist John Blacking's assertion that musical activities (for instance) are essential for a balanced personality and for community growth, reflecting 'patterns of human relationships' since 'the value of a piece of music as music is inseparable from its value as an expression of human experience' (in Malloch and Trevarthen, 2018, p.2).

Nevertheless, since the NACCCE report was published in the early days of the former Labour government, policy makers have incorporated the ideological, *integrational* concept of creativity into the design of curricular and assessment frameworks as an implicit social (rather than educational) goal, i.e. it's a nice thing for everyone to have access to but not essential enough to teach properly. Successive governments have positioned creative thinking, doing, teaching and learning under the overarching banner of 'creative and critical thinking', rather than as a specific set of practices or processes. As such, what 'high-quality' creative practice looks like has never been clearly delineated (beyond basic arts subject skills), although many arts education organisations and researchers have attempted to pin these down (Runco *et al.*, 2014). The vagueness of such an ideal has led to much confusion over the concept of creativity, what it looks like in practice, how it can be accounted for and what (or whose) different standards of quality should be used to measure its progress (Benton and Craib, 2011).

Furthermore, the recent primary and secondary curriculum changes, the exclusion of arts subjects from the E-Baccalaureate and therefore many universities (Cultural Learning Alliance, 2018) and the focus on empirical testing mechanisms as opposed to cumulative modular assessments have left creativity in an educational vacuum.

Although socially and culturally well intentioned, and notwithstanding the many educational settings which have the training, skills and understanding to embrace the arts and creativity to high standards, I would propose that two decades of ideological thinking about children's creativity has been embedded at the expense of a deeper cultural focus or even a recognition of its origins in the aesthetic or imaginative domains (Brėdikytė, 2011).

There is little doubt that creativity as a state of mind or practice is accessible by anyone; research shows that very many people have creative capacities from birth and, what they do not find naturally or easily can be learned (Treffinger *et al.*, 2002; Runco *et al.*, 2014). This is why creativity is often emphasised as a 'universal capability' (often referred to as '*little c creativity*'), in order to rescue the concept from being seen as the preserve of famous artists or geniuses alone (often referred to as '*big C creativity*') (Craft, 2002). But in some ways, the discourse has become synonymous with more popularist, adult-oriented definitions such as 'safe' risk-taking, emotional intelligence or resilience, which could describe many states and are only loosely related to the original theories of creativity.

It is not that artists hold a monopoly on creativity, which is clearly an important faculty in every field or industry (Runco, 2003), but that this fundamental channel for artistic and cultural identities to be explored and expressed seems to have been forgotten in the race for academic and economic supremacy. In other words, I believe that the empirical research into creativity over the years has created a false binary concept portraying two types of creatives: those who are artistically or creatively gifted – *big C* creatives, which is out of the reach of most people, and those who have 'everyday' levels of creativity – *little c* creatives (Richards, 2007; Runco, 2016), otherwise known as the distinction between creative *achievement* and creative *potential*.

This is what most educational and cultural policies are now geared towards, creating a dangerous precedent of homogenising (making uniform) and over-simplifying the intrinsic human capacity for creativity and devaluing the range and heterogeneity (diversity) of creative behaviours possible in contemporary society. I am a strong advocate of an approach based on accessibility insofar as finding ways to facilitate everyone's creative experiences, opportunities and imaginative capacities, and there's no doubt about the beneficial investment in culture and arts education made during the golden years of the Labour administration prior to the severe austerity measures that started in 2010. But the short-term nature of that investment did not leave enough time for the rewards of that work to be reaped, or for creative cultures to become embedded in curricular practice. With the onset of the recession, those last-in changes were also first-out, the arts once again were portrayed throughout policy as a non-essential factor in the health, care and education of millions of children.

As a result of this political de-prioritisation, lack of arts training and lack of embedding in the curriculum or assessment frameworks, the vast majority of educators without an arts background are left with a simple, basic understanding of the arts as a set of technical skills and low-level activities. As eloquently expressed by early childhood play consultant Janet Moyles over a decade ago, 'Practitioners need to regain their artistry in teaching, for in the past decade or so this has increasingly taken a back seat to conformity and a technical construction of teaching and schooling' (in Craft, 2002, p.viii).

I cannot help but wonder, did this political turn to 'universalise' creativity inadvertently turn back on itself, reducing creativity to an everyday event and replacing imagination specialists with cultural generalists?

Perhaps there is an alternative approach to curricular design. I believe that creativity exists on a continuum which takes into account 'degrees of creativity' (Kaufmann, 2003, p.239), the journey through which is anything but linear and may change radically from one day to the next (Runco, 2016). This creative continuum theory allows for a more nuanced understanding of the possibilities that our creative characteristics might encompass, including (and prioritising) imaginative play, spontaneity and intrinsic motivation (e.g. following children's lines of enquiry or creative expression). I propose this is a better model for creative as well as artistic opportunity in the early years curriculum as it can be represented in many forms and languages, integrates well with most other subjects and can be observed and assessed reliably using both qualitative and quantitative methodologies.

REFLECTIVE QUESTIONS

* How much creativity is involved in your day-to-day life – how many times each day do you need to think, act or communicate creatively (outside the box) in order to achieve something? Keep a note of these times just for one week – it might surprise you!

* How can you help parents and carers understand the importance of their children's creativity not just for their being and learning now but for their future security?

* How could we move from a fixed focus on implementing rights (that may or may not be equal) towards an ethics of care, responsibility, stewardship and relationship for the creative humanity of our adults and children, wherever they are at?

* If you are an arts or cultural provider, how could you share the creative ways you use to survive with other small arts businesses, to strengthen the range of values-led approaches?

* What business models or partnerships are working well across different scales, economies, sectors and supply-driven or demand-led providers? How could funders encourage these?

* Is there a third way that enables the social, health and educational benefits of the arts to be equally valued with the innate, aesthetic experiences of artistic training? Can we bring artists and educators together in partnerships that are mutually purposeful and beneficial?

* How can you embed a creative continuum that raises the status of the arts and meets different needs in diverse ways in your setting? (Clue – read Chapter 9 onwards!)

Chapter 6

Testing for Creative Traits

The evolution of identifying creative traits

Natural scientists will often talk about the need for empirical evidence which confirms a truth beyond doubt about any specific hypothesis on creativity. For instance, Darwin's half-cousin Francis Galton (1822–1911) believed 'genius' (the 19th-century definition of creativity) to be a biological trait arising through one's genetic heritage, so he would conduct quantitative intelligence quotient (IQ) tests on his research participants to gather 'irrefutable' data on his hypothesis. Galton[1] designed one of the first psychometric tests to assess IQ criteria as a way of building logical and categorical evidence as to the level of zeal (passion or motivation), adaptation (problem-solving), sensory functioning and diversity (divergent thinking) in the minds of gifted people.

However, as we have discussed previously, while these traits might be considered some measure of creativity, we need to bear in mind that 'the complex and multidimensional nature of creativity cannot be captured

---

1   Galton, as it turns out, lived the latter part of his life and died (17 January 1911) in my aunt's house in Surrey.

effectively and comprehensively by any single instrument or analytical procedure' and requires the studying of 'both quantitative and qualitative data' (Treffinger *et al.*, 2002, p.xi), which was not the method of the early creativity theorists.

These traits can also be identified as measures of other faculties, such as intelligence which, it could be argued, could be achieved without an ounce of creative thinking! In fact, several eminent psychologists now regard creativity and intelligence as virtually independent processes, the former being more associated with novelty and originality (for the person being creative, at least) and the latter being defined by analytical reasoning (Kaufmann, 2003).

Nevertheless, empirical, quantitative testing gave Galton the chance to study the development of creative productivity over a lifecycle, giving rise to its predictability and probability for people displaying certain dispositions. Many scientists, psychologists and educationalists were influenced by his work but, ultimately, the net result of all studies into hereditary genius was that there was no correlation between creative dispositions (or abilities, as they saw it) and eminent achievement.

Galton's greatest contribution to creativity research was in the study of human differences, which led to eugenics studies in an attempt to scientifically (and literally) *breed* talent into future generations by selecting eminent families to reproduce, and minimise uncertainty in natural selection in Britain (Sternberg, 1999). However, in later developments of his research, it became clear that creativity was not the preserve of the higher classes but possible across all populations.

Eminent clinician and psychologist Catharine Cox (1890–1984) extended Galton's theories across much larger sample sizes and examined exhaustive biographical data of the subjects, to discover that creativity emanated from a complex correlation of several traits, not just a few. These included persistence, intrinsic motivation and autonomy, all of which are still considered valid to this day (Sternberg, 1999). She also found that creativity was not exclusively linked to high IQ, nor to a specific behavioural type, nor did it emanate from the unconscious, nor exist for a single purpose of productivity, as had been previously thought. Most importantly, Cox discovered that creativity played an important role in building personal identities and conscious abilities to adapt, i.e. creative abilities could be learned. Since then, many bodies of research have highlighted that, for all the differences of those considered highly creative in the world, the most influential factors were not IQ but developmental and family differences (Sternberg, 1999).

And so these discoveries have moved us closer to the need for more qualitative, descriptive methodologies, the linchpin of the social sciences birthed in the 20th century. All of which suggests the need for a more nuanced approach to understanding creativity as being demonstrable along a continuum of possibilities rather than through a stark set of binary options.

Early creativity testing with children

Creativity as a specific domain (apart from IQ) was not widely understood, or scientifically studied in universities, until a century ago when, in the late 1920s, the discipline of psychology took it under its wing as a unique expression of human nature. Up to this point, it was regarded in terms of unusual personal traits such as giftedness, madness or supernatural intervention from the muses! The history of creativity testing for psychoanalytic, cognitive, behaviourist and humanistic purposes is well documented (Craft, 2002; Runco *et al.*, 2014; Sternberg, 1999), so I will simply outline a few of the key contributions here.

According to Dr Paul Torrance's excellently kept records (2004), Kirkpatrick (1900) might have been the first psychologist to organise basic imagination tests with young children using inkblots. These were considered reliable as evidence of creativity except for the fact that responses were dependent on verbal competency, which precluded many younger children. Psychologists, including McCarty (1924) and Abramson (1927) produced creativity tests based on drawings and inkblots, with limited success, and others created tests using drawing and transforming objects, whose reliability was again dependent on a child's motor skills development.

After many years of observation from which she concluded that all 'normal' children had creative imagination (Torrance, 2004), educational psychologist Elizabeth Andrews (1930) developed the first in-depth psychological tests for imaginative play, measuring:

- imitation

- experimentation

- transformation of objects

- transformation of animals

- acts of sympathy

- dramatisations

- imaginary playmates

- fanciful explanations

- fantastic stories

- new uses of stories

- constructions

- new games

- extensions of language

- appropriate quotations

- leadership with intention

- aesthetic appreciation.

Andrews's observations of children took place between ages two and six, and she found that the optimal creative imagination period was between three to four years but then taking a significant dip at five when the child entered primary school (Torrance, 2004), not surprisingly.

Psychologist Elizabeth Starkweather (1964) then pioneered creativity tests that did not rely on oral-, verbal- or drawing-based responses. In fact, her first tests also focused on divergence from 'conformity', problem-solving, risk-taking and originality of thinking, using colour wheels from which children would rank all 13 colours by preference. Five of these would then be selected (from across the preferences) to form the colour schemes for simple pictures of animals, each one printed in the same colour as one of the five selections. The child would then be shown three identically coloured pages (e.g. three cows on a red background) and told that her friends had chosen these pages. She would then be presented with two coloured pages – one the same as her friends' and one different, and asked to choose the page she most preferred.

The idea was that a conforming child would choose the colour her friend had chosen, whereas the non-conformist would choose the colour they most preferred. There were several variations of this sequence that were carried out to ensure that no bias was involved, and the test was done with 200 children from 30 months to five years old in both experimental and control groups. Two versions of the test were carried out on all children, including the opportunity to conform to peers and the opportunity to conform to parents. The former showed the opportunity to conform to parents was more potent than the opportunity to conform to peers. The hypothesis that strong likes and dislikes would influence a child's conforming behaviour was shown to be true and the test was considered a valid measure of what became known as convergent or divergent thinking. However, the expense of the equipment and materials involved, which were bespoke for every child, together with Starkweather's untimely death, precluded this approach from being widely taken up.

In 1956, psychologist J. P. Guilford started scientifically examining the traits of divergence and convergence, considering the former a distinguishing feature of creativity, leading to the development of a multidimensional model for measuring intellectual abilities, called the Structure of the Intellect (SOI).

The divergent thinking element of the SOI had four scoring measures, which influenced the subsequent Torrance Tests for Creative Thinking (TTCT), published in 1966 by Torrance:

- originality or novelty – the uniqueness of the ideas or perspectives

- fluency – the number of interpretable ideas in response to a stimulus

- flexibility – the number of different categories of ideas produced

- elaboration – the continual exploration and embellishment of an idea.

(adapted from Clapham, 2011)

To these were added further characteristics after more refined tests revealed their repetition in highly creative thinkers, but these were not agreed on by all test researchers during this era, which the above four generally were:

- resistance to premature closure

- emotional expressiveness

- storytelling articulateness

- movement

- Synthesis

- analysis or evaluation

- unusual visualisation

- internal visualisation

- humour

- richness of imagery.

Torrance had already trialled various creativity measures with children and adults through the 1940s and 1950s, primarily in response to various challenging students he encountered as a teacher, whose unorthodox behaviours he viewed as 'something very valuable and precious' (Hebert *et al.*, 2002) that were gradually harnessed through creative activities and turned into highly engaged learning behaviours. These students eventually went on to secure high-ranking positions, which sparked the start of Torrance's research into whether different levels of creative potential could be predicted when certain aptitudes, attitudes and behaviours were identified.

He felt that, in order to support children's natural creative talents, a test appropriate to their age and stage of development was required to find out what conditions would enhance those talents. The test needed to have several indicators to increase its reliability, enable one-to-one support for children who 'test as more intelligent individually than in a group' and take little time to administer (Torrance, 2004, p.354).

Torrance conducted several longitudinal trials of children's creative potential which started in 1958 (Hebert *et al.*, 2002). Torrance's two most popular tests were *Thinking Creatively with Words* (1966) and *Thinking Creatively with Pictures* (1966). Outcomes of these, combined with his longitudinal trials, resulted in his first comprehensive test for early years children, the *Mother Goose* test, released in 1968, which included the following:

- Problem Solving Test

- Construction Test (using LEGO blocks)

- Originality Test, asking for unusual images associated with different shaped wooden blocks

- Question Asking Test, calling for questioning responses to Mother Goose prints, stories and poems

- Just Suppose Test, based on original drawings of unlikely situations.

(adapted from Torrance, 2004)

This was adapted to become more kinaesthetic and less verbally dependent and to reflect natural experiences rather than test conditions. It was eventually replaced by the *Thinking Creatively in Action and Movement* test in 1981. Based on simple imagination and movement activities that children of three to five years would have been familiar with, the reliability of this test was found to be very high. The test consisted of four activities:

1. How Many Ways? – used to observe the child's ability to move in alternate ways across the floor.

2. Can You Move Like? – invites the child to move like animals or a tree.

3. What Other Ways? – asks the child to place a paper cup in a wastebasket in alternate ways.

4. What Might It Be – involves the child coming up with a variety of uses for a paper cup.

Assessing the kinaesthetic and verbal responses, the tester would use a scoring guide to score the children based on their fluency and originality (tests 1, 3 and 4) or their imagination (test 2), the results of which were gathered and analysed using quantitative assessment methods.

Torrance recognised the strength of human motivations at work, as a force in children's creativity, and adjusted his measures of creativity to take into account:

- novelty and value

- divergence from previously accepted visions

- being true, generalisable and surprising for the child's knowledge at the time

- involving persistence.

He also insisted on gathering from parents biographical and socio-cultural contextual data about their child's interests and hobbies to give educators the best clues as to how to nurture their creativity. Torrance recognised that 'the creative behaviour of preschool children is characterised by wonder and magic' (2004, p.352) and his measures were an attempt to capture and compare this in a way that was valid in praxis, i.e. both theoretically and practically.

The results of this work, together with the Rorschach (inkblot) test – now established as a useful tool in psychotherapy circles – went on to influence the final development of the TTCT in 1974. Torrance was careful to research the most appropriate measures that would not discriminate or favour anyone based on age, gender, language, race or socio-economic status or physical disability, acknowledging the agency of even the very youngest child. His checklist of behavioural indicators of creative strength was widely heralded, versions of which can still be seen in creativity frameworks today.

> Preschool children are experts in creative learning because by the age of two to three years, they have acquired considerable experience in learning by questioning, inquiring, searching, manipulating, experimenting and playing to find out, in their own way, the truth about things. (Torrance 2004, p.352)

One of the drawbacks of creativity tests was that they were focused on testing for signs of divergent thinking (the ability to come up with novel, creative answers to problems that exist), which is not the same as creative potential (the ability to imagine problems or ideas that might not yet exist, and consider new horizons), and were often conducted in test-like environments. This meant that even the most divergent of thinkers would under-perform in these tests just by the very nature of wishing to meet expectations and score highly, which led to more conventional, less original responses to the tests. According to Runco, divergent thinking tests became much more meaningful when carried out in playful, game-like environments where children could 'explore wide associative horizons and consider unconventional and original ideas' (2016, p.100). Runco adds that the other reason why divergent thinking tests are unreliable is because we forget that authentic creative behaviour requires spontaneity. Therefore, there is no such thing as a 'test' with time and other constraints that can indicate a true level of creativity; it can only provide estimates of creative potential.

Modern creativity testing in education

Fast forward to creativity researchers of the 21st century and many of these core characteristics have been embedded in contemporary tests, pointing to their reliability over time, albeit using more sophisticated methods. Most researchers agree that creative thinking involves two key stages – a generative stage and an exploratory or problem-solving stage – which provide the foundations for the creative actions that follow. Creative thinking frameworks usually include specific techniques for ideation, problem-solving and evaluation, not necessarily as a linear process, such as the Six Hats method designed by Edward de Bono, especially useful for group creative thinking (although this is an experiential method of creative thinking rather than an empirical test for creative traits).

Treffinger and colleagues propose four creativity characteristics that can be both taught and nurtured since 'no one person possesses all the characteristics, nor does anyone display them all the time' (2002, p.viii). These four characteristics, derived from creativity research mainly based on adults, have since been developed by the Center for Creative Learning[2] into a more holistic assessment framework for educators in schools, recognising the important role of educators in helping students become creative thinkers and makers. Translated into an early years context, it might look something like this:

1. *Openness and courage to explore ideas* – a supported environment presenting carefully chosen, intelligent and open-ended resources or ideas for exploration and discovery without predetermined outcome or time constraints.

2. *Generating ideas* – environments for testing, theorising, problem-solving, problem-creating and risk-taking with those resources or ideas, with appropriate provocations to enable children to explore from all angles and perspectives that are relevant to them.

3. *Digging deeper into ideas* – more complex techniques or resources added to enable children to access more richness, plus sensitively scaffolded starting points or connecting ideas offered to help children access deeper levels of thinking about their ideas and interests, and to try out new ideas where they occur to extend existing knowledge and understanding, which is recognised and celebrated. Carried out over time and in space.

4. *Listening to one's inner voice* – supporting children to trust in the richness of their own ideas, allowing long periods of time to think (together and apart) and explore artistically in more depth and complexity. Respecting, acknowledging and responding to non-verbal languages in non-verbal and intuitive ways, encouraging children to participate in choice and decision-making, critical and evaluative thinking, and enabling their multimodal languages to be heard, felt, seen and appreciated.

Where this framework is less suitable for early years use is in its assessment methods which, despite attention to include more generative, qualitative measures, still rate performance on a scale of four parameters: not yet

---

2   See www.creativelearning.com

evident; emerging; expressing; excelling. This has the effect of creating hierarchies based on extent and quality of performance, which threatens to undermine its stated intentions to recognise the complex and changing nature of creativity over time and context. This is undoubtedly the limitation of any performative or behaviour-based assessment method.

However, it may be an effective way of measuring progress in artistic skills, and some creative thinking techniques at least, and enables educators to observe when to extend their own methods of scaffolding to increase levels of complexity and challenge for different children and provide truly differentiated teaching. Some renowned researchers such as Amabile (1996), Finke, Ward and Smith (1992), and Isaak and Just (1995) also highlight the importance of removing obstacles in order to develop higher-level creative characteristics but, by and large, this only addresses cognitive constraints (internal ways of thinking) as opposed to social, cultural, political or economic (external) constraints, which I have addressed in Chapter 12.

The main questions that empirically focused creativity researchers have been asking themselves since the early 1900s are: 'What is creativity? Who has creativity? What are the characteristics of creative people? Who should benefit from creativity? Can creativity be increased through conscious effort, i.e. can it be learned or is it some kind of innate, genetic gifting?' (Sternberg, 1999, p.25). These are not to be marginalised as unimportant questions and I hope this book offers some clues, specifically in relation to young children.

However, the social scientists among us who care about the 'who' in our world are also interested in the bigger picture of where children have come from (socially, culturally, genetically), who or what has contributed to who they are now in terms of their agency and potentiality, and how we can shape interactions and environments that cultivate and celebrate this. So, I would also add a further key line of enquiry which is to ask, what generative conditions or environments stimulate a child's creativity, as a fundamental element of who they are?

REFLECTIVE QUESTIONS

* Are you interested in observing children's creative traits through a set of parameters, such as an imagination or creativity test and, if so, what would you do with the results?

* What are your thoughts on eugenics (i.e. *breeding* certain traits such as intelligence or creativity into future generations)? Is it foolish or wise? Do we effectively do this already in our 'choice' of partners or is mutual attraction more nuanced than that?

* Do the characteristics developed by Andrews, Starkweather, Guilford, Torrance and Treffinger help you form a clearer sense of what creativity might look like in young children? Is there anything missing from these that you would expect to observe in a creative thinker?

* How much room for spontaneity and magic is there in your practice?

* What generative conditions or environments in your setting might stimulate a child's creativity, as a fundamental element of who they are?

Chapter 7

Creating the Conditions for Creativity

Can we define the optimum conditions for creativity?

What all researchers seem to have agreed on in the last two decades is that creativity is complex – it is not one single measurable aspect of human nature, but several definable elements working together to different degrees depending on internal and external influences. Eminent psychologist Mihaly Csikszentmihalyi designed one of the most influential systems theories of creativity based on three conditions that influence an individual's access to their creative elements:

- *Domain* – the body of knowledge that, as it becomes well known to the individual, it becomes internalised.

- *Individual* – the person who acquires the domain knowledge and produces variations on the existing knowledge.

- *Field* – other experts (both producers and audience) in the domain who offer insights, inspiration, new perspectives, critique and judgement on what works and what constitutes creative 'quality'.

Csikszentmihalyi (1997) held that the optimal creative state could be achieved when an individual was most highly motivated and in a state of 'flow' with all three elements being fully integrated. He reached these conclusions over many years by studying the conditions for optimal experience in adults, i.e. what combined elements provided people with a deep sense of enjoyment, fulfilment and intense focus, where the intrinsic rewards outweighed the extrinsic motivations. He discovered the one thing in common with all intrinsically rewarding experiences was that their owners reached a state of highly creative consciousness – the state of flow. In this state, people were rewarded by the feelings that arose from the very act of being creative – immersion in the process itself and the freedom this gave them – rather than any promise of a goal at the end. This underpins my hypothesis of creativity not just as a set of aptitudes and skills that can be learned, but also as an essence, or *noumena* (ideas, feelings and perceptions that cannot be articulated easily through words) that may be expressed across the whole body, mind, spirit and soul and that, once accessed, facilitates a deeper state of being.

Other researchers have extended these elements to reflect a wider view of social, cultural and individual influences on creativity (Amabile, 1996; Sternberg, 1999; Runco *et al.*, 2014) and subscribe to Csikszentmihalyi's view that sustained creativity requires a level of mastery, knowledge and tools, and forms of expression to activate these three aspects successfully, and that this is available to all who wish to learn, not just to those who might be genetically gifted. This theory significantly influenced the development of the contemporary frameworks for cultivating creativity.

What is important to note is that most of the accepted theories identifying the conditions for creativity to flourish are not culturally sensitive. They reflect a western concept of cultural development which favours innovation and individuality, based on a capitalist economic system (Craft, 2002). This concept, or worldview, positions creativity as a source of development for, and from, the economy. Public funding is made available to support the growth of creative and cultural policy and practice for the public good, and private investment promotes an agenda of creativity aligned to productivity in the workplace. This concept is not sensitive to the constructive and collaborative practices of eastern cultures or more community-oriented western cultures.

Nor does it reflect the values behind much early years creative practice, where the purpose revolves less around growing economic futures and more around cultivating children's *present sense*, in partnership with parents and caregivers. Our focus is perhaps better directed towards exploring theories of creativity that seek to engage with a child on their own terms, intrinsically motivated, rather than imposing a set of teachable creative behaviours for a political objective which may well result in extinguishing the creative flame anyway. The problem is, how do we know what creative elements we are looking for when cultivating children's *present sense*?

Can children's creativity be observed?

Children tell us all the time when we are nurturing their brains and bodies through their *observable behaviours* (Bruce, 2005a). We can see that they are intrinsically motivated when they demonstrate higher levels of interest in objects or activities and talk about connections with their personal life. They might display increased concentration, alert postures or particular facial expressions such as curious looks or tongues sticking out while deep in thought, for example when absorbed in drawing from their imagination. They may be deeply immersed in a state of 'flow' with ideas that are sustained over time, when deeper connections are made between existing and new knowledge, such as role playing an idea that came from last week's story.

They might exert more energy and higher levels of motivation to explore something that captures their interest, or use a new technique or resource, for example a baby learning to handle a rattle or exploring their reflection in a mirror, especially where this presents a challenge to the child requiring persistence or precision. Young children feel successful and competent when they fulfil a task they have chosen for themselves, and this emerging mastery is important for the child to feel in control, able to conquer their fears and build their competences.

Children's satisfaction is often clear to see, as are their frustrations, but sometimes it is harder to spot the more complex emotions and responses, which is why listening to all their languages is crucial, especially in the case of babies and non-speaking children. Their choices, acts and behaviours are purposeful and driven, as Bruce explains:

> Children do not act randomly but in ways that are patterned, through the influence of their genetically predetermined biological development and also through the way socio-cultural influences interact with their biological make-up. Beneath the apparent randomness and chaos in a child's behaviour there is order. (Bruce, 2005b, p.70)

The last two decades have seen many examples of how organisations have set about measuring the observable behaviours related to children's creative acts (Brėdikytė, 2011; Craft, 2002). Sense-based criteria are often used to capture ways of measuring observable creative behaviours such as curiosity, risk-taking, adaptability, ingenuity, empathy, flow, joy, wonder, deep concentration, sustained thinking, confidence, perseverance, independence, self-regulation, reciprocity, empathy, playfulness and excitement (Nutbrown, 2011).

Confusingly, these observable behaviours might show traits of creativity but are also traits shared with other dispositions for mental or physical wellbeing, intelligence, social and emotional development (Hughes, 2010). These traits are, therefore, not necessarily stimulated by creative acts nor reliant on the imagination. Some sensations can also emerge in response to the nervous system which, when generated and intensified, increases dopamine production in the central reward centre. This leads to peaks of motivational behaviours such as having a brainstorm of ideas in quick succession, which can be mistaken for creativity but may originate more in biochemical reactions (a bit like a sugar high) than in sustainable creative thinking (Kaufmann, 2003).

Not surprisingly, many of these traits are reflected in Gardner's (2011) multiple intelligence theory, which identified nine intelligences, including musical, kinaesthetic, interpersonal, linguistic, logical/mathematical, naturalistic, visual/spatial, intrapersonal, existential.[1] Gardner's multiple intelligence theory was widely used by educators and creative professionals alike to identify preferred learning styles, although some neuroscientists now consider this theory a neuromyth due to the lack of neurological evidence to validate the claims about preferred learning styles (Thomas, 2015). Interestingly though, Gardner's theory mirrors the domain-based behaviours of many highly established ('Big C') artists who identify as having preferred sense *channels* through which they are creative (Robinson, 2010), for example musicians who think musically, dancers who think kinaesthetically or artists who think visually. Since young children use multimodal channels to create memory and expression, this distinct domain-based framework is perhaps not the most useful for observing their creative behaviours, and also because it relies on identifying competencies and skills rather than senses. As Bruce maintained, observation of children's states of play appears to be the best way to identify their deeper modes of imaginative being (Bruce, 2005a).

Vygotsky (2004) highlighted the role of play in nurturing 'the most authentic, truest creativity' by developing the imagination and ways of sense-making in order to have a unique understanding of the world. In true constructivist form, Vygotsky described children's play not as a reproduction of social experience but 'a creative reworking of the impressions he has acquired', which are used 'to construct a *new* reality, one that conforms to his

---

1   See http://thetutorreport.com/howard-gardners-9-types-intelligence

own needs and desires' (2004, p.11, in Brėdikytė, 2011). In this way, children are recreating and discovering for themselves what the world is made of – something that is original and useful *to them*, if not to the wider community (Kaufmann, 2003). In fact, Vygotsky argued that 'absolutely everything around us created by the mind and hand of man is the product of human imagination' (Brėdikytė, 2011, p.43).

This begs the question that if creativity – or imagination – is an 'essence' that exists in everything as well as requiring certain dispositions, can it be observed by educators without personal experience or who cannot 'accurately identify their own creativity' (Runco *et al.*, 2014, p.390)? And can we differentiate between dispositions for *being creative* and just, well...*being*?

Is there room for a creativity schema?

Phenomenologists Weber and Schutz were among the first scientists to develop 'schemas of interpretation', which were an attempt to set aside preconceived knowledge and trace the processes by which we give meaning to the world – to find out exactly what influences our meaning-making. In order to identify the different conditions and explanations for social phenomena such as consciousness, motivation and action, their research considered internal motivators such as purpose and emotion as verifiable scientific data, as opposed to the positivists' view that only what could be seen could be counted. The idea was to strip back everything that could be known to its natural beginnings and start to identify how knowledge is categorised and connected, such as how the individual artefacts of grass, trees, sky and clouds become organically, biologically, physically and socially connected to develop relationships that produce complex outcomes such as rain and crops.

The *phenomenology of the social world* was the phrase coined to describe Schutz's work on 'ideal types', which identified how we build up 'typifications of people, classifying them into types with particular qualities, from whom typical courses of action can be expected' (Benton and Craib, 2011, p.83). For the first time in social science, agency and rational choice were considered core elements of meaning-making, rather than assuming behaviours were simply a response to the surrounding conditions and materials. Schemas have since been designed to account for patterns of behaviours on many levels of science and are useful to show a range of possibilities depending on the influences and conditions on them. However, they can also be problematic in setting benchmarks from which external behaviours can be judged without fully understanding the surrounding influences.

Influenced by Frobel and Piaget's schematic thinking, Chris Athey (2007) identified schema in young children as patterns of repeated thought and behaviour that describe how young children subjectively organise knowledge, leading to 'logical classifications' (Nutbrown, 2011, p.14). Although Athey's schema are often used to observe biologically determined growth patterns, Athey stressed the importance of not studying schema in isolation but alongside other contexts for learning and development, including socio-cultural influences, that may affect children's behaviours at different times (Bruce, 2005a). Athey emphasised that children's schema are constantly changing and are just one lens through which we can observe what children do, not necessarily giving us the full picture of who they are.

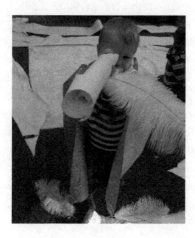

Athey proposed that schema are explored at four different levels, through which children express how things work and how they feel, enabling them to reason why:

1. Action – physical and sensory exploration without significance (embodied, tacit knowledge).

2. Symbolic representation – where meaning is then assigned.

3. Functional dependency – identifying cause and effect and relation-ships between things.

4. Abstract thought – where deeper thought and ideas are supported and extended over time.

Through observing the regular actions of children, Athey identified many typical patterns of behaviour (and educators are constantly discovering more in response to contemporary cultures) that happen when children are examining the cause and effect of their actions, the results of forces on things, the relations between things or how things can be coordinated to work together. Athey identified schema within static or dynamic movement categories, such as transporting (moving from one place to another), trajectory (watching motion and the direction of travel, often in straight lines), rotation (circular movements), connecting, positioning, mapping (exploring journeys from a fixed starting point to an end point), transforming (such as mixing colours or materials to watch their properties change). Athey confirmed that children sometimes focus on a single schema and at other times explore a 'cluster' of schemas simultaneously, for instance in drawings, role play and movement narrative (Athey, 2007, p.57).

Like Schutz, Athey's schema provide a framework through which we can observe conditions that give rise to certain behaviours, even though children's approaches to the same schema will be different. For instance, a *connecting* schema in one child involves tying everything up in string, whereas another will join train-track pieces together; a *trajectory* schema for one child will involve throwing a ball to watch the power of its movement from one point to another, whereas for another child it will involve switching a tap on and off repeatedly to watch water fall down in a straight line. Schema help us understand how children experience the power of agency triggered through their decision-making and actions on an object, combined with the forces around the object, leading to highly mathematical, scientific and creative thinking (Athey, 2007).

Athey's schema revolve around the intentional actions of children in experimenting with how the world works so this framework of thinking may not explain subconscious responses, or *noumena*, that we see when children respond from their inner, creative drive. It is constructive insofar as children respond to the materials, objects and relationships around them. For each child, their reality is the only one that exists until they witness another child's actions achieving a different outcome, from which children learn and develop more of a socially constructed awareness of reality (Brėdikytė, 2011).

But these schema do not necessarily explain the intra-responsive relationships between human and more-than-human agencies, such as the way certain materials and people attract a certain response or behaviour towards them that is not within our conscious control. Is it possible to isolate creative essence, thought, agency and action processes into a 'creativity schema' by which these elements could be observed or sensed objectively? This would mean finding a way of identifying a universally agreed set of symbols that describe the intrinsic nature of children's creativity, including unconscious responses, rather than its extrinsic effects and affects, which strikes me as being impossible.

Social psychologist and educationalist Graham Wallas (1858–1932) proposed a particular sequence of four stages that would lead towards creative fulfilment, including *preparation* in terms of information collation and identifying problems, *incubation* involving time to think about the idea or problem, *illumination* where a sudden insight or realisation occurs as new knowledge, builds on existing knowledge and starts to make sense, and finally *verification,* where the solution is tried out, applied and resolved (Runco *et al.*, 2014). However, we very rarely see a child (or adult) working in such a linear fashion and, although these stages make sense in theory, understanding creative process as a series of mechanisms (optimal conditions) and interactive processes is probably more realistic in practice.

In short, I propose that any attempt to define a creativity schema is virtually impossible because of:

- the subjective nature of value judgements in the creative sphere

- the complex language required to accurately interpret children's somatic, mental or ethereal expressions, 'perceptions, feelings and attitudes' (Crotty, 1998, p.75)

- the inability to completely disregard the observer's own inherited prejudices

- the lack of space or time within any target-driven educational setting for careful anthropological approaches to observation, and the tendency to resort to simplistic explanations of causality where behaviours are complex and opaque (Denzin, 1992).

Indeed, as with all instrumental frameworks or assessments of creativity relating to a set of changeable aptitudes, there are a number of common problems (Clapham, 2011):

- Different testing criteria are borne of, and result in, different concepts of creativity. Without identical constructs being used, there is little comparability between tests.

- Similarly, test scores can often be interpreted in different ways with divergent thinking being taken to assume creativity, when it is actually only one aspect of creativity.

- Ensuring the suitability of different tests for their target audience based on developmental assumptions is problematic and yet crucial for validity.

- Measuring current levels of creative performance is not the same as predicting someone's future creative potential, which critics argue is very difficult to do. A number of factors will come into play in the future which have no bearing on the present abilities.

- Engaging in creative actions is not a linear process but a continuum of different stages (ideation, incubation, evaluation, extension, reflection, etc.) that are visited repeatedly and in different orders throughout the creative process. Those who are more aware of their creative processes may be able to recognise where they are on the continuum and intentionally move between stages without destroying the spontaneity that generates and embeds further creativity, but that is not a given.

Clearly, there is no one 'right way' to be creative and perhaps we can only objectively use schema to observe the external expressions of creativity, experienced in real, material, bodily or ideas-based form rather than in a more ethereal form. However, since experiences and meanings are subjectively created in the context of children's social, emotional, cultural, gendered, biological, spiritual and cognitive development (i.e. there is no one truth that describes all children's creativity), in observing measures of external creativity, we only see part of a child's story.

What we may, in fact, need to talk about is a new more-than-human methodology, not bound by age or experience (but somehow fixed in time and space) that allows adults to enact the *least adult role* (Mandell, 1988) through which we can experience the world as a series of whole body and mind sensations in order to come close to recognising the intrinsic experiences of a child. This gives us an opportunity to consider a new materialist dimension to children's creativity that transcends traditional boundaries, often referred to as their 'otherness' (Benton and Craib, 2011, p.74), not in the sense of being alien or deviant but in the sense of celebrating their uniqueness by 'paying attention to particularity and difference' (Benton and Craib, 2011, p.74). In doing so, we need to find methods of observation that are expressed not within a standardised framework but through dynamic thinking that tries to resist neat, transparent, simplified explanations and encourages the opening up of complexity (MacLure, 2006), and possibility thinking, which may not even be consciously motivated (Craft, 2002).

Indeed, Runco's more recent research into a theory of personal creativity, focusing on the subjective originality of children's creative thinking, is showing an interesting move away from decades of quantitative hypotheses (which form the basis of his widely used battery of creativity tests (2014)) towards a more socially nuanced, qualitative understanding;

> It is nice to be objective, to have validity for one's claims, yet not if it means children whose creative skills are not yet expressed will be overlooked, not if it takes us to educational practice with which we fail to recognise potential. (Runco, 2003, p.323)

To explore this further, we need a critical look at what is understood by the *conditions for creativity* in this context.

Conditions and stimulus for creativity

Rather than relying on specific elements to observe in children's creativity due to the problems in pinning down its rather ambiguous nature, many arts education models of measurement prefer to address what constitutes the most generative conditions for creativity to flourish.

These are the conditions that enable different relationships and connections to emerge that trigger new ideas, creations, viewpoints, reflections, meanings and understanding (Prentice, 2000). In setting these out, we are seeking to specify not what specific creative products (objects or ideas) will emerge from any particular activity but trying instead to 'maximise the probability of the occurrence of creative performance' or action (Kaufmann, 2003, p.237).

Over the years, most assessments or frameworks designed to cultivate the conditions for creativity focus on the *Six Ps of Creativity* (the last two of which have been added recently as a result of emerging research).

THE SIX PS OF CREATIVITY

* *Products* – specifying the types of creativity expressed or displayed in objects (tangible, material products) or ideas (non-material products). However, products reveal little about their creator, aesthetic intentions or processes used.

* *People* – identifying the qualities associated with creative individuals, including interests, attitudes, skills, values, biographies that lead to creative performance, heredity and personality traits such as openness to experience, perseverance, autonomy, humour and being adventurous.

* *Processes* – examining the cognitive functions of, and dispositions for, creativity, observed during the varied stages of creative activity, such

as curiosity, ideation, critical thinking, experimentation, production and evaluation of ideas.

* *Environmental pressures (also called 'Place')* – determining the environmental conditions that either inhibit or enhance creativity, and the relationships between environments and people that provide optimum creative opportunity.

* *Persuasion* – identifying the amount of influence held by an agent (e.g. person, material, object, environment or combination) to inspire or stimulate creativity. This links to Csikszentmihayli's systems model of influences on the direction taken.

* *Potential* – addressing the latent capacity for creative thought and action to be realised to increasingly higher levels providing certain conditions are in place (e.g. technical training, opportunity or emotional support).

Runco (2003) stresses the need for creative *potentiality* as a vital condition that enables the construction of personal meaning as opposed to creative *performance,* which is outwardly expressed and can be measured unambiguously against larger norms. It requires competent scaffolding that facilitates creative thinking slightly beyond a child's ability, towards a potential they can achieve with support.

This concept of 'scaffolding' was developed by early childhood psychologist Jerome Bruner (1915–2016). This is where young children's thinking and ideas are supported to focus on key information or knowledge through intuitive questioning as they play, thereby enabling children's competence to be extended beyond what they were capable of doing on their own. As the child forms the knowledge and understanding, the amount of 'scaffolding' required is gradually reduced, just as with scaffolding around a house, until the skills or understanding of a particular concept are complete.

Scaffolding is an important part of building independent thought, self-regulation, critical awareness, memory recall and imagination (Bruner, Ross and Wood, 1976), and is empowering and effective as a way of bringing new ideas, objects and materials to life – so much so that cultural centres often employ facilitators, enablers or educators to help children and their families make the most of their experiences. As children lead their own play through an exploration of exhibits and resources, facilitators help to scaffold their play and draw out relevant connections and ideas, resulting in deeper thinking, exploration and ownership of the experience by the child. This element of democracy, or choice, is a fundamental concept in the process of being creative (Bruner, 1990).

In actively seeking opportunities to stimulate and promote children's own ideas through scaffolding, co-constructing or following their lines of enquiry, we are not just validating children's own thinking about objects, but we are also nurturing positive learning dispositions, such as confidence, curiosity, negotiation, risk-taking, self-esteem, enjoyment, independence, self-control, reciprocity, empathy, sustained concentration, spontaneity, imagination, critical awareness and scientific reasoning (Duffy, 2006). Cultural learning has an important role to play in this process of engagement and, where trust is high, in modelling it for parents and caregivers.

This is reflected in the arts-based methodology of creative collaboration (otherwise known as co-production or participatory methods), where the carefully crafted propositions of others can significantly extend our own creative thinking, ideas and solutions and significantly mature our creative competence. Bruner's scaffolding approach was built on Soviet psychologist Vygotsky's theory of the Zone of Proximal Development (ZPD), which is the distance between one's actual and potential level of development. This theory remained unfinished before his untimely death in 1934 at the age of 37.

Vygotsky (in Vygotsky, Veresov and Barrs, 1933) asserted that the ZPD is the space where a child can achieve more with someone's help than they could have achieved without that help, where they are challenged and inspired to develop their thinking and actions without being too frustrated (because it's too hard), and without being too bored (because it's too easy). With the right amount of scaffolding, children in their ZPD are observed moving beyond what they thought they were capable of by being more creative, and so it is useful to consider as a condition for creativity.

Vygotsky developed this theory to counteract the growing practice of adult-led didactic education that teachers were taught to embrace in the 1930s. With the introduction of curriculum assessments and testing, Vygotsky felt strongly that this was not an effective means to measure intelligence, and in fact held that it was positively obstructive to innate creativity.

Runco goes further to suggest a two-tiered approach to achieving deeper levels of creativity (see Figure 7.1), which is not a linear progression but a constant and unequal interaction between tiers. This strengthens my argument to view creativity as being on a dynamic continuum. Runco's approach (2003) suggests that the first tier in developing creative capacities involves the combination of motivation (both intrinsic and extrinsic) and knowledge (both declarative, explanatory knowledge and tacit know-how).

Once those are in place, it becomes much easier to access the second tier of creativity, which involves problem-finding (problem identification and definition – also known as problem discovery), ideation (fluency, flexibility and originality of imaginative ideas) and judgement (critical thinking, evaluation and valuation of the ideas).

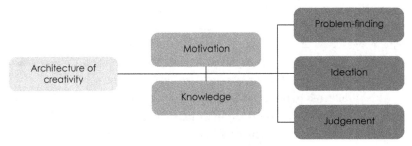

Figure 7.1: Runco's (2003) two-tiered systems theory of creativity (author's illustration)

Note that Runco's thinking has moved on from the traditional view of problem-solving to problem-finding, as it is now thought that problem-solving resides in the domain of convergent – not divergent – thinking. Problem-solving is more aligned to finding patterns or solutions that make the whole rather than deviating from the norm or constructing new knowledge, which is a key characteristic of creativity. Piaget refers to problem-finding as 'invention', without which he felt an individual would 'simply be memorising information, but not understanding it' (Runco, 2003, p.318).

However, in my view, the one crucial element missing from most creativity theory models, which is vividly expressed in Csikszentmihalyi's model and is accounted for in the 'Persuasion' element of the Six Ps, is the influence of external people and partnerships on the individual's own creative concepts. Without this collaborative approach to creativity, the individual is limited by his or her own experiences and encounters as the frame through which to view the realities of the world, which, as we know, is not how young children construct meaning on the whole.

Expanding these dimensions for cultivating (and perhaps assessing) creativity and taking into account the plethora of research in this field (NACCCE, 1999; Prentice, 2000; Hughes, 2010; Brėdikytė, 2011; Runco *et al.*, 2014), we can consider that the ideal conditions for young children will include:

- *familiar objects*, tools, materials, techniques and ideas to be experienced in unusual contexts, outside of the bounds of routine

- *spontaneity* or unexpected outcomes

- *reflection* and critique

- *time and space* to play with materials and ideas

- *technical mastery* and confidence

- *deep and relevant thinking* to practise creative modes of thought

- *the child being in control* of their own creative endeavours.

Brėdikytė (2011) refines this further to five conditions for stimulating children's creativity:

1. *Arts experience* – a long period of social and participatory arts experiences such as puppetry, theatre, painting, drawing, modelling, dance, music, singing and storytelling.

2. *Environment* – with open-ended, intelligent (not ready-made) play materials.

3. *Independence* – self-organised activity (adult intervention being facilitative rather than directive).

4. *Time* – the optimum amount being from 40 minutes to two hours, allowing for new knowledge, constructed on existing knowledge, to create context and meaning (Duffy, 2006; Ackermann, 2004).

5. *Place* – self-chosen 'special' spaces (e.g. dens, houses or castles behind the sofa or under the table).

According to Vygotsky (2004), the ability for children to imagine the world is crucial to fill the gap between experience and understanding. Several educational theorists consider make-believe or role play, which combine evolving memory with imitation and curiosity, as the basis for training the cognitive, kinaesthetic and visual *muscles of the imagination*. Through these arts-play processes, children make images in their minds of situations, people, objects and environments to:

- order and think about them, often in abstract ways and from unconventional perspectives, in order to explore the essence of a phenomenon

- become engrossed in the flow and joy of their creative concepts or fantasies

- reach a state for optimal creative potential

- regulate their naturally strong and real emotions and feelings

- communicate novel ideas about their experiences, translating the imagination (or images) into creative expression of some sort

- enable emergence of speech where specific words are often designated to ideas in the mind in order to empower and liberate them.

Perhaps a combination of these conditions would more authentically shape a creativity schema than the list of performative behaviours that could as easily be applied to identifying characteristics of physical development, mental wellbeing or engagement in learning per se.

REFLECTIVE QUESTIONS

* What things in your social environment, background culture and personal aptitudes make you more or less open to creativity?

* Can you identify what gets you into a state of 'flow' where you have a deep sense of enjoyment, fulfilment and intense focus?

* Can you see creative thinking in your children's patterns of behaviour (schema) where they experience the power of agency and forces through their choices as they explore the objects and spaces around them?

* What dynamic methods of observation could you use to identify creative thinking that is less visible or tangible in your children?

* Using the Six Ps as a guide, can you identify what might be the most generative conditions for creativity to flourish in your setting?

* How could you encourage children to sense their own creative potential as well as their existing creative abilities and aptitudes?

Chapter 8

Can Creativity Enhance Early Brain Development?

How the brain's shape and size is determined in the early years[1]

Babies' brains are amazing powerhouses. Research shows that babies are born with around 100 billion neurons and with about a quarter of the connections, called synapses, already made between them during gestation in the womb (David *et al.*, 2003). By comparison, a fully grown adult brain only has an estimated 86 billion neurons, of which 83 per cent develops in the first two years of life (Finnegan, 2016).

In fact, babies' brains make billions of new connections with everything they experience as they contextualise and make sense of it using all their senses. This process is called synaptogenesis and happens most prolifically

---

1 Adapted with kind permission from the Museum of London from an article written by Ruth Churchill Dower for their Early Years Toolkit: www.museumoflondon.org.uk/supporting-london-museums/resources/early-years-toolkit

between the ages of birth and three years old. By the age of two, a staggering 700 new connections are formed every second (National Scientific Council on the Developing Child, 2007).

It would be natural to assume that our genetic predispositions to certain interests and strengths (our DNA) are what cause these connections to be made. However, with the help of neuroimaging techniques,[2] neuroscientists are discovering that synaptogenesis is as much influenced by the environment in which children are brought up and their real-life experiences in the early years as their DNA (Finnegan, 2016; Van der Kolk, 2015). The field of epigenetics is now rapidly growing to explore these environmental phenomena.

Neuroscientists Shonkoff and Philipps demonstrated in their research that positive personal, social and cultural experiences are more critical in the early years for the development of healthy brains and well-rounded personalities than at any other time during the rest of childhood and adulthood (David *et al.*, 2003). These critical experiences help children to make meaning, hone skills and deepen their understanding of themselves and the world around them. Severe disruptions to these experiences early on lower children's chances of thriving and reaching their potential later in life (National Scientific Council on the Developing Child, 2007).

This combined influence of nature (DNA) and nurture (environmental experiences) sets out the blueprint for each child's personality for the rest of their lives. It is what makes us uniquely who we are, mentally, physically, spiritually, biologically and psychologically, in the same way that DNA makes us uniquely who we are genetically.

So why is it that the adult brain has fewer connections than a baby's brain? After all, adults have a lot more experience than babies. One of the reasons is that between the ages of (approximately) three and adolescence, the brain starts a process of pruning out billions of weak or underused synapses to make room for the stronger ones to grow. Just as with a rose bush, pruning clears out the 'dead wood', which stimulates a greater concentration of nutrients to the stronger connections and makes the brain more effective. Once this process is complete at the end of adolescence, the brain's size and shape hardly changes again and our ability to grow new synaptic connections is reduced, although not impossible. The brain's plasticity (i.e. its adaptability, flexibility and ability to reorganise itself especially during sensitive periods

---

2   Neuroimaging scanners are broadly designed either to capture functional imaging or structural imaging. More details at www.st-andrews.ac.uk/psychology/research/brainimaging

of growth), allows for repair and regrowth of fundamental neural pathways even after adverse experiences (Bergen and Woodin, 2017).

Interestingly, these sensitive periods, which appear to provide the optimum conditions for plasticity, were observed by scientists, doctors and teachers centuries ago, even though the knowledge of early brain development was only developed through behavioural observation then. It was discussed in the 19th century by Dutch geneticist and botanist Hugo de Vries, then later by physician and educator Maria Montessori, who asserted in 1949 that sensitive periods for early learning occur when 'an irresistible impulse urges the organism to select only certain elements in its environment, and for a definite, limited time' (Bruce, 2005a, p.25). Montessori developed her 'scientific method' involving particular materials, exercises and approaches that were seen to maximise those periods, specifically including arts methods such as clay, drawing and painting.

The plastic nature of the brain enables development in response to both nature and environment, but the prime window of synaptic growth for building connections and making meaning is between pre-birth and three years. Recent research demonstrates how the synaptic connectors which hold the key to each child's personality are linked to the development of both mind and body (David *et al.*, 2003) and that, when babies experience joyful play-based activities, there is a blooming of synaptic connections. Conversely, anxiety and stress result in the pruning of vital synaptic connections (Gerhardt, 2004).

This is why scientists are increasingly promoting the importance of exposing children to a wide range of positive, creative and secure opportunities in the first three years of their lives. During this period, the foundations for their personalities are being established and the synapses that are predisposed to faculties for love, communication, curiosity, reciprocity and creativity are more likely to grow strong and connected. Many educational neuroscientists now believe that all educators and parents should have a basic understanding of neuroanatomy so that they can make their own evaluations of teaching or parenting resources and so they can 'realise how important healthy environments and positive early experiences are for optimum brain development, and to support practices that make such environments available to all children and adolescents' (Bergen and Woodin, 2017, p.2).

What disrupts healthy brain growth?

In situations of adverse childhood experiences, the synapses that are predisposed to those faculties may not grow strong, and some do not connect at all. Exposure to continuously neglectful, abusive or repeatedly violent circumstances (sometimes referred to as 'toxic stress') can result in 'the permanent disruption of brain circuits during the sensitive periods in which they are maturing' (National Scientific Council on the Developing Child, 2007, p.8). In these cases, the stronger synapses that remain after pruning might be the ones predisposed to negative emotions and behaviours such as insecurity, mistrust, fear, lack of self-control and aggression. This is not an irreversible situation but it is a reality for some children and can permanently damage their ability to recover quickly from stressful events, which significantly shapes their longer-term worldview (Gerhardt, 2004).

Based on the fMRI images of young babies' brains, and on patterns of behaviour studied by psychologists, it is understood that neglect and other adverse experiences in the early years can have a profound effect on how children are emotionally 'wired'. Early neglect has a direct correlation with increased levels of cortisol (a stress hormone) throughout later life as the brain and body adapt early on in order to survive its circumstances (National Scientific Council on the Developing Child, 2007). Short bursts of cortisol are healthy to enable us to be alert to danger or build resilience in adverse situations. However, long-term build-ups of cortisol can cause unusually high levels of fear, inability to regulate emotions, lack of self-control, loss of memory, links to obesity and heart disease and the suppression of the 'soothing' neurotransmitter, called serotonin. Low levels of serotonin in stressful situations can lead to anxiety disorders, depressive illness and aggression in adulthood (Van der Kolk, 2015; Gerhardt, 2004).

This can deeply influence children's emotional responses to events, their ability to build relationships or to empathise with other people. Extreme cases of emotional and physical neglect have led to such heavy pruning that the brain becomes smaller as the child grows (Gerhardt, 2004).

The impact of social interaction on early brain development

Babies are born both vulnerable and competent; they are biologically programmed with certain types of behaviour to ensure their survival. Some behaviours are more developed than others at birth, such as eating and exploratory, communication and attachment behaviours. These are designed to attract a response from the main adult carer to provide protection, security or nutrition for the baby and ensure they will stay close (Schore, 2000). Unsettling verbal or physical behaviour may demonstrate an unmet need in the baby, and whether or not (and how well) this need is met can determine how strong their relationship will grow, and how attuned the baby and caregiver become to each other.

Attachment theorist John Bowlby proposed in his seminal research on *Attachment and Loss* (1969) that a baby's emerging social, psychological and biological capabilities are species-specific and cannot be understood except in the context of their relationship with the mother. This relationship is built through physical, emotional and social interaction, much of which is highly creative (exploratory, spontaneous, provocative, immersive, imaginative).

Bowlby held that a mother responds to her baby's cries by offering physical comfort such as close cuddling and dancing, emulating rocking movements such as the baby might have experienced in the womb. She comforts and calms her baby using singing and vocal noises that mirror those made by her baby, building a shared creative language between them. She builds emotional attunement by timing her responses to meet her baby's needs or even anticipate them (Malloch and Trevarthen, 2018). She offers social interaction to further develop her baby's competence and confidence, for example focusing on a toy or object the baby might like to explore, watching the baby's responses to spot signs of happiness and interest, communicating through call-and-response as she helps her baby play with the object, and understanding when to step in and 'scaffold' further exploration or when to remove an object if the baby shows signs of danger, distress or disinterest. The same would be true for a father or other carers, including health professionals, educators and childcarers.

Strongly attuned relationships provide a secure base from which a young child can develop their individual and community identities, and their competence and confidence to explore the world around them, knowing that they can return at any time for nourishment and comfort. The more secure and stress-free the relationship, the more the baby's brain (and body) can focus on fulfilling its higher order needs such as curiosity, imitation, communication, meaning-making and self-control. The theory is that neural connections bloom through positive emotional relationships, and a well-bonded, attuned relationship increases a child's confidence and competence to explore the world around them. This sets the scene for developing other skills, such as language, coordination, proprioception, and senses such as imagination and creativity (Schore, 2000).

However, while this theory is what underpins most clinical and educational models of caregiving for babies and young children, what it does not account for is the complexity of relationships and diversity of families into which babies are born. Not all caregivers are mothers, and not all caregivers are in a position to offer care to a particular standard that is the dominant 'norm' in society, for a whole variety of reasons. Neither are they in a position to be a child's sole, or most influential, carer. The political inferences on the role of the parent, particularly the mother, encourage a social burden of responsibility, guilt and judgement, i.e. that the caregiver is not a good enough parent if they cannot fulfil the 'ideal parent' role or that the child's long-term satisfactory development depends entirely on one or two people, who themselves represent the 'ideal' family unit, as if such a thing could exist without belittling other models of care.

While the intentions for strong attunement, happiness and security are shared by most caregivers, the theory is problematic in setting up expectations that the caregiver (mainly a mother) should feel a natural disposition of love and attachment to her baby, even though the skills for this are mostly learned 'on the job', after birth (and are often not taught at all). All of these messages can be damaging in terms of reinforcing feelings of inadequacy for caregivers who do not fit the model, having to defend their perceived role as an *abnormal* family unit, and being exposed to possible adverse psychological and physical effects through exposure to subjective societal judgement.

Impacts of creative environments
on early brain development

Neuroscientist, Marian Diamond (1926–2017) – the first to investigate and report on the make-up of Einstein's brain – was pioneering because she asked different sorts of questions from most scientists to try to work out what the most important environmental influences were on the brain. Through her groundbreaking studies, Diamond demonstrated five key factors for a healthy brain, including *diet, exercise, challenge, newness* and *love*. Once the intelligence and learning capability of rats was realised, and the evidence that rats and human brains develop in quite similar ways, Diamond's experiments with rats were illuminating. She demonstrated statistically significant structural changes in the brains of rats who were given a range of novel, play-based objects in their pens (in *enrichment*) compared with those who were denied a playful environment (in *impoverishment*). The rats who played in enriching environments grew a thicker cerebral cortex, which is linked to higher levels of consciousness, choice, memory and intelligence, and this was the first finding of its kind to highlight environmental influences on the brain (Diamond and Hopson, 1998).

Then, Diamond started to test for structural changes in the brains of rats who were given playmates, then physical care through daily petting by humans, and so on. All these experiments produced increasingly impressive results highlighting the positive (life-lengthening, in some cases) impacts of enriching experiences for rats. Rats with brain damage also demonstrated significant healing and growth in the brain when placed in these enriching environments. Conversely, the brains of rats put in stressful environments (including overcrowded pens, hourly changes of toys to over-stimulate and splitting up families) were found to have significantly reduced cerebral thickness and over-production of the stress hormone, cortisol, which was discovered to inhibit cerebral growth. Diamond was able to produce repeatable, reliable evidence of the brain's plasticity – its ability to change in response to appropriate environmental stimuli, including creative novelty and love. Diamond went on to apply her findings by working to support malnourished children in Cambodia through the Enrichment in Action programme, with positive results in terms of progression in education, creativity and wellbeing. She has since influenced many education programmes around the world using play, drawing, colouring, visual arts and music to help young children, their parents and teachers learn about the power of enriched creative environments on their brains (Diamond and Hopson, 1998).

Given the enormous impact on brain development that all early experiences have, it is not surprising that only a few longitudinal or large cohort studies have isolated the positive, long-term impacts of creative interventions in particular (Hardiman *et al.*, 2019; Bergen and Modir Rousta, 2019). The few that exist highlight how creative activities that encourage social development such as positive relationships, high self-esteem and better mental health can also support cognitive development such as memory retention, higher order thinking and transferable problem-solving across domains.

Many studies suggest a strong correlation between the creative intervention and the rapid blooming of synapses at particularly sensitive periods. However, we need to bear in mind that the impact of different experiences on different parts of the brain (and body) is incredibly complex, and goes far beyond what existing research has revealed. In fact, what we currently know about early brain development is minute compared with what we do not yet know. Australian online education platform Open Colleges has produced a fantastic interactive map of the brain which gives us some idea as to its complexity.[3]

In addition, scanning the brain requires complete stillness in an unfamiliar, noisy and potentially scary environment. For a baby or young child, this usually means having to be anaesthetised, which is a complicated procedure and a potent chemical to introduce into a young body – one that sometimes muddies the brain, making interpretation challenging.

The interpretation of results is more difficult in young brains due to the high proliferation of synaptogenesis in early childhood. It is exceedingly difficult to isolate brain changes that happen due to a creative intervention rather than any other influence. Most creativity tests are based on measuring one or more of the Six Ps identified in Chapter 7 and, of those, neuroimaging can really only examine 'Process' as the others are dependent on functions that are not exclusively brain based. But as Bergen eloquently discusses:

> Presently many creative thinking qualities cannot yet be distinguished from brain processes that also underpin non-creative thinking. Thus, these terms may need to be further defined to identify what, exactly, is creative about them. For instance, the famous incubation phase often hypothesised as important in creativity could be studied as 'mind wandering' in brain studies. (Bergen and Modir Rousta, 2019, p.66)

---

3   See www.opencolleges.edu.au/informed/learning-strategies

However, there is hope on the horizon. A new breed of mobile brain scanners is emerging that require neither stillness nor chemical intervention and are ideal for little ones, but some require significant financing and training of professionals and so, as yet, are not widely available. The cheapest and most accessible for scanning electrical and biometric data is the electroencephalography (EEG) wearable cap system. These products are now commercially produced as much for gamers and psychologists as for clinical use, which makes them more competitive and accessible to researchers. The electrical signals captured can be translated via algorithms to measure the wearer's cognitive states in real time, including excitement (arousal), interest (valence), stress (frustration), engagement/boredom, attention (focus) and meditation (relaxation), as well as biometric measures such as heart rate, respiration, blood pressure, blood volume flow, skin impedance and eye tracking.[4]

Also widely available and fairly inexpensive is the functional near-infrared spectroscopy (fNIRS) scanner, which can also be worn like a cap, enabling normal movement in familiar surroundings for any child. It works by measuring changes in the properties of light as it shines through the skull and is refracted back to the sensor. It has limitations in only being able to record surface level and frontal brain activity rather than any deeper-level or anatomical activity, plus it picks up superficial scalp noises, making it harder to interpret and less reliable. However, it is becoming more and more widely used for interdisciplinary studies such as this one to identify the association between humour and creativity by detecting changes in the brain.[5]

More recently, a mobile, lightweight magnetoencephalography (MEG) helmet has been designed to imitate much of what the current fMRI scanners can pick up, but without the bulky freezers required in fixed fMRI machines that cool the magnets down to minus 269°C. Instead, these mobile scanners can work at room temperature to record the tiny magnetic fields generated by the brain and can be placed directly on the scalp, which greatly increases the signal they can pick up. While the scanning functionality is fully developed, the design of the full-face helmet is still being adapted towards more of a cycling helmet style which will be easier for a younger child to wear.[6]

The other main reason for lack of investment in creativity-based brain studies is money. The majority of financial investment into brain-based research tends to revolve around genetics, epigenetics, artificial intelligence

---

4   An example of an EEG system (but others are available) can be found at www.emotiv.com/epoc-flex

5   See https://nirs.stanford.edu

6   See www.ucl.ac.uk/news/2018/mar/new-brain-scanner-allows-patients-move-freely

and other big ideas that the world's science communities are grappling with in response to large-scale health and economic challenges. Studies of the effect of creativity and its importance have not caught the attention of financial backers in the same way. The few rigorous studies that do exist tend to revolve around the effects on cognitive development of specific art forms such as music or drawing but, as we have discussed earlier, these often don't tell the whole story when using only quantitative measurements.

One such study that has achieved an interesting interdisciplinary and cross-methodological mix with powerful results and significant implications for the way education is designed, delivered and assessed has been produced by the School of Education and Center for Talented Youth at Johns Hopkins University in Columbia, Maryland. This research focused on investigating what effects arts-based teaching could have on the long-term retention of science knowledge in primary school. Their methodology was hugely rigorous and still very creative (although did not include brain scanning), and the results quite surprising.

The research team took 11 teachers and taught them how to sing their chemistry texts, draw the results of their biology experiments, make collages of environmental science and create dances to describe the connections in particle physics. They ensured that all teachers were highly trained, competent and confident in arts and science, as well as teaching methods, and had worked with their children for at least two years.

Then they took 350 year 6 children (10–11-year-olds), assigned them to randomised control groups of which two were allocated arts-based teaching and two were allocated conventional teaching methods. The groups were swapped around after a term to repeat the experiment and exclude teacher bias. The results were measured carefully using quantitative and qualitative methods.

The research team discovered statistically significant improvements in the learning progression of struggling readers, for whom the multimodal cues and modalities provided through the arts helped children conceptualise, store and recall information from their long-term memory. There were also significant differences in retention of science content in the arts-taught classes compared with the control classes, which indicated that teaching through the arts was as good as, or better than, teaching through conventional methods.

They also discovered that children who received arts-based teaching in the first term performed just as well (or better than expected) when receiving traditional teaching in the second term, suggesting there may be transfer effects where creative problem-solving skills and the acquisition of art skills and competencies enabled more understanding and memory of big ideas.

The researchers concluded that arts-based teaching is as effective as, or better than, conventional instruction for long-term memory of science content, and that children performing at the lowest levels of reading achievement benefit the most from this pedagogical method and remember more of what they learned. This begs the question as to why the 'arts is not used more as a pedagogical tool to address the performance gap that continues to challenge educators looking for viable and scalable solutions to differentiated instructional approaches' (Hardiman *et al.*, 2019, p.31). The next stage of this research would be to use wearable neuroimaging devices and investigate what's happening in the brain when arts-based teaching helps to open up multimodal avenues to learning that make sense to children who otherwise would have struggled to imagine, store and recall content.

REFLECTIVE QUESTIONS

* Could you imagine some of the things that might have been pruned in your own brain, such as skills or dispositions you would like to have now but find difficult to achieve (e.g. learning languages)?

* Conversely, are there skills or aptitudes you have developed in adulthood that weren't there when you were younger, or that might have developed as a result of overcoming adversity? What do you think might have contributed to this from your genetic heritage and from your environment?

* What is the best combination of things (e.g. from diet, environment, challenge, health, relationships, play time) that helps you to feel most ready to learn? Could you do specific things to help put this optimum combination in place more often both for you and your children?

* What could you do to help the parents, carers, educationalists and other professionals better understand the different ways their children's brains and bodies grow?

* Could you integrate facts about the anatomy and function of the brain from the Open Colleges interactive map[7] into your sessions with children so they can also learn more about how they work as a human?

---

7   See www.opencolleges.edu.au/informed/learning-strategies

Part 2

Chapter 9

Using Different Art Forms in Early Years Practice

Choosing an arts or creative approach to explore

All people have creative abilities that can be expressed in different ways. Sometimes these abilities need to be 'discovered' before they can be nurtured. Maturity happens not only by providing the innovative ideas and stimulating environments, but also from having the knowledge and skills to follow children's lines of imagination and take their creativity to the next level of expression.

Some, but by no means all, art forms will foster a creative response in young children. Children create, store and recall their knowledge as memories which are articulated sometimes immediately, sometimes many days or weeks after they have been created, and sometimes never. But whether articulated or not, all of their creative experiences will help to form a contextual tapestry of meaning through which existing knowledge is joined to new knowledge as children make sense of the things around them (Mukherji and Albon, 2018; Bruce, 2005a). Different art forms can play different roles in helping babies and young children to explore, discover and communicate their meaning-making, as well as flexing their imagination muscles.

Through these modes and channels, children will communicate their feelings, emotions, ideas, questions and perspectives on the world around them to other children and adults they interact with. They may not yet have the capability to express these things in a verbal language, so the arts provide fantastic resources to help children represent what they mean using movement, colour, texture, gesture, sound and image. Because of this, it is important to explore different art forms, materials and approaches that help stimulate the most imaginative responses and facilitate deeper levels of learning and creativity for different children.

Some children will have been brought up with a heritage of storytelling in their cultures, something significant that reinforces the ways in which their caregivers express their love and their lives through story. This is an important part of their family identity that will feel familiar and exciting to those children on a deeper level. Others may have well-refined motor skills which naturally dispose them to manipulate and make things using crafts or malleable materials. For others, a physical expression such as movement and dance is what unlocks a creative spark, especially for some boys whose cognitive engagement may come more easily through exercising their locomotion skills (Daly and O'Connor, 2016). Others still may have an aversion to the textures of some materials (such as rough cloth) but enjoy the textures of others (such as clay slip) due to different levels of sensory integration. Some of these things will be obvious, others less so.

As well as making symbols or patterns on an easel, children will also be fascinated by how different colours look when mixed together, how slimy paint feels when it is applied to the hand, how PVA glue peels off the fingers in little sheets when applied liberally and left to dry, or how gracefully ribbons can encircle them when whizzed around using the whole body. All of these activities, which might cause a bit of mess and annoyance to adults, are actually part of a generative learning experience on many levels, not least in enabling children to tap in to a deeper aesthetic appreciation of materials, and their possibilities, which might never be experienced through conventional areas and methods of learning.

While having their artistic senses fired up, children will be exploring and learning about science through the properties of materials. They will be learning about maths through the patterns and shapes they are creating. They will be extending their own language through the vocabulary they use to describe these strange sensory, physical and tactile experiences they are having which will not be found in any phonics book. They will be developing physical coordination and fine motor skills in holding paint brushes and glue sticks and applying them using different forces, as well as developing their tactile and locomotion intelligences through the proprioceptors in their fingers (Daly and O'Connor, 2016). They will be making choices and decisions on what materials, colours, shapes and patterns to use in order to express their inner thoughts and feelings in very specific ways. The important thing is to spend time with each child finding out what matters to them and encouraging them to take risks with materials.

Finding what arts activities a child enjoys doing most, or what techniques they are good at, is a great starting point for engagement. It builds self-esteem and the confidence to be able to take risks down the line. But, while it is important to spend time developing technical expertise in particular art forms or materials, it is also important to introduce new opportunities rather than sticking to the same preferences every time. This gives each child different chances, as they grow, to strengthen brain and body connections in the areas they excel in and still create new connections in areas they may not have been ready for before.

In addition, different children's skills will be more or less suited to different materials, which is important to consider when choosing which materials to make available, offering always a depth of challenge as well, since, 'as they mature, children's recognition of the materials' potential expands, and when their technical skills live up to their expanding conceptions of what they what to create, the quality of their artistry increases' (Eisner, 2005, p.80).

We primarily receive and perceive the world through our senses, whether this is through light, sound, texture, shape, smell, location or movement. Therefore, possibly the most important aspect of choosing a creative focus lies in the recognition of young children's multimodal natures. This means offering opportunities to perceive the world through sensory modes and represent and express this through symbolic modes using any one or combination of verbal forms, such as sound or language, and non-verbal forms, such as gestural or body language, making marks, using artefacts, or through digital means.

Children may also have been born with a genetic predisposition towards certain art forms such as music-making or singing, even if this is not apparent in their immediate home environment. Genetic traits can be passed on through every generation or they can skip generations, as we often see in the cases of twins. It could be that a love of dance is perpetuated through the cultural heritage of several generations in one family, for instance, and becomes encoded into the brain and body of future generations (Schore, 2017). That is not to say that specific genes have been identified relating to being 'musical' or 'artistic' for instance, but that there are likely to be 'genes that support component brain structures and, thereby, by extension, component musical [or artistic] behaviours' (Levitin, 2012, p.634) such as hand-eye coordination, auditory memory function, rhythmic sequencing, visual and spatial awareness and so on. Although, as Levitin points out, it is most likely that practice is the key variant that distinguishes between who becomes an expert musician or artist and who does not, regardless of genetic traits.

We simply do not understand the neuro-bio-psychological complexities of what might constitute an artful mind and body at birth. But we can observe its positive effects on the whole child. Therefore, it is important to ensure that children in educational settings are exposed to a wide variety of arts opportunities to stimulate and nurture genetic traits that might be predisposed to grow into creative or art-form inclinations and may develop over time, especially if their caregivers do not practise them at home.

So far, I have advocated for a purposeful breadth of opportunity; however, I should emphasise that the way to do this is not to bombard children with every art form and creative activity possible, and certainly not in quick succession. Rather, we should tune in to children's thinking and preferences by carefully setting up simple, creative provocations that might extend their interests and increase their enjoyment. These could be a small but carefully selected set of materials or resources that do not predetermine the full purpose or activity a child might use them for. Selection criteria could include materials that enable children to build on specific interests they have displayed, or to try out new techniques, to stimulate expression using a different sense or part of the body, or to be challenged to extend their existing knowledge and skills without becoming too frustrated or bored.

We can observe how different children respond to different opportunities, which ones spark their imagination in new directions, deepen their lines of enquiry, encourage curiosity, open up new modes of thinking and expression, cause delight and surprise, break through obstacles to interaction, build relationships with peers, increase communication or extend play in the most unusual ways. In these ways, the arts can take learning to a new level not previously experienced because 'creative insight often occurs when new connections are made between ideas or experiences that were not previously related. This happens across as well as within different modes of thinking' (NACCCE, 1999, p.40).

To provide some ideas on exploring with different art forms from a new materialist perspective (see the Philosophy Glossary at the end), the following sections offer some theoretical and practical ideas on using the art form to help inspire greater confidence. I have by no means covered all art forms but have focused on the ones that already have a fundamental presence in young children's lives, and that will provide a relevant springboard for most other forms.

Drama, role play and storytelling

Stories describe our diverse lives and relationships with the world around us. They are a hugely important mechanism for children to understand how people and things work in relation to themselves, and the variety of ways they can choose to respond to them. Children often act out 'plots' they have experienced at home or seen on the screen in order to try and make sense of them, just as adults do when thinking or talking through a dramatic event.

Even when re-enactments are exaggerated or become fantasy versions of real life, children are still using their own imaginations to ask important questions such as, 'What happened there?' or 'What might happen if…?' or 'What happens next/What should I do?' It is a powerful route to problem-solving for young children trying to make sense of their complex emotions, how and where they belong, their multiple identities and fragments of incomplete memories. And by assuming different roles, they can investigate the boundaries of these issues and emotions in a safe environment.

The importance of meaning-making, puzzling through issues and gaining some sense of emotional control through dramatic play can be missed in a structured classroom, and yet it is fundamental to children's social and emotional intelligence. It is the place where stories attempt to bridge reality and the imagination and where space is required to unfurl and make connections between the two. This is particularly the case where children are living in an increasingly directed culture and need ways for their imagination to be stimulated beyond the functionality of everyday toys or apps (Ackermann *et al.*, 2010). That is not to say that children's fantasy worlds are not real to them. Mental spaces and non-material stories are as real as any physical object we can observe or handle, and should always be taken as seriously in order to validate and cultivate children's creative thinking.

Like music, drama and role play can stimulate the same synaptic connections that are fired up in using spoken language (Sousa, 2006). Language is practised on several levels through the simple act of hearing different characters speak in stories, role play and dramas and in children's internal narratives. For many children, the act of creating or listening to stories is what helps them feel attached to, and positioned in, the world. The gestures, facial expressions, body language and vocal tones of a story reader will provide a rich language relating to the codes and symbols of human emotions, helping to ground children in their own languages, symbols and codes of belonging and being.

Children love to have their stories documented verbatim by adults. As well as being a symbol of validation and of being taken seriously, having their stories written down and retold enables children to listen to their own words and to recognise their own voices in a protected space. It also opens up the joy of watching the expectant concentration and curiosity of other children listening to their stories, building recognition, attunement and bonds between the group.

In her wonderful book, *The Boy Who Would be a Helicopter* (1990), American early childhood teacher and researcher Vivian Gussin Paley talks about the importance of the imagination in the stories children tell through play, showing how children often express deep and significant ideas and feelings through their many different modes of expression. Whether verbalised or not, an important aspect of this is that the stories, and the meanings behind them, are 'owned' by the children themselves and not subject to adult translation.

Paley explains, 'A day without storytelling is, for me, a disconnected day. The children at least have their play, but I cannot remember what is real to the children without their stories to anchor fantasy and purpose.' With each story, Paley continues, 'I am a step closer to my vision of connecting everything that happens in this nursery school classroom. My habit of drawing invisible lines between the children's images is, I think, the best thing I do as a teacher' (Paley, 1990, p.3).

Role – or dramatic – play in particular is an excellent way of learning how to work together as part of a team, helping develop children's self-regulation as they learn when to speak and when to hold back and create the space for other speakers in the story. Drama is a unique art form in helping children learn how to relate to each other and how to interpret different emotional signals because stories are often based on relationships between people and situations.

For educators, however, referring to children's socio-dramatic play as 'drama' can conjure up fears of constructing staged performances at Christmas centring around a devised script with enough characters for each child to have a go and lots of chances to dress up. There is understandable anxiety associated with the stress involved in coordinating the logistics around Christmas per se and meeting (some) parental expectations for angelic, grand-scale productions. However, outside the more stressful times of the early education year, children's performances can be incredibly rewarding experiences, especially when enacting improvised or impromptu dramas which give us an insight into the unfettered imaginary worlds of our little ones.

Structured performance can be an ideal starting point for learning technical skills such as voice projection (which is different to shouting), memory strengthening through line learning, vocal and physical expression, portrayal of emotion, suspension of disbelief (i.e. knowing that you are pretending but still portraying an absolute belief in the reality of the character) and stage management skills. All of these require a level of planning, practice, responsibility and performance at a certain time and are what might be considered 'transferable' skills that are hugely useful in many other domains throughout life.

What can surprise some is that, whether children are at the stage of the abstract and symbolic or the stage of realistic representation, most children's dramatic play has a plot, a narrative structure and a set of characters (or one, at least). Even if just representing ideas visually, children's artworks will often still have narrative structure and meaning to them (Eisner, 2005).

There are many different forms of drama and story-making that exist as possible starting points for children's creative expression (as well as social, emotional, cognitive and physical skills), which share some common elements. As with other art forms, supporting children's agency and enabling a more open-ended, less structured approach can be the key to unlocking their amazing creative gifts. Having the adult take on the role of the unknowing, somewhat helpless, non-expert can spark a much higher sense of agency in children to be able to take responsibility, where they feel secure and confident to do so. For instance, pretending to be a story-maker who has lost her book of stories, or a magician who has run out of magic, is a good starting point to generate children's power, ownership and control in designing and deciding the trajectory of the drama. It provides space for children's imagination muscles to be exercised, as anything becomes possible when liberated from the normal rules of an adult-imposed structure.

That is not to say that chaos will reign (although a creative pedagogy should make room for a bit of chaos, to play with ideas before a clear story emerges). Children understand that the rules of story-making and role play are largely built around fantasy – they know the difference between the space for make-believe and the space for reality, and when it is time to return to this – so a well-facilitated session will include the ability to return to a more structured environment when required. Children are masters of improvisation so role play should be allowed largely to emerge from their ideas rather than relying on over-prepared scenarios that may simply be irrelevant to what they are interested in on that day. This will become obvious with practice as imposed scenarios will fizzle out very quickly.

Using props and costumes can bring an added level of complexity to children's story-making by inspiring actions and narrative that might not otherwise have taken place. However, just as with objects in a museum, it is the novelty of such objects that stimulates the most diverse imaginative forays and leads to a deeper level of creative thinking than might otherwise have been possible with predictable props or costumes that have a predefined purpose or are overly familiar. Children are kinaesthetic thinkers – they think with their hands, bodies and minds simultaneously. Therefore, the act of handling props, hats and costumes engages them on a deeper level in story creation. The novelty of unusual props and costumes can trigger a more thorough mode of narrative questioning in order to identify what this object is and how it relates to them (Piscitelli *et al.*, 2003).

For children who may not be quite so confident in divergent thinking using props, a useful starting point might be to use a trigger technique such as Mr Benn's Museum or Mr Benn's Hat Shop (loosely based on the 1970s children's TV programme, *Mr Benn*, by David McKee[1]). During this session, children can be asked to choose an object or a hat and observe it closely with their eyes and hands. It is important to create an atmosphere of expectancy and magic in which the imagination has the space and focus to flourish. To do this, a physical space can be demarcated with masking tape or a long ribbon laid out in a big circle, inside which the children sit with their object. Children can be asked to close their eyes and their concentration can be deepened by asking them to listen to the sounds around them, then to the sounds inside them. Once focusing internally, they might be asked to imagine a world around the object or hat using any of the following prompts:

- What does it look/feel/smell like?

- What is it for?

- Where does it come from?

- Who owns it?

- What did they do with it?

- Where has this object travelled?

- Where might it go next?

- Why?

For younger children, the simple *triadic question* routine of 'Who? Why? How?' is all that is needed to spark off an imaginary adventure.

Open-ended props – especially from secondhand shops – are great to spark new ideas for a story, including hats, shoes, umbrellas, and a range of flexible accessories such as bags, sunglasses and thick belts, all of which will have a story, an essence, a history, an agency of their own that comes alive through the minds and bodies of a young child. From a new materialist perspective, we might well ask, where do the stories of these objects come from? Each object that is secondhand (i.e. has had a previous life elsewhere) comes with an essence – a smell, a particular shape, textures or wrinkles from being used, rips or tears from overuse, repairs of some description, a particular weight to it that is unfamiliar but somehow may be comforting (such as the weight of an old leather bag or jacket), unusual zippers or buttons, mysterious pockets or hidden compartments. Allowing children to explore them in different ways through different scenarios, the unique

---

1   See www.bbc.co.uk/news/av/entertainment-arts-27536659/as-if-by-magic-mr-benn-reappears

agency of a prop or costume accessory can spark a whole lifetime's worth of stories.

While children take this naturally in their stride, adults may be surprised at being attracted to a certain prop or material and wonder if the material is choosing them. This *aesthetic-affective openness* to materials is described by Rautio as an 'attentiveness to and sensuous enchantment by non-human forces, an openness to be surprised and to grant agency to non-human entities' (2013, p.395). In most cases, the educator could name a specific reason why they had been drawn to the material, which may be to do with the process of something being created and 'becoming' or to do with the object or story.

These elements of surprise, of the unknown, of the changeability of the materials should be embraced as an opportunity to reflect differently and take an alternative perspective through the props or objects. Having some*thing* in hand with which to do this can be very comforting and help remove the feeling of exposure for a child to think up a story. The more unusual the prop, the more likely it will carry the storyteller down unusual avenues of thought, one thing leading to another, enabling a playful process of discovery of self, the process and the object. Sometimes, the not-knowing can be a little scary for children. But as long as they are in a safe and supported environment, there is merit in this, as identified by developmental psychologist Seymour Papert and explained by his former student, now esteemed psychologist Edith Ackermann: 'diving into unknown situations, at the cost of experiencing a momentary sense of loss, is also a crucial part of learning' as this dance of immersion and dissociation to adopt different perspectives is how 'a dialogue can begin between me and my artifact', and where 'the stage is set for new and deeper connectedness and understanding' (2001, p.10).

Children build on the stories they already know so it is important to extend their repertoire by offering props and costumes that do not just reinforce the roles they are already familiar with. There are only so many things a fireman, policeman, Disney character or princess can do in a day, whereas a range of hats that have no particular character assignment (e.g. a wedding hat, top hat, woolly hat, trilby, large felt hat, flat cap, large straw sunhat, sombrero or conductor's hat) can open up their inner worlds in a way that more familiar hats may not. By consciously selecting a range of unusual hats and costumes, educators are also taking an important step towards preventing the reinforcement of stereotypes such as male or female roles, hierarchies of power, class systems and racial stereotypes, which are sometimes implicit in shop-bought costumes.

Some children may have strong imaginative muscles and choose to wander all over their fantasy worlds with these props and apparel. However, some children may stick to the same costume, prop and story for several weeks with many repetitions of the same themes being acted out. There may be many reasons for this, from the sheer enjoyment of the feel of one particular accessory in the hand, to the excitement of a story that unfolds over time, to the need for control that a particular character or scenario offers, especially if their situation at home is consistently challenging or stressful in some way. This child will still be working things out and may need time to do so – an observant and attuned educator will not rush this stage.

While being externally expressive in many ways, story-making and role play can also mask an array of subtle emotions or more complex feelings that children are coming to terms with as they grow. Drama is a valuable way of allowing space for expression, but sometimes this is an internal expression of feeling and not immediately visible to educators. Therefore, while having a broad offer available, it is not advisable to make a child 'wear' or 'be' a particular thing or character for the sake of extending their learning about an issue if it does not come from their stories. Children will always be aware of other possibilities, observing and learning to understand what other children are feeling, through the stories and play of children around them. For shy children who prefer to observe rather than perform, this will help them build confidence in knowing that other children feel similar emotions and that it is okay to feel like this. Their own stories will move on when they are ready to do so, especially when they feel secure and supported by an attuned adult.

Puppets are also a great way to offer children alternative opportunities to make sense of more complex emotions. By projecting some of those emotions on to third-party characters, children can observe how those characters deal with their feelings in response to familiar situations, within an emotionally safe space and without any threat of exposure themselves. Being in control of a puppet puts them in an empowering position that enables a child to try out different voices, movements and emotional responses through the puppet without concerns that they might not know what to do, run out of words, be exposed or that they might get into trouble for expressing strong emotions. It is a super opportunity to learn about how to be and how to relate to the world.

Indeed, several studies have emerged that focus on the relationship between participatory arts and regulation, where the ability to manage emotional affect and expression has improved significantly, along with their ability to function during and after arts interventions (Lonie, 2010; Brown and Sax, 2013; Eisner, 2005). Many of these studies also show correlations between the arts intervention and children's ability to achieve higher levels of self-motivation and self-esteem, both of which are essential skills for life.

In the educational setting, we should be prepared to make spaces flexible enough to change with the children's growing ideas. This will ensure that investigating, problem-finding and learning do not become limited to, or inhibited by, the furniture or a psychological fear of moving something that 'should' be in a particular place. Things can always be put back afterwards, which is a good way of symbolising the end of the fantasy world enactment (where anything was possible) and the return to reality (where we are relatively safe).

Books can also be excellent stimulants if they are linked to children's interests and ideas, especially if role play emerges naturally from books with which the children are already engaged. However, just as with over-structured scenarios, be careful to avoid over-using the 'book of the week' for the sake of slotting in a lesson on vocabulary or phonics. It is likely to close down the imagination, which is one of the main purposes of role play. Dramas that are allowed to flourish and be practised over time will be full of rich language, interesting and new concepts and complex evaluations of life which, if observed sensitively, will provide plenty of substance for practising language, literacy, numeracy and other areas of learning at appropriate times. It is so important to protect the times and spaces where the imagination is allowed to flourish without walls so that children acquire a robust balance of learning approaches and methods, structured and unstructured, full of reality and full of potential, within their educational experience.

Further activities, research and resources

https://earlyarts.co.uk/story-telling-role-play
https://earlyarts.co.uk/theatre-research

Key prompts and starting points

o   Is there a good balance of book-based stories and children's own stories in the setting to encourage children to use their imagination as a source of content?

o   Are you confident to start off, scaffold and open up children's fantasy worlds?

o   Are there enough unusual props, costumes and accessories to extend creative thinking?

o   Do children feel safe enough to take risks in their stories and role play?

- o Is enough time and support given for their own explorations of emotional issues?

- o Are we purposefully shifting the power-base to privilege their agency in story-making?

- o Are we validating their stories and building confidence through documentation and reflection?

Malleable and modelling materials

While the thought of using messy, malleable materials such as clay, mud, plasticine or dough, may fill some educators with horror, there are some well-researched benefits for choosing to use these art forms over others at certain times. The same with textiles, modelling and sculpting materials such as boxes, tubs, tins, cardboard, pipes, fabric, fibre, rubber, tubes, rocks or blocks. Many young children are offered neater, cleaner two-dimensional (2D) materials with which to express themselves, especially in the home where access to arts materials may be limited. However, for so many young people, the movement of the world is what brings it to life for them – you may notice that some young children find sitting still very hard to do and, in fact use their whole bodies to do things that adults would stand or sit still to do. They wriggle their bottoms while washing their hands; they do little squats up and down while drawing; they lie on their backs and dance their feet around while reading a book. It is such a strong part of their innate drive to explore and connect their somatic knowledge (what they know physically and through their senses, also referred to as embodied cognition), that some of the less tactile, 2D, rigid objects and materials (especially plastic) simply do not offer the opportunities a child needs to be able to fulfil this urge for movement, or kinaesthetic thinking.

Remember, at this stage a young child is mostly exploring the properties and potential of materials and, if we are lucky, they will express and share their stories as the sensory nature of the materials triggers ideas, emotions and memories. But they are not necessarily intending to make 'something'. Therefore, if the focus of material exploration is to extend their ideas, articulate their stories and build on their interests, then a child's natural drive for movement will be very much a part of this process. Very young children will joyfully express abstract ideas on paper, which they will not expect to look exactly *like* something, because in their minds it *is* that thing. What may appear as a scribble to the adult is actually a dancing frog, or daddy on his bike, to the child. They are not trying to represent what the actual thing looks like but more the action or the emotion of the situation, or what it means to them. The movement of something may be represented by symbols such as long, streaky lines or continuous circles on the sheet. Daddy on his bike may look like a big smile on three raggedy circles. While we may perceive there to be no perspective in an artistic sense, in fact the child will show their understanding of perspective by enlarging the thing that is most meaningful to her in the picture, such as a smile being twice the width of the face, or the long wiggly line showing the actual movement of the car as the child felt and saw it. But some materials are just too limiting to explore or capture the essence of movement.

Imagine a child wanting to tell you about a horse they saw on holiday. To start with, a horse up close is a huge animal to a little person, with its unique animal smell, its great sense of presence and bulk, its strange noises, soft nose, big eyes and, if cantering or galloping, its tremendous motion of a hundred legs – or so it would seem. The sensory experience would be enormous for a small child, and difficult to articulate in words for sure. But the child will happily represent this creatively – not through an actual picture representing a horse but instead the sensory experiences they felt, heard, saw, smelled and perhaps tasted. Imagine the differences in trying to capture this on a piece of paper, in a painting, through a clay sculpture, in a dance or in song. Each art form presents its own possibilities and limitations – some are more dynamic, others more fixed and stable. As Eisner explains:

> What you are able to achieve will depend on what you are able to do with the material. This doing represents a transformation of the material into a medium. Materials *become* media when they mediate. They mediate the aims and choices the child makes. In this sense, to convert a material into a medium is an achievement. (Eisner, 2005, p.80)

Until a child has developed an understanding of representation (i.e. expecting images to look like the same things in real life) then trying to represent actual forms (lines, shapes, textures, icons, colours) on paper can be a frustrating exercise, especially if the ink does not flow well from the pen, or the crayon is too thick, or the pencil is not sharp enough to draw the fine lines of the fluttery wings. Materials matter hugely to the quality of the child's expression. Malleable and 3D modelling materials will offer a greater sense of dynamic shape. They can reflect the mass, matter, bulk or presence of the thing. They can show movement that is constantly changing and represent the motion of a real, live event, even if the 'performance' or recreation of that event is over within a few seconds while the child plays with the clay and forms it into different shapes as they recall their memories.

According to Lowenfeld (1987) children do not conceive actual subject matter in their artworks until they start naming things. Therefore, its often better to avoid asking 'what is it?' or assuming that the creator has a product in mind as they may just as easily be exploring the movement, texture, matter or mass through their tactile senses in relation to an idea or memory they have, especially if there are mosaic materials and small tools available to create patterns and decorations. To scaffold the exploration further, if needed, questions or comments that help children observe more closely or reflect on their achievements are more constructive, such as 'Isn't it interesting how you made those patterns in the clay?' or 'Can you show me how you joined these pieces together?'

Clay and dough are heavy materials and likely to create challenges in trying to form shapes and structures that defy the forces of gravity, especially when soft. A respectful approach is to offer an extra pair of hands to support the child's design concept as it emerges, without offering any 'helpful' suggestions on *how* to do it, all the while ensuring the child remains in control of learning about how clay works as a medium. Whatever malleable material is used, these are often excellent 'slow burners' because of the challenges they pose to little fingers and muscles, and it can take a while to find out how the material responds well to inputs. A gentle approach to time and space for this will help the child enjoy manipulating the material without feeling the pressure of it having to 'be' something. Clay in particular tends to have a calming, grounding effect on young children, partly because it is so somatic – engaging the upper body and most of the senses – as well as the mind (it is a great material to explore with few clothes on so that children can really interact with its smooth, cool textures on their skin and, after play, all it takes to clean up is a wet flannel). As a result, they will be rewarded with an immersive experience, increased confidence, long periods of concentration, technical problem-solving skills and a deep knowledge of how to explore or express their theories of the world through this medium.

Whatever the materials used, 3D modelling is a great way of helping children investigate the skills needed to manipulate and manage the properties of less malleable materials. Ensuring a wide range of containing and connecting materials, such as large cardboard boxes, round tubes, pipe cladding, shoes boxes, tubs, paper, fabrics, wools and ribbons, will guarantee children practise both fine and gross motor development as well as many other cognitive and physical skills.

Because of the very practical nature of sculpture and construction (i.e. children having to use their hands to act on their thinking and work out how things fit together – the ultimate do-it-yourself or DIY), problem-solving through construction also stimulates critical thinking, which affects everything in life. It enables children to be able to be independent in their decision-making. It means they are not always asking for help or expecting someone else to work out the answer. Instead, they can ask themselves 'What is the purpose of this?' or 'How does it work?' or 'Can I do this?' or 'What might happen if I do this?' Far more than simply cutting, joining and sticking materials together, these critical thinking skills are crucial for taking control of many other problems in life.

Experiencing the work of artists through gallery exhibitions or artists' visits to the setting can open up children's appreciation of the visual world by offering opportunities to see and respond to professional arts in situ. Not only does this offer children an insight into the imaginations of professional artists, which may stimulate their own aesthetic responses, but it also helps them understand that art doesn't come in neat boxes and can be anything they want it to be using any materials that help them express their ideas. It also helps them develop a visual, spatial and tactile awareness by seeing things they would not normally see in everyday settings, and heightens their awareness of visual forms within their environment.

President of Reggio Children[2] Carla Rinaldi points out that, while children are highly competent in making their own meaning, having this validated by peers and adults through the *reciprocity of listening* helps develop a sense of independence, surety, confidence and mental wellbeing. Children's use of multiple *symbolic languages* to express their ideas and thoughts, feelings and concerns, raise questions and construct theories about the world is how

2   Reggio Children is the foundation dedicated to promoting the Reggio Emilia approach and the work of its founder, Loris Malaguzzi. More details at https://reggiochildren foundation.org

they create their identities and understanding. Using children's natural art forms allows opportunities to 'represent their mental images to others' and, as they do so, to 'represent them to themselves, developing a more conscious vision (interior listening)' (Organisation for Economic Co-operation and Development, 2004, p.12).

In committing to mutual and creative listening practices and tuning in to others' intentions and agencies (human and non-human), the spaces for individual and community voices arise. These are spaces for our collective thinking in action, a verbal and gestural playground without fear of judgement or being labelled and put in a box marked 'done' (tick). As Rinaldi puts it, 'If we need to be listened to, then listening is one of the most important attitudes for the identity of the human' (Rinaldi, 2001, p.3).

Therefore, space and time to practise using their 'hundred languages' of expression through different art forms requires that we, as adults, have a level of knowledge and familiarity with such art forms to ensure that we can support a child to a high quality of creative experience (Dewey, 1934). This means taking the time to go deeper and for longer with fewer creative resources – less is more! As Lindsay (2016) asserts, this is a challenge for some modern practices where multiple, task-based arts activities are provided in a short space of time to motivate, entertain and keep children from 'getting bored'. Ironically, the more superficial the approach to engaging in arts and creative processes, the less immersed, enriched, challenged, independent, thoughtful or stimulated a child will be and the more activities and attention they might request.

Dewey frequently stressed the importance of the quality of the experience. So, if the creative process is simply a way of filling time with a fun activity with little thought (or preparation) for the children's interests and ideas, lacking time to enable a depth of exploration into different modes of enquiry or lacking relevance that can extend the existing learning taking place, the experience will have limited usefulness. In these situations, while the activities can be fun, Dewey uses the metaphor of the child 'forever tasting and never eating' and never having the 'organic satisfaction that comes only with the digestion of food and transformation of it into working power' (Dewey, 1902, p.16, in Lindsay, 2016).

Lindsay maintains that quick-fire, close-ended, entertainment approaches to learning may have their place in taster workshops or commercial play venues, but in an environment where the intention is to provide quality education and care, this approach can limit rather than extend children's potential. It can encourage a desire for superficial experiences that, through their novelty, trigger a chemical reaction in the brain's reward centre without building the structure required for sustained, resilient learning. It's like having a sugar high – such experiences feel great for a short period of time, but leave the person feeling even emptier inside after the novelty has been quickly digested – the high turns into a low – and set up expectations to be re-entertained. Rather, avoid short-shelf-life activities and focus on much more open-ended materials, such as clay, that can offer a deeper, richer and much longer experience for the children. In doing so, their thinking and expression – their hundred languages, as Reggio Children founder Loris Malaguzzi described – are drawn out in many surprising and unusual ways. Without these opportunities, early education gives the impression of wanting to 'separate the head from the body' or to 'tell the child to think without hands, to do without head, to listen and not to speak, to understand without joy' as expressed in the *Hundred Languages* poem by Loris Malaguzzi (translated by Lella Gandini) (Reggio Children, 2001).

Further activities, research and resources

https://earlyarts.co.uk/clay-modelling
https://earlyarts.co.uk/recycling

Key prompts and starting points

o   Are we offering a range of modelling materials that stimulate kinaesthetic thinking?

o   Are we creating enough time and space for sensory exploration of malleable materials?

o   Do we know how to sensitively scaffold and model to help develop technique?

o   Have we invested in our own training to understand different techniques and materials?

o   Are we selecting materials and encouraging language that helps children discuss the properties and visual qualities of materials (e.g. line, shape, weight, texture, feel, colour)?

o   Are we paying attention to children's emotional and imaginative responses to different materials, to see which ones provide greater value for their creative explorations?

o   Can we help children see, feel and talk about what is distinctive about their creations, including what is mysterious or symbolic and not immediately apparent?

- ○ Are we inviting in artists and designers who can help inspire children's creative vision?

- ○ Can we build a relationship with a local art gallery or museum to extend children's aesthetic experiences and artistic intelligences?

Mark-making and drawing

Similar to malleable, modelling and other visual arts materials, mark-making and drawing are valuable communication channels for children which, according to Eisner (2005), resonate deeply with a child's expressive and emotional drive, providing a jumping-off point for communication and interaction. Through this method, children can test out and create symbols that signify the meaning of whatever they are feeling or wanting to communicate, for which words simply cannot provide a satisfactory outlet on their own (and sometimes not at all).

In addition, drawing is a very physical activity, with many children preferring to use more challenging implements to make their marks, such as sticks in sand, feet in paint, brushes and water on concrete slabs, in order to relish the physicality of the experience.

Listed below are the six stages of artistic development proposed by art educationalist Viktor Lowenfeld (Lowenfeld and Brittain, 1987) which were considered to be a ubiquitous, global progression for all children up to the age of five based on both biological and psychological growth, although Lowenfeld held that the stages are dynamic rather than linear, with some overlapping and encompassing movement in both directions.

Scribble stage (2–4 years old)

- Kinaesthetic activity and manipulation of tools/materials
- Accidental marks made, including dots, slashes, scribbles, open shapes
- Rapid sensory and motor development leading to closed shapes
- Eventually beginning to use imaginative names for shapes

Pre-schematic stage (3–7 years old)

- Beginning to understand symbolic representation, and actual objects are recognisable in drawings, though shapes are constantly changing
- Tadpole human figures, eventually with body and arms added
- Drawing from mental or sensory perception, not observation
- Size and position of objects reflect their importance to the child
- Letters and numbers appear, no ground or baseline for objects

Schematic stage (7–9 years old)

- Highly individualised schemas (repeated concepts) or invented symbols appear to represent humans and objects in the world
- Human figures are fully formed, often with facial features and stacked geometric shapes for body parts, still lots of movement
- Drawing from mental perception, not observation
- Colour becomes meaningful and important to distinguish features
- Ground, sky, air and baselines for 2D perspectives are incorporated
- X-ray drawings often showing profile with front view or elevation or inside, plus outside in same picture to capture a detailed narrative

Drawing realism stage (9–11 years old)

○ Previous schema replaced with more realistic representations

○ Internal subjective ideas combined with external objective views

○ Starting to explore horizon line and 3D perspectives

○ Preoccupation with depicting realistic detail without subtleties

○ Loses the flexibility of movement and action of previous stages

○ Human figures are more holistic, with sexuality and personality identified

○ Social identities are much more apparent, belonging to certain groups

○ Desire to express emotional intensity and creativity – this can cause frustration until adequate techniques and outlets are mastered

○ Sense of self-critique and awareness (fear) of quality judgements

○ Perseverance leads to rich sense of fulfilment and self-expression

Age of reason stage (11–13 years old)

○ Increasing self-critique and frustration marks end of creative spontaneity; focus is on naturalistic products to 'adult' standards

○ Those who overcome this crisis will unlock a world of new creativity with skilful techniques and complex visual ideas

○ Subtleties of atmospheres are added, including light and dark, shading.

○ Attempts to include full 3D perspective in pictures by proportional sizing of objects

○ Drawing from observation, not memory

○ Attention to realistic colours and experimentation with materials

Period of decision stage (14–17 years old)

○ Art usually only continues with conscious decision to refine skills

○ Depictions of human form and mind emerge, revealing inner drive

- ○ High critical awareness of immaturity of drawing skills, easily discouraged unless introduced to non-representational forms (e.g. architecture, urban design, interior design, crafts)

- ○ Space, colour and design elements well understood and portrayed

- ○ Individualistic styles emerge driven by social or emotional issues, experimentations in materials and concepts motivated by meaning

The age groupings within this framework are largely based on what children might be capable of but, as we know, this is often not the same as what they want to do naturally. Children never move abruptly from one stage to another and their progression is possibly more influenced by how much encouragement and opportunity they experience in the home and other environments than their ability to draw. So, just as I would urge caution with any developmental framework based on ages and stages of ability that might single out some children for not being as 'good' as others, the same applies here. However, it was eminently clear from Lowenfeld's writings that his intention was not to design this as a reductive mechanism but rather one of immense encouragement and support for children's unique experimental and creative expressions. The important motif throughout is to resist judging any artwork from the perspective of realism but instead to look for the originality and expressiveness of its nature. Lowenfeld was a great believer in exposing children to the work of contemporary artists to highlight that there is no right or wrong way to express ideas or portray objects and space in drawings.

In children's drawings, one can clearly see examples of their schema as described by Athey (2007) in Chapter 7, where the form (lines, shapes, spaces, connections, icons, symbols, textures, etc.) is often created in a consistent style from picture to picture whereas the content is what changes and 'depends on the richness and extent of a child's experiences' (Deguara and Nutbrown, 2018, p.2). This recurrence of a unifying form is what Nutbrown (2011) discusses as showing the 'threads of thinking', reflecting the many connections between a child's concepts of the world and how they know these things. In other words, drawings can express the links between 'what children do and think' and 'the process of learning' (Nutbrown, 2011, p.35).

For instance, a young child makes marks on paper as a visual narrative depicting a trip to the park, whereby she appears to scribble shapes – mainly circular or u-shaped lines – and 'filled in' textures. She accompanies her drawing with a verbal narrative describing her experience of 'zooming' round on the roundabout, and 'whooshing' up and down on the swings, and the actions of her pencil on the paper represent the feelings or movements experienced during this event, rather than depicting what she actually did or saw. A year later, the same child draws a view of her family by placing each member of the family in size or age order, reflecting her fine motor skills in connecting lines and shapes, her knowledge of mathematical concepts as well as concepts of familial connections. She draws large circles to show much bigger heads than bodies, with more emphasis given to the expressions on the faces than anything else, such as big smiles or tears, describing her fascinations with faces and emotions. Her pictures retain a similar schematic form of circular movements, even though her content has changed considerably.

Due to the small spaces in many settings, we often find early years activities restricted to small-scale projects, A4 pieces of paper, a limited number of colours and brush sizes, or a tiny area within which to 'do' the creative activity. Sometimes playing in a small space can be great for focused attention to detailed work, but when these restrictions are removed, it is common to experience children responding quite differently to the activity, drawing or painting, with much more vigour and vitality.

Children whose brains and bodies need to explore the world in a more physical way might be encouraged to paint in large scale on long rolls of paper using long brushes attached to sticks. This dramatically changes the way they both make and see their creations, looking from a distance where they can take in an overview of the whole thing, rather than only seeing small details at once.

This kind of embodied expression in the process of creating can be tremendously liberating, especially for children with active legs and little fingers who may struggle with smaller tools or detailed, focused work at an early stage. Large scale also releases children with movement-based schema to physically describe their preferred patterns of action (e.g. using paint, ribbons or flexible materials), reflecting what they like to do with their whole bodies as they find out how things work and fit together. Indeed, working on the *cusp of chaos* when you do not know what the outcome might be can be liberating for educators as well. This is where the complexity of children's learning often comes out in the messiness of the creation as it is no longer limited by our 'neat' concepts of what learning *should* be taking place at that time. This has implications for daily practice, planning and preparation, and also for adult self-regulation in standing back and allowing children's ideas to take their own course.

It is interesting to note that children's drawings are often an externalisation of their thinking processes and, as such, may not contain a complete meaning, or explanation, of a situation by themselves. Children's verbal and gestural narratives that often accompany drawings are critical to enable a fuller understanding of the processes of learning that they are applying, as well as the understandings they are reaching through this visualised thinking (Deguara and Nutbrown, 2018). Therefore, when children's drawings are put on display, it is important to carefully consider whether or not additional documentation might help the child's meanings to be expressed more fully and to help resist adult interpretation to suit their own needs, such as looking for a psychological interpretation of their child's state of mind, or a signifier of their child's cognitive skill development. Additional documentation might include the child's verbalised narration in written form or their gestural expressions in photographic form, with respect for the multimodal nature of the story creation.

Having said this, it is worth bearing in mind that a retelling of the story often does not capture the intended meanings of the drawing at the time and, for many children, displaying their artwork on a wall can seem to be superfluous. As Wright (2010) points out:

> After-the-event stories are a pale imitation of the vitality of the child's running commentary that is so central to a visual narrative… It is separated from the 'soul' of the composition such as the child's in-situ facial expressions, expressive vocalisations, dramatisations, gestures to illustrate enactment and personal engagement with the creative act of meaning-making. (Wright, 2010, p.47)

However, that is not to say that every picture a child draws will contain a specific meaning in and of itself. While children are certainly very intentional in exploring meaning through their actions, drawings (and most embodied art forms) can also express meaning-making on another level – simply in terms of experiencing (and making sense of) the feelings and emotion that drawing can illicit, i.e. the joyful exuberance, or the calming focus that is felt through the art form itself. This may be to do with the satisfying expression of form or content, but it may as easily be to do with how the actions, sounds or shapes of drawing feel in the body, or the surprise of exploring specific colours next to each other, or the challenge of making shapes in a certain way, or simply appreciating the beauty of the creation as it emerges.

This transcendental, emotive sense often felt through drawing (and music and dance) is not so easy to identify through a schema that describes repeated, physical or somatic actions. There is no doubt that children draw because they love to draw, they love the feelings it gives them. It is not clear from current research what those more-than-human experiences are caused by but this takes me back to my question in Chapter 7 of whether a schema could be created that helps describe and identify any sort of correlating patterns in these transcendental creative behaviours or senses.

Drawing happens before children start to write, which has many benefits not least in giving children a true voice to their feelings and expressions through meaningful pictorial signs. As Wright observes, 'The act of representing thought and action while drawing actually strengthens children's later understanding of literacy and numeracy' (2010, p.7). Unfortunately, however, many traditional systems of schooling suppress children's *free composing* through drawing in favour of *teaching* the more rule-bound, structured symbol systems of numeracy and literacy because of the perception of 'letters, words and numbers as a higher status mode of representation' (Wright, 2010, p.7). And yet, thinking in symbols and connecting concepts – what Dewey (1934) describes as a central facet of the arts – is one of the most sophisticated forms of critical thinking and meaning-making. In fact, Harvard University psychologist Howard Gardner stresses that 'so pervasive is symbol use in human culture that it is difficult to designate an area of human expression where symbols and symbolisation are not entailed. Moreover, symbolisation seems to play an especially important and prominent role in the arts' (Gardner, 1982, p.113).

Traditionally, scholars have promoted two approaches to interpreting and measuring symbolisation. According to Gardner (1982), the first is the cognitive approach, advocated by educational theorists such as Bruner and Piaget, which considers symbolic activity as an intellectual activity through which children will understand symbolic meaning the more they develop their cognitive capacities. The other approach, favoured by psychologists, revolves around the development of emotional capacities, or affect. This perspective assumes that children can create and understand symbols, and the job of the professional is to understand how they use symbols, and how or why this affects their social and emotional development. Gardner admits that there is still a way to go before an adequate description of symbolisation is reached that encompasses the multiple, diverse influences on symbolic meaning-making.

Either way, to 'judge' a child's drawing on the basis of its technical or aesthetic skill, or to consider only the psychological insights it might offer into a child's mind in isolation of the child's own storytelling, is to privilege a spurious adult authority over the child's original intentions. The authentic purposes for drawing, as we have discussed, are often more to do with the journey of making sense of the world, to play with movements and emotions and for the enjoyment of self-expression than to achieve an aesthetically high-quality product, or to reveal deeply emotional intentions. In fact, most of these acts would assume the need for an audience, which is not the primary reason young children draw until they enter the primary school environment where their perception of creating art for a specific, externally imposed outcome becomes much more refined.

More recently, neurologists have been exploring their own theories of drawing as well. Drawing and painting stimulate the visual processing system that recalls memory or creates fantasy, and the limb-to-eye movements associated with observing and creating shapes, lines, colours and forms link to the development of coordination and muscle memory in conjunction with motor skills (Sousa, 2006). Interestingly, a new body of research called Child of the New Century (CNC), run by the Centre for Longitudinal Studies at University College, London, is recording the lives of the generation born at the turn of the millennium. The purpose of the study is to understand the whole picture of people's lives individually, and of a generation as a whole. In the UK cohort study CNC surveys completed so far, which were gathered at ages three and five, mothers were asked how often they helped their child with reading and writing, and activities such as drawing and painting. The surveys found that children who had these types of interactions in their preschool years displayed better behaviour and moods, and higher ability in reading and maths (Kelly *et al.*, 2011).

Nevertheless, it is without doubt that the core benefits of drawing and making symbols lie in a much more nuanced purpose than purely academic impacts. As Howard Gardner (1982) illustrates:

> An artistic medium provides a special, even unique, avenue for grappling with important and complex issues [...]. Indeed it may be this paradoxical, ambiguous quality that, more than anything else, conveys the special power and fascination in the drawings of the young child.

Further activities, research and resources

https://earlyarts.co.uk/drawing-painting-mark-making
https://earlyarts.co.uk/visual-arts-research

Key prompts and starting points

- Are we encouraging children to be inspired by the imaginative art of real artists so that they can see the validity of individual expression rather than trying to recreate photographic realism?

- Do children have a wide range of high-quality materials and resources to use?

- Are we stimulating and supporting a diverse range of concepts and techniques in drawing?

- Have children got enough space and large paper to think and draw with their whole body?

- Are children encouraged to tell the story of their drawing and name their scribbles?

- Do children's intended meanings accompany their drawings when on display?

- Are we helping extend children's repertoire by using drawing as a tool for describing thinking across all areas of learning, such as maths, science, language, understanding the world?

- Have we provided drawing materials for outside games, walks, investigations and play?

Movement and dance

Physical movement starts in the womb and relies both on the development of the brain and the body together in a natural order. Until the larger bones, muscles, primitive reflexes, tendons and ligaments are developed, the smaller, more complex and refined ones that control fine motor skills and attuned sensory perception and articulate language cannot begin to form properly (Daly and O'Connor, 2016). Child development expert and founder of Moving Smart[3] Gill Connell attests to this by confirming that the best way to improve children's handwriting skills is to 'put your pencils down and go play on the monkey bars' (Connell and McCarthy, 2014, p.135). Larger physical activity like this has the effect of not only strengthening the body ready for fine motor, coordination, language and sensory development, but also inhibiting the primitive reflexes designed only for the new-born stages of life.

These include the Palmar (grasping) reflex where a baby grasps hold of your finger, hair, clothing or any object placed in its hand; the rooting or sucking reflexes designed to help the baby find nourishment (breast or bottle) from day one; or the Moro (startle) reflex that happens where a baby's head, legs, arms and fingers jerk up and are outstretched before retracting into a state of crying in response to being startled. These reflexes can become detrimental to the control of other body parts if not inhibited, which happens naturally between 5 and 12 months. Creative movement play is one of the best ways to encourage this inhibition and refinement of reflexes by strengthening connections in the frontal lobe, which naturally inhibits the primitive reflexes originating in the brain stem.

Children's self-control of their bodies grows stronger as healthy development happens, so it should come as no surprise to realise that their behavioural, psychological and social regulation also grows as a result of increasing physical control. Each time they try, and succeed, at a physical challenge, their brains store the memory of this in the hippocampus, closely linked to the reward centre. This leads to the release of the neurotransmitter dopamine, which is also closely linked to affect in terms of sending positive signals, positioning this activity in the amygdala (emotional centre of the brain) (Berrol, 2006). The memory of this positive experience is stored in readiness for the child to repeat and refine their achievements, in correlation with the joyful emotions and self-regulation experienced at the same time, all of which motivates repeated activity.

---

3   Moving Smart was founded in 1997 by educator and author Gill Connell to help teachers and parents better understand the role movement plays in early childhood development.

As humans, we are all creatures of habit. From the early stages within the womb, we form patterns of repetitive behaviours that satisfy basic instincts, such as thumb-sucking, kicking, turning and dancing. From birth, a child mirrors the movements, facial expressions and gestures of their caregiver to elicit further response and satisfy desires for attachment, attunement, mutual affection and expression (Malloch and Trevarthen, 2018; Schore, 2000). As our body and mind learn how to function, we build sensory movement schemas in order to help our bodies function more efficiently, faster and stronger and achieve and fulfil our needs, whether that be sucking milk from the breast or bottle as a baby or feeding ourselves with a spoon as a toddler. The older we grow, the more established those movement routines become for any one of a thousand actions in everyday life. Unless we break them...

> Habits, including those of movement, gesture and posture, afford us a sense of security and safety in that they are implicit 'proven' adaptations to particular environmental conditions, designed to produce optimal outcomes. To be playful and creative is to challenge habitual responses in order to move, think and feel in new, unfamiliar ways – to seek out and grapple with the risks that enliven us by their unpredictability and expand our windows of tolerance. (Ogden, 2018, pp.92–93)

Movement habits enable us to predict and adapt the actions we will need in the future based on what has been successful (or not) in the past. As movements become learned, adapted and established, they become intuitive and higher order cognitive processes are no longer needed to regulate them. This leaves the mind and body free to experiment, explore and engage with novel ideas and situations without being overwhelmed by such novelty. In other words, the more intuitive their core sensory movements become, the more creative and resilient children will be with their bodies, senses, minds and new situations, without being overwhelmed or frightened. Regular movement programmes help children feel safe, in order to then take risks. Unusual movement programmes (such as contemporary dance or music and movement) help children improve their creativity by pushing beyond the familiar and finding out what else their body can do outside the learned routines. That level of challenge is exciting for children and necessary for healthy growth.

There are several reasons for this. On a physiological level, dancing that extends everyday movements has been found to increase the number of capillaries in the brain, which facilitates blood flow and therefore oxygen to the brain, thereby impacting on cognitive performance at the same time as supporting a child's healthy, physical development (Daly and O'Connor, 2016; Sousa, 2006).

Lakoff and Johnson (1999) maintain that children's intuitive, embodied experience underpins all cognition and is demonstrated through their sensorimotor systems. For example, children often describe spatial concepts physically (e.g. moving and adapting blocks or drawing in the sand with sticks to delineate the boundaries of a space) or try to solve sequential problems through gestures (e.g. specifying shapes, distances and other numeric concepts by drawing in the air). This seems to aid the choice and sequence of words spoken, and the ability to make themselves understood, as the visual, gestural, facial and verbal cues are received and interpreted by the listener. In situations of collaborative play or co-constructed learning where much is yet to be imagined in the conversation that will be had, the language of movement plays a vital role in establishing reciprocity during this two-way approach to meaning-making, creative challenge, call-and-response and joint problem-solving.

> A resilient movement vocabulary enables us to welcome appropriate risks and respond to novelty in imaginative, life-enhancing ways. Our [children's] response to novelty becomes ever more creative and playful when we can help them challenge their physical habits and develop expansive, innovative, flexible, and fluid movement vocabularies. (Ogden, 2018, p.108)

From a young age, children often experience fairly structured movement routines, usually to music, at their nursery, playgroup or stay-and-play sessions. Learning the actions to nursery rhymes is a great way to help co-ordination, balance, motor and muscle growth and strength building. However, just as important are more spontaneous opportunities for children to play with movement – to explore the limits of their bodies by running, jumping, rolling, climbing, stepping, crawling, wrestling, skipping, sliding, hopping, drawing, fiddling, shaking, squeezing, flicking, wiggling, tickling, twirling and sometimes colliding! The opportunities here for putting language to movement are numerous, especially enjoying how onomatopoeic words *feel* in the body, which is just as valid a way of aiding memory retention. But being spontaneous does not mean that these actions are without purpose.

The opportunity to be spontaneously physical underpins the process of how children's brains and bodies learn to connect important neural pathways, linking the cognitive, social, emotional, physical and creative aspects of their whole being. It is when children are given space to move their bodies freely that they are learning to make sense of the world around them, thinking about how things work, understanding cause and effect, trying out new techniques, feeling positive and negative emotions and understanding how to respond to each one. Routines definitely have their place, but spontaneous movement play is crucial to help a more creative occurrence to happen.

This sort of movement enables children to think in more creative ways, and to express and communicate their inner thoughts and feelings. It is child-driven, often self-initiated largely in reaction to their environment at the time, especially when they have the freedom and permission to explore, interact and discover the limits of that environment (and themselves) through their own physical expression. It also gives us a fantastic window into children's inner lives – their hand or foot gestures, finger waggles, facial expressions, eye contact and subtle movements or flickers of small limbs tell us what is happening for them and how they are feeling.

To limit young children's expressions to writing exercises, or using verbal speech, is to deny that important gross motor activity is taking place in order to develop the fine motor skills required for writing and speaking. Worse still, it disrespects the natural predispositions young children have for physical expression, it disempowers them from moving their whole bodies to allow their neurons to connect properly, which can lead to later problems with health disorders (such as obesity, self-image, communication, anxiety, balance, ability to develop practical, hands-on skills) and it prevents the very essence of who they are from flourishing.

The current educational emphasis on teaching writing and speaking skills at an age that research shows to be too early for appropriate physical development pressurises children to 'use their words' to express feelings when they are too young to be able to articulate emotional reasoning (Daly and O'Connor, 2016, p.17). This, together with the trend of measuring learning progression only through verbal articulation, results in children's main form of (non-verbal) expression at this age being largely ignored or misunderstood. This risks inhibiting both who they are now and in the future.

Young children need to be able to move in big ways, which is sometimes a challenge in the small rooms in which they live, play and learn. Creativity offers wonderful opportunities for that essential large-scale play that engages the whole of their bodies, strengthening their gross motor skills, coordination and balance before the small-detail play of fine motor development is refined. Painting the outside walls using large brushes and water, painting with absorbent materials (such as sponges) on large rolls of wallpaper, drawing with chunky chalks on the pavement, swirling to the sounds of the birds singing using silky scarves, being gently dragged along the floor or slowly swayed in lycra hammocks: all these are examples of unstructured, creative activities that introduce children to their physicality and help them explore and express it as much as they possibly can using their whole bodies.

For many children who are either too young to have clear verbal speech, do not have English as a first language, are shy or simply cannot speak due to an anxiety or physical health difficulties, understanding and correctly interpreting their body language is a crucial step towards having their needs met, their ideas validated, their potential recognised and their feelings fulfilled.

Just as with their innate musicality, children are born with the languages of sensory perception and recall that are highly physical and lead to embodied cognition through repeated actions, or schema (Daly and O'Connor, 2016). Yet educators are trained to reduce physical language assessment to motor and locomotion skills which, together with speech, are easier to measure using empirical frameworks. But what is 'listened to' through statistical measures does not tell the whole story of a child's being and knowing (Denzin and Lincoln, 2013) despite being used to interpret and label children's identities in terms of health and education. It is interesting to note that increases in the awareness of sensory processing disorders over the last decade may point, in part, towards the heavy reliance on language for interpretation of children's needs, interests and progress to the detriment of embodied knowledge (Grace, 2017).

Rinaldi (2001) endorses cultivating a pedagogy of listening, where educators encourage responsibility-taking to explore the more creative and critical responses often experienced by listening more thoughtfully. In doing so, the dominant signifier of words is replaced with music or move-ment to enable the affective flow of expression, which opens up whole new languages to the child, not determined or limited by the mastery of speech. However, where pre-recorded music is used, it is worth bearing in mind that music is culturally specific and can cause as many obstacles to sensing as opportunities, influencing both children's and adults' responses to materials, objects, movements and stories. The careful choice of music by the educator is important so as not to skew and even manipulate responses to the movement experience. In fact, it is worth experimenting with bird song which is considered a universally value-minimal stimulant (Gardner, 1982).

Touch is one of our core senses, and it is there for a reason. As well as using their physical languages to communicate with us, children also need us to respond and communicate with them physically, not just in our facial or bodily gestures but also through holding, stroking, hugging and other appropriate and sensitive tactile gestures. Human touch is essential to the cognitive, physical and emotional wellbeing of children, not just for bonding, reassurance, validation, comfort and care but also to help embed positive learning dispositions and self-regulation that will support children through life. At the core of our tactile interaction is the sense of security that we are giving our children. As we gradually decrease the number of things we do for children, and help them increase their physical independence, balance and strength, we are also helping them increase their emotional independence, balance and strength. Of course, as well as observing safe and sensitive practices regarding touch, it is imperative to also listen to a child's response. Just as with adults, sometimes children do not wish to have any tactile interaction, or some interactions are preferred over others. It is essential to respect children's wishes to build trust and mutuality and ensure that children feel secure and able to develop socially and emotionally.

The largest organ of our body is our skin, with its thousands of nerve endings that detect and process information about touch, pain, pressure, temperature and the space around us (proprioception). We can train these nerves to grow fully by helping children experience tactile sensations that also help to connect the neural pathways to other sensory centres that are crucial for learning across the brain, such as the amygdala (emotional memory), Broca's area (language processing centre), visual cortex, auditory cortex, motor cortex and several other key systems.[4]

For the many children who do not have a secure foundation and have not received responsive physical attachment or emotional attunement from their caregivers, the growth of vital nerves and the subsequent move to independence can take longer, or not happen at all. Related mental and physical health problems can become evident early on, especially at key transition periods where children are separated from their primary caregiver, such as starting school.

Dance and movement provide a unique opportunity to help temper the negative effects of such situations by releasing young children from the limitations of their physical or mental 'containers' (such as car seats, pushchairs, lack of self-confidence or the over controlling of caregivers). Opportunities for free movement may also effectively support many physical disabilities, neurodevelopmental delay (such as retained primitive reflexes) or neuromotor challenges that are restricting movement. The earlier we can intervene with creative movement play activities, the easier it is for a child's body and brain to adapt to these challenges.

---

4   See Brainfacts.org's excellent interactive map of the brain to find out how each area relates to another: www.brainfacts.org/3d-brain#intro=false&focus=Brain

Further activities, research and resources

https://earlyarts.co.uk/dance-movement

Key prompts and starting points

o Are we helping children's sensory responses to become intuitive so that they can explore the bounds of their bodies with more unusual movements?

o How expressive are we encouraging our children movements to be through music, drawing, flexible materials and so on?

o Do children have plenty of opportunities to be spontaneous as well as learn dance or movement techniques?

o Do we actively encourage children to take risks and extend everyday movements, to reach for things up high, climb larger steps, run around winding paths and undulating ground?

o Are we paying attention to the subtle, little gestures and movements that tell us what is happening for them and how they are feeling?

o Are we consciously putting aside our inhibitions so that children don't develop theirs?

o Are we encouraging nerve connections across the body and brain, as well as emotional assurance and validation, through affirming and attuned touch?

o Are we getting excited about movement and the huge range of opportunities for communication, language, maths and social and emotional development it offers?

Music and singing

As a ubiquitous global and cultural phenomenon, music is a significant part of our lives and is all around us every day. In fact, it is also a biological reality – babies are born with an inherent musicality across all cultures, which underpins all forms of learning and communication. For many children and adults, there is no doubt that music is a deep source of identity, expressing the innermost self and what it means to be human. It brings a sense of joy and vitality in both inward and outward expression, lifts our spirits and brings resonance to our limbs, manifesting across mind and body. From the moment the heart starts beating in the womb there is the potential for a sense of pulse to begin. Indeed, research shows that, in utero, the unborn baby processes sounds as early as 16–20 weeks, with motor responses to sounds becoming evident at 24 weeks. Malloch and Trevarthen (2018) also illustrate the highly intelligent kinetic and musical attunement that happens naturally between adults and even very premature babies when they become synchronised to each other's breathing and vocalising rhythms.

They assert that babies have an innate *communicative musicality* by which they mean the 'habitual patterns of action' through which infants' bodies explore their environment, vocalisations and movements in moments of intimacy between adult and child. These communications are shared narratives of meaning, with gestural, vocal and musical structures that underpin many art forms, including dance, theatre, music and storytelling. Of course, young children love to play with sounds. Whether it is listening to the same tune again and again as they become familiar with its words or rhythms and enjoying the positive feelings it elicits, or improvising a tune to describe their thoughts as they play, music plays a really important part in children's development. Because of its origins pre-birth, music is a natural and significant way for children to express themselves, their feelings, their emotions and their creative ideas.

Children whose physical expression is stronger in the early stages might especially enjoy banging drums, hitting xylophones, strumming guitars, shaking beaters around and striking bells. The physicality of this expression brings an immediate gratification that such a loud sound, vibration or dynamic effect can be produced by themselves. For children who are not yet able to verbalise their thoughts and ideas, this can be a welcome release for their emotional responses and communications. Although sometimes challenging to the adult, having a safe and welcoming environment where strong sounds can be expressed as well as softer ones can ensure that children who enjoy these instruments will feel more fulfilled. Making a range of percussion instruments available outside is also a great way for children to find a sound, a pace and a rhythm while moving in big spaces, or responding to the environmental music experienced from the trees, the wind, birds or other children playing.

Making music inside works well in groups, and experimental sound does not need to equate with unruly noise. Call-and-response activities, musical animation of stories or a simple conducting exercise in a group, for instance, can give each child in turn opportunities for control and experimentation. Being able to lead the actions of other musicians, improvise with sound and movement ideas or turn the volume of the group up or down can give children a tremendous sense of satisfaction and ownership, not to mention surprise at the interesting experimental effects they might have caused. At the same time, the act of listening to others' making music is equally as rewarding, with exciting sounds, rhythms and vibrations stimulating new ideas and sensory perceptions.

Musicality is a complex combination of physical, social, cognitive and psychological skills or traits, some of which are unique to music production and reception, others of which are shared with other processes. While there has been evidence of the cognitive and social benefits of music for a few centuries, neuroscience research (although in its infancy) is beginning to reveal how music activates several areas of the brain, with different neural circuits responsible for the various components such as pitch, volume, timbre (sounds of different musical instruments) and pace (Levitin, 2012). Some of these circuits are the same ones that are also activated during mathematical processing. It appears that early musical training begins to build the same neural networks that are later used for numerical tasks, such as creating patterns and sequences, counting and discerning shapes, understanding ratios and proportions, contextualising facts and solving problems (Sousa, 2006).

Language development is also influenced by music-making patterns where notes, chords and rhythms are created, which help children to hear and create the harmonic sounds of vowels and consonants as well as sequencing words and movements as the air vibrates through their bodies. Malloch and Trevarthen refer to this as the 'raw material for cultural forms of music and the rules of grammar and syntax' required for a mastery of language (2018, p.9). Just as with music, speaking involves melodic rises and falls, strong and light breathing patterns and rhythmic elements, which make use of up to 36 muscles just by saying one sentence! A large body of evidence demonstrates how music-making in early childhood can develop the perception of different phonemes and the auditory cortex and hence aid the development of language learning as well as musical behaviour (Lonie, 2010). Some of the more well-known music education methods, including Suzuki, Kodály, Orff and Dalcroze are particularly well designed to support children's auditory and kinaesthetic development from very young ages. The In Harmony programme (based on Venezuela's El Sistema programme) is a good example of how a large-scale approach to music-making in the foundation years can lead to engagement in learning as well as enhanced academic achievement, especially for children with special educational needs or those for whom music opportunities would not otherwise have been available (White, Lord and Sharp, 2015). As Lonie reminds us, it is worth remembering that young children experience a broad diversity of musical landscapes and have 'a high degree of agency in their musical choices…to decide what kind of music they wish to be exposed to as well as engage in' (2010, p.10) and the context of these experiences should be considered when integrating their music-making more effectively.

The high degree of precision required in auditory processing means that reading is often enhanced in musically trained children, who are better able to distinguish sounds, shapes of letters, memory storage, recall and concentration. According to Levitin (2012), the act of listening to music not only activates higher cognitive functions such as attention and memory, but also stimulates the reward and pleasure circuits which, in turn, generate higher musical expectations (i.e. tonal, harmonic and rhythmic expectations) that are fundamental to the enjoyment of music. Some studies have also shown correlations between musical creativity and the creation of serotonin (healthy levels of which can help regulate mood and suppress anxiety, among other things) and oxytocin, a neuropeptide that has been shown to enhance social behaviours such as empathy. In fact, many studies have shown how listening to and making music develops a phonetic awareness that enables children to pick up the nuances of speech and read the subtle changes of emotion in people's voices (Royal Conservatory, 2014).

Similarly, singing is an art form that enables a child to experience almost all of their senses at once – they hear the sound their voice makes, they feel the breath rising in their body and coming out of their mouth (and sometimes feel their body move to the sound of the song), they can taste things while singing as their tongue is usually fairly active around their mouth and they are often observing or imagining the things they are singing about, especially if they are immersed in song while playing. Smell is probably the only sense not experienced during singing or humming due to the nasal passages expiring rather than taking in breath while singing. The physical action of moving large volumes of breath from the chest or the diaphragm (above the stomach) to the mouth is a great way to re-awaken the brain. It stimulates blood flow to the head, neck, chest and other parts of the body and enables a very sensory response to a cognitive or emotional stimulus.

If we believe that the essence of creativity is like a sixth sense then we could contend that children who are deeply immersed in song are experiencing their sixth sense in expressing their inner spirit and individuality without inhibition or limitation. This is very similar to when we see children immersed in dance as if they are in a daydream (and indeed, the two art forms often go hand in hand).

Children often express their inner thoughts while singing, bringing to the fore thoughts, conversations, sights and feelings they are trying to make sense of. Often these are expressed in a fantasy language, as if they are extending a story into song and, by doing so, giving it an extra creative and magical quality. Pre-verbal children are especially competent in expressing their feelings through the tone and pitch they choose to use when singing sounds and making noises. When we listen to them carefully, it can be surprising how much sense their sound-stories make.

We see this with parents and caregivers who are tuned in to their babies, engaging in frequent mirroring or call-and-response games where they mimic and respond to the other's sounds. The interaction not only provides reassurance and strengthens their attachment but also elicits positive emotions by sharing a set of understandings about each other through such an interaction. Babies can express their delight and sorrow in ways that are fairly evident but sometimes get misinterpreted as caregivers learn how to synchronise communications with them. The older a child becomes, the more complex they are in both their emotional make-up and the methods of communication they choose. Whether infant or toddler, we need to listen to their songs carefully to determine how we can best encourage them, interact with them or step back and let them be alone in the delight of their fantasy or sensory worlds.

In a twist of biological genius, singing with our babies ensures their tongues, lips, vocal folds and vocal chords are being strengthened ready to create the shapes required to form words when they are ready. There are not only significant physical benefits but also social and emotional ones. One study in the USA used data from *The Early Childhood Longitudinal Study – Birth Cohort* preschool wave, which is a nationally representative dataset of children born in 2001. This study showed that children whose parents interacted creatively with them – such as singing to or with them or playing with construction toys and building blocks to create sculptures – at least three times per week had a higher likelihood of developing strong and sophisticated social skills, such as pro-social behaviours, compared with parents who reported interacting creatively with their child fewer than three times per week (Muñiz *et al.*, 2014).

Indeed, several studies have emerged that focus on the relationship between singing participation and emotion regulation, where the ability to control emotional affect and expression has improved significantly, along with children's competence, self-esteem and independence (Young, 2003; Brown and Sax, 2013; Schore and Marks-Tarlow, 2018; Kelly *et al.*, 2011; Trevarthen, 2002). So there are lots of reasons why music – and singing in particular – should be prioritised equally with language in the education system.

Children's rhymes are often written in a major key, and go up or down the scale in thirds and fifths (i.e. jumping up or down three notes or five notes at a time). Because of this musical pattern, which is common in everyday language and in nursery rhymes, they put the brain into what is referred to in neuroscience as the positive emotional affect (PEA) (Boyatzis and Hazy, 2015). Songs such as *What a Wonderful World* or *Twinkle Twinkle Little Star* both demonstrate these patterns of thirds and fifths that can result in the PEA state in both singers and listeners (otherwise known as emotional contagion). Singing these songs using patterns that reflect and reinforce everyday speech can make it easier for children to develop language.

Singing is a form of play that encourages children to practise a wide range of sounds and make sense of language through action and movement, not to mention the tremendous sense of joy that is shared when people sing together. Lots of familiar songs can be easily adapted, such as *Here We Go Round the Mulberry Bush*, which can be tailored to *Now We are Cooking Fish for Tea* or *What Shall We Eat for Lunch Today?* or other words that children make up. Singing is wonderful. It creates beauty and everyone can take part. It helps children learn how to work together effectively and requires no equipment so can be done anywhere. It is cheap, and generally makes you happy. Sadly, with the decline of school assemblies, children rarely sing together as a large body, but singing is important in making everyone feel included in a joint activity. Singing at a rugby match, singing the national anthem or singing in a community choir are strongly emotional and uniting events.

Feversham Primary is in Bradford and its headteacher, Naveed Idrees, took the school from being in special measures to achieving a 'good' Ofsted judgement in just three years. Feversham is now in the top 10 per cent nationally for pupil progress in reading, writing and maths, with its results for disadvantaged pupils being well above the national average.

When asked how this was achieved, Idrees revealed that at the heart of his visionary leadership was a practical programme of reform, not of systematic numeracy and literacy teaching, but of singing teaching. Supported by his music coordinator, Idrees implemented a programme of six hours of music every week for every child based on the Kodály approach (using child-centred singing and movement games to sharpen skills in concentration, listening, memory, rhythm, improvisation and play as well as musicality) with remarkable results. Feversham's music coordinator, Jimmy Rotherham, extolled the virtues of the programme for their 510 children, 99 per cent of whom speak English as an additional language, in an interview for *The Guardian*:

> The focus on creativity has improved results across the school, not just among the musically gifted. It is demonstrably more effective than drilling SATs papers. My hope is that headteachers…will read about our school and realise that creative subjects are not mere add-ons but essential for the progress of all pupils. (Rotherham in Halliday, 2017)

There are many excellent practical resources available with plenty of ideas for collaborative and individual music-making which do not need to be duplicated here, but what should be stressed is the importance of adults engaging in communicative musicality with their children as a way of building relationships, attunement and confidence as musical communicators. Early childhood music specialist Dr Susan Young (2003) emphasises this notion of 'mutuality' as a way of sharing possibilities, building trust and learning from each other at the same time as enhancing essential skills such as negotiating and networking with others. Young points out the profound musical competences and sensitivities shared by parents and caregivers or educators and children when making music together. These are often hidden behind a fear of inadequacy or lack of musical confidence but become apparent in the interactions between them. Their musical reciprocity conveys the 'strong traditions of adults incorporating music into the upbringing of their babies and very young children. Indeed it is intuitive to the caring role [but has] long been overlooked and devalued' (Young, 2003, p.11).

This may be partly due to the fact that, unlike visual art forms, musical creations with young children are often transient and not preserved unless they are recorded in some way. Therefore, it is easy to forget how amazing a musical interaction was, or to reflect on how it was reached, how it made the collaborators feel and what happened to their communication and attunement as a result. At the end of the day, tuning in to children's communicative musicality involves offering a range of thoughtful opportunities to synchronise our musical senses, whether vocal, physical, visual or multi-sensory, engaging mind and body in a reciprocal act of understanding and expression. All of us have an innate musicality and educators or caregivers do not need to be music specialists to be confident and competent communicators with their children. All it takes is to be willing to have a go at developing your musical languages, in order to open up a world of rich meaning and possibility and share many beautiful moments of joy and laughter with your children.

Further activities, research and resources

https://earlyarts.co.uk/music-singing
https://earlyarts.co.uk/music-research

Key prompts and starting points

o How open-ended are our musical activities?

o Are we actively listening and responding to children's musical explorations?

o Are we building on the ideas and interests from previous sessions?

o Are we introducing new sounds and techniques when appropriate?

o Are there opportunities for children to lead the music and make choices?

o Which sounds (vocal or instrumental) might add value to a session, and which will not?

o How will we ensure that all adults are comfortable to interact musically with their children?

o Are we documenting children's creations and becoming more aware of their musicality?

- ○ Is there anything deterring us becoming more attuned and communicating musically?
- ○ Are we investing in our own musical training?

Photography

Photography is a great example of a creative language that can easily be shared due to the universal and diverse impressions that can be taken from an image, whether or not we can express our ideas in words. Because of this, it is ideal as a communication tool to unite parents, caregivers, professionals and children. Photography positions children more centrally in having ownership and sharing the experience of what's important to them with each other. Many settings use photography as a consultation tool, inviting children to express the things they do and do not like about their environment. In many ways, this helps adults to see the world through the eyes of their children and better understand where their ideas, inspiration and creativity come from.

Many also use photography as an advocacy and relationship-building tool to communicate the many exciting things children are doing during the week to their parents and carers, and to extend the learning experience from the setting into the home. Most online learning journals that include parental access have the option for uploading photographs and making it easier to portray actual activities or events. Conversely, some educators invite children to introduce family and community members into the setting through images and share aspects of children's home cultures, relationships and identities that may not otherwise be visible in the setting. These are great starting points for children to express their worldviews and their theories on people and places around them.

In fact, all of these uses of photographs have specific benefits in terms of validating children's identities, representing real images of who they are, and who they are in relation to others, in their sometimes very different worlds – at home, with extended family or friends, in the setting, outside, on trips and so on. But we have an enormous responsibility in understanding the deeper ethical implications of using photographs in the setting, not just in terms of who images are taken of and how these are stored, accessed, protected, deleted and so on, but in terms of how we use them to portray a sense – an image – of who our children are to themselves, to their educators and to the world around them. Sometimes in the business of the day and the need to meet all the various regulations, a setting can inadvertently create a token exercise so that a child's cultural identities are *represented* only in images and not *actively embraced* in the day-to-day culture of the setting. Sometimes those representations are reduced to the occasional image, sometimes to none. This can serve to subtly reinforce the 'otherness' of the child instead of moving towards inclusion and validation, which requires paying close attention and getting to know our children and their families. This may require cultural and pedagogical changes within the heart of the setting, not just on the displays or during the EYFS activities on 'understanding the world'. It requires a systematic shift in the way we relate to and communicate with our families that is more than just the odd training session, open day or parents evening (although these are all great). It requires thoughtful planning, intentional communications and creative ways to build understanding between caregivers and educators.

Photography is one of the easiest ways to invite families to become more involved in the setting, documenting their home cultures and sharing them with the children in the setting if possible. If taken by the child, photography offers them opportunities to be acknowledged as an expert of their own lives, locating this expertise in the home *and* in the setting. It gives children a chance to explore this expertise by deciding what is discussed or shown visually and provides a very immediate starting point for children to explain their interests and ideas, even if not directly evident in the picture being shown. Taking photographs in collaboration with adults helps children negotiate the sharing of expertise and equipment with their main carer and, importantly, it positions the adult as an equal learner in the experience, raising the self-esteem, confidence and synergy of both (Rinaldi, Giudici and Krechevsky, 2001). Displaying children's photographs in story books, on posters, in learning journals, in portfolios and all around the classroom gives children and their families a strong message of inclusion, ownership and belonging.

Some settings create slideshows of the children's activities to run in the background as parents and caregivers arrive to pick up their children. It's a great starting point for conversations with parents about what has happened during the week, or how this addresses themes from the curriculum, and can be continued with their children later at home. A single photo can often open the flood gates of conversation for a child, and provide an effective way to build relationships and language.

The practical aspects of learning how to use a camera can require a little more thinking through than is apparent at first. As a way of co-learning, a technical play-with-the-kit session is a great way to unite adult and child in a period of trying out, having a go, researching the tool itself and evaluating how well it can be used for certain tasks such as consultation, storytelling or documentation. Certainly, there are enough basic cameras on the market to allow little fingers to have complete control over the shutter button and review screen, giving children some great opportunities for choice-making and ideation. But how many education settings undertake training in how to really use the camera as a specific lens on life rather than a generic tool to record events? Photography can have a much deeper impact by taking time to learn how to look, observe, listen, select the most appropriate image to take (rather than having a scattergun approach and hoping one image will *come out okay*) and then using that individually chosen image to reflect carefully on moments of learning, of action, of relationship and of being.

Children can be very discerning and, especially when seeing this modelled by adults, will quickly grasp how to stand back, observe the scene, decide what they are aiming to achieve with the camera for that day, which image(s) should be captured forever and why. They may know what they want to say about an image often before they have taken it because they are looking carefully at things, and the image often serves a very particular purpose, in which they are more than happy to talk about once captured. What looks to us like a bunch of holes in a drain cover is an amazing discovery of a geometric pattern that the child believes will unlock a secret cave if the pattern can be pressed in the right order – a beautiful insight into their imagination, appreciation for mathematical concepts and ability to make connections between ideas that could be taken in numerous directions.

What seems to be a random image of a broken stone in a wall, to the child is the hidden doorway to the ants' house. And, sure enough, if you look more closely you can see the army of tiny ants (huge to a three-year-old) marching across the wall in a straight line, some with bits of leaf in their mouths – a whole biology conversation right there. What looks like a silly photograph of the half-inside-half-outside of a reddish-pink nostril is actually the view a child has of her big sister's face every time she gives her a hug and looks up closely at her. It's a view she knows well and finds fascinating – where does that hole go? Why are there two? Why is it red inside when you shine a light on the outside of the skin? This is how these children see the world. It's an incredible place of intrigue, exploration, curiosity, questions and answers that only they hold the key to as they scientifically and creatively put the pieces of the jigsaw puzzle together.

We can often miss the small things that are so important to children, and digital documentation can help a child to show the journey of their thinking. Their photographic interests can be further extended through books, materials and drawing, which will have the effect of integrating their modes of understanding as well as practising their skills, language, self-confidence and ability to articulate themselves. Documenting learning helps children convert their internal ideas and discoveries into external artefacts that are visible, valued and appreciated. It helps to provide starting points for active questioning and scaffolding, for example asking children what they think of a particular issue or what is going on for them in their image. In doing so, we are encouraging a reflective process, which leads to a deeper level of critical thinking and better decision-making for children.

Photographs are full of clues as to who our children are as intelligent, purposeful beings, with wonderful powers and agency to understand the world in lots of different ways from us as adults; ways that can either be opened up, shared and celebrated or limited or, sadly, closed down with a skin-deep, superficial approach to photography. The trick is for the educator to find out how to use cameras to add value, such as using children's imagery not just for descriptive talking *about* the image but as discussion points to sustain possibility thinking or transformative enquiry *beyond* the image. Photographs help us understand the links between children's interests and questions they might want to explore about the world, if we take the time to listen to those questions lurking in the stories behind their photos. Having cameras freely accessible in the setting means being open to using different methods of observation through the lens, considering how we might think about scale from the point of view of a child in relation to our environment, activities and resources, and helping to create worlds which are scaled to, and by, their imaginations.

Young children are exceptionally good at thinking visually and seeing what is right in front of them not only for what it is but for what it could be. They have the knack for capturing through the lens exactly the things we miss in our day-to-day business and drive for efficiency. Children can see the unexpected, surprising aspects of life. For instance, if asked, they would have little difficulty in taking a picture that conveys the sound of running water, or the smell of a flower (without photographing the object itself). They might need to think about it for a while, but it is more straightforward for children to find a way to represent interconnected senses because they use multiple senses in everything they do – they are past masters at immersing themselves body and mind, senses and spirit, in activities they enjoy.

So, it is more natural for a child to *see* what sound or smell looks like, even though this might feel almost impossible for adults whose brains have developed into more discreet areas. Children will happily show us how! By trusting children's ability to be imaginative and capture unexpected connections in the world, and learning how to tune in and listen to their rich expressions and cultures, we help to instil a deeper sense of confidence and self-awareness in both our children and ourselves. It becomes very satisfying for staff to discuss the world on these levels because it is clear to see the progress of children's knowledge and skills in this way. It helps educators to relate to children more authentically, to document learning more fully, and helps parents to understand a little more of what goes on in their child's minds.

Photography is a great aid-memoire, so it is easy to record everything that happens in a period of time, and then spend a long time editing the images down to a select few that might reflect a particular learning journey, behaviour or learning outcome, and consider this adequate documentation. It is the easier (if time-consuming) approach but not necessarily the most meaningful, nor will it make the biggest difference to our knowledge, understanding, teaching and learning. This is because the intention is to find one image (or more) that will demonstrate evidence of an outcome, of what a child can do (it could be any child) rather than to learn more about who *this* child is. Just as with story-building and drawing, children can express deep and significant ideas through images without needing complex verbal languages. Used as a way of actively engaging an audience, *digital listening* can really add value as a pedagogical asset more than just another technique to fulfil technology 'outcomes' in the EYFS. All photographic documentation taken by children should be accompanied by their words and stories as a reflection on the activity, rather than a description of it. In other words, taken seriously, photography is a way of co-communicating, building deep and strong relationships, nurturing creativity and sharing who children are in ways that will support them for a long time to come.

A plethora of literature is emerging to discuss the most effective ways of developing children's digital literacies. Photography has a strong role to play in this in terms of helping children to organise (and make visible) their knowledge and using innovative methods to 'encourage repositioning learners as co-producers of knowledge who partner in the definition of problems, formulation of theories, and the application of solutions in the learning environment' (O'Byrne, Stone and White, 2018).

Over the last few years, there has been an explosion of digital storytelling applications and software, alongside the hardware available in still and video photography. Many of these are over-designed, complicated to use and not particularly intuitive for young minds. Therefore, it is important to keep things simple so as not to let the technology get in the way of the creative, investigative or storytelling process. In fact, the very presence of photographs on their own is powerful enough to achieve all the story-building, language development, shared narratives and insights required in children's learning, without the need for any storybook software in which to display them. Often uploading photos to online platforms removes their flexibility because their purpose changes to one of displaying prior knowledge rather than being able to use them flexibly in shared discussion, questioning, generating new ideas or building on existing knowledge. So, it is important to be clear about what an app can bring to the experience that a still photograph can't already provide.

Further activities, research and resources

https://earlyarts.co.uk/digital-documentation

Key prompts and starting points

- Are we giving enough time and space for children to observe their surroundings and choose to take photographs slowly?

- Do children take the lead in deciding what to take pictures of, and how they want to share them?

- Are we supporting caregivers and other adults to scaffold children's photographic play at home or share their home cultures in an inclusive way in the setting?

- Is our feedback for each child's photography specific enough to raise their confidence, skills, curiosity and self-esteem, and motivating enough to help them continue?

- Are there opportunities for children to work together on collaborative photography adventures, both in taking them and in explaining their different perspectives afterwards?

- Are children encouraged to take pictures of unusual concepts such as smell and sound?

- Are we taking a 'digital listening' approach to documentation to learn about each other?

- Are cameras available for children to use whenever the inspiration takes them?

- Does a child's story accompany any displayed picture verbatim rather than the adult interpretation?

- How can photography help children express their own views, opinions and aspirations?

Technology and creativity

Arts, creativity and technology have always had an interesting relationship. As well as the obvious areas of cinema and animation, technology has featured in ways that enhance, make more useful, more accessible and more inspiring the work of artists. Recently, Tate Modern invited gallery visitors to experience via a virtual reality headset the life, culture and identity of the artist, Modigliani, from his perspective. Although still only a voyeur, this immersive experience of being inside Modigliani's chaotic, bohemian, Parisian studio bedroom, complete with the sounds and sights surrounding him during the final months of his life, was revelatory in seeing how the incredible shapes, iridescent colours and elegant lines of his paintings and sculptures were inspired and achieved among abject poverty, almost 100 years ago.

According to Tate's International Art Curator Nancy Ireson, the Tate team conducted forensic and scientific testing of his work and researched, x-rayed, analysed pigments of, photographed and filmed every object and aspect of that bedroom, which no one alive had ever been inside, in order to bring this intense experience to modern-day viewers. Technology, in this case, was instrumental to achieving a deeper experience and understanding of something we would not otherwise have had access to and gave us an opportunity to have a cognitive, aesthetic and sensory response to this artist and his work.[5]

Technology offers these opportunities in many subjects, not just the arts, but the interactive nature of this technological experience means that the viewer is not just a passive recipient of someone else's interpretation of culture, but an active participant in their own experience of it, as if it were happening in the here and now. It enables the participant to respond from their own cultural context and make new connections to understand the context of this influential period of art. That is where technology really comes into its own – when it goes beyond the passive brain download to inspiring action, out-of-the-box thinking, new perspectives, interaction, recall and response, and from a whole community, not just one person at a time.

Technology not only acts as a tool, making access to the arts more open, interactive and fulfilling on a global scale, but it also makes new forms of expression possible. It may be a musician, theatre designer, choreographer, animator or dancer using a particular piece of software to compose or design a new work, and then express this through special hardware designed to enhance their performance in one way or another (such as a performance by world-renowned dancer Kaiji Moriyama, using sensors to track his movements and translate them into piano music[6]).

Or it could be someone attending, watching and receiving the performance and sharing their critique, ideas and responses afterwards through social media, blogs, vlogs, ebulletins and so on. Technology is providing both the tools and the creative space for sharing our ideas, expressions, processes, products and messages of our heart and our art in ways that can reach an enormous community in one go – ways we would never have thought possible even only ten years ago.

Since even our youngest children already inhabit a technological world that affects their personal, social and educational lives, it is hard to imagine a future

---

5   See *The Making of Modigliani VR: The Ochre Atelier* at www.youtube.com/watch?v=CdYLscE6kE0&ab_channel=Tate

6   See www.youtube.com/watch?time_continue=316&v=tLFe2AzCodk&ab_channel=YamahaCorporation

that does not intensify this phenomenon. While being wary of what we already do (and do not) know about screens and social media, as educators, parents and caregivers, we must surely recognise the opportunities of technology to help children express their potential in creative ways. The challenge is how to harness this in a way that enables children to achieve a growing control over their tools, technical skills and materials to become increasingly active protagonists in their own creative worlds, not just passive participants of ours.

> New technologies are providing new means for creative thinking and achievement and new forms of access to ideas, information and people. Young people's command of new technologies will be enhanced by experiencing them as tools for creative achievement: rather than as ends in themselves. (NACCCE, 1999, p.62)

In the early years, technology can not only help children to explore new ideas, make new connections and build their understanding, but it can also help with their communication, language and literacy development, used appropriately (i.e. as a tool for storytelling and relationship building rather than a replacement for interaction) and in the right context (i.e. relevant to the child and extending their play and learning during that session).

Children's learning is deepened when adults interact, support, extend and take an interest in the learning that is happening and join in with their play, and this is hugely important where technology is concerned so that it does not become an isolating or limiting activity. Children gain more from using an app when an adult helps them explore and reflect on their experiences. Plus the positive sensory messages about safety, attachment, validity and care are all communicated during that time when an adult watches, reads and discusses the online story or game together with the child. During these periods, children's spindle cell neurons try to tune in at lightening speeds to the emotions of the adult, so that they can subconsciously mimic the adult's calm, positive behaviours in a basic human process that neuroscientists call *emotional contagion* (Boyatzis and Hazy, 2015).

In order to explore digital tools through a creative lens, a good starting point before using the new software or hardware is to ask ourselves, How can this technology help us discover/experiment/play with different arts and creative forms? Or, how can it help us explore our ideas more creatively? Being familiar with the technology makes it easier to use it as a tool for learning rather than becoming overly focused on the technology as the objective in itself. Once adults and children are familiar, then focusing on storytelling, role play, dance, drawing, painting, photography and so on helps to ensure that the technology is just used as a tool to enhance children's ideas and expressions.

Many software programs are so tightly defined that, for little fingers, even a drawing or paint programme can become a frustrating exercise in mouse control, which has very little to do with creativity. In real-life drawing or painting, a child experiences an embodied action through direct interaction with the art materials (i.e. it takes many different parts of a body working together to draw a line or paint a shape), together with sensory responses as they feel the materials working and changing form in their hands. In trying to control the mouse to 'draw' a particular line or add shapes, colours, textures, words and graphics to an image, the child is focused on holding down a mouse button to drag the cursor around the screen; they are not looking at the effect of their hand in control of the paintbrush or pencil. The activity is not stimulating brain-eye-hand connectivity or coordination in the same, more direct way as when a chalk or paint brush is held and felt through the senses so that lines and shapes can flow, stutter, jump or rotate in perfect accordance with the child's ideas. Despite the many digital software titles that include the word 'creativity', the actual tasks involved are much more functional and less creative than they may at first appear, being partly limited to motor skills and hand-eye coordination where young children are concerned.

The magic of creativity can also be lacking in software programs where mixing colours, textures or shapes becomes rather limited to the pre-programmed solutions offered, rather than discovering (and – importantly – being in control) for themselves of the surprising ways in which different paints, chalks, crayons, clay slip or other materials react and feel when squelched together, layered over each other, mixed up in different proportions and so on. This element of surprise is an important part of learning, stimulating deeper levels of motivation in the child's reward centre in the brain to such a positive effect that it then triggers and retriggers a desire to continue this journey of independent learning and discovery for themselves. This is because the brain rewards the process of positive discovery with a release of the neurotransmitter dopamine, which reinforces the process towards, and memory of, the reward achieved in this activity.

It is thought that excessively high levels of dopamine release can lead to addiction in certain environments, where the brain wants to experience the same reward over and over again (Boyatzis and Hazy, 2015). However, the level of dopamine released by a creative action is nowhere near the levels generated by the regular intake of sugary foods or alcoholic drinks (for instance), partly because it is very difficult to exactly replicate the results of a creative action more than once, and partly because creativity is not made up of biological and chemical reactions alone. While there is no doubt that we know of many unique individuals with a passion for the arts and creativity, I have never heard of scientists being worried about children becoming addicted to creativity!

Software programs are generally not culturally specific; do not encourage individuality or the expression of multiple identities; are not great at providing opportunities for social integration (or opportunities are limited in early years for safety reasons), relationship building or asking relevant, thought-provoking questions; and can take a lot of adult time away from listening to children. Having said this, digital platforms are excellent channels through which to learn technology skills, with personal photos making story-building much more relevant, motivating and engaging than impersonal ones. Plus they open up wonderful avenues of communication for children with learning or physical difficulties for whom other verbal or embodied methods are not available.

According to O'Byrne *et al.*:

> This [digital] medium and the associated tools incorporate higher order thinking skills while also strengthening social connections in and out of the classroom. In particular, this provides more insight into the use of digital technologies and their effects on the child's motivation to write, create, and share their stories within the classroom community. (2018, p.12)

This research highlights how, generally speaking, educational and gaming software for digital storytelling becomes much more relevant at primary age onwards where it can be used more effectively for research, analysis and visual and textual learning, as well as cognitive, social and emotional and literacy development, but still not so useful for physical or imaginative creative development.

In addition, the sensory and emotional experience at the heart of many creative encounters is all but lost in using a mouse, where the learning achieved is largely about the skill of manipulating the technology rather than being creative. That's not to say it is not a valuable skill to have or that it does not engage the imagination or emotions. Some programs, such as *Woebot*,[7] help children to explore and express their emotions in more positive and constructive ways. Others, such as *Story Creator*,[8] can trigger very imaginative responses and put the child in control of their creative learning. But there are plenty that limit the imagination to a choice of predetermined actions. Some will also cause greater isolation for young children at a time when learning about their relationships to, and interactions with, other unpredictable humans is an essential part of learning to thrive. At this age, a focus on generating social languages of creativity is important. So even if a software program is entitled *Creativity Suite Pro*, it can only be as imaginative as the people who created it and should not be confused with the complex, mysterious, wonderful, analogue powers of creativity within our own brains and bodies.

Further activities, research and resources

https://earlyarts.co.uk/digital-documentation

Key prompts and starting points

o   Do children have opportunities to learn how to use recording/documentation/communication devices of one sort or another?

o   Are we familiar and confident in understanding how to use digital tools and how they can add value and extend learning?

o   Have children got access to iPads, cameras, microphones and recorders, headphones and audio recorders to capture their stories?

o   Have children got access to a small range of other technologies that enhance play, such as finger torches and larger torches, overhead projectors or light boxes, digital keyboards and shiny fabric or sequined materials?

---

7   https://woebot.io
8   https://itunes.apple.com/us/app/story-creator-easy-story-book-maker-for-kids/id545369477

- ○ Are all staff members clear on safety procedures and able to carry them out effectively?

- ○ Are we actively engaging families to use digital tools in the home for enhancing creative communications and relationships rather than functionality?

- ○ Are we supporting and extending children's spontaneous creations using the technology?

Chapter 10

Creative Practices

Environments for creativity

Research shows that children thrive when they express themselves through the arts in a relaxed environment, not under pressure to achieve a certain standard (NACCCE, 1999; Daly and O'Connor, 2016; Grace, 2017). Exploring an arts or cultural space is often a novelty for young children who may wish to run around on entering a gallery, theatre or museum space. This apparent rushing around in seemingly random fashion from doorway to window, or corner to middle, helps a child orient themselves in the space and carry out what's called 'cognitive mapping', and afterwards feel able to settle down more easily (Piscitelli *et al.*, 2003). Having oriented themselves, a child will then be able to slow down and explore the materials or objects more purposefully and at their own pace, often not following the curated route that is intended but following their own interests.

Children think with their bodies, therefore, whether in an arts space or an education space, kinaesthetic thinking happens a lot in thoughtfully designed hands-on spaces, where resources lend themselves to being touched and explored by young hands and bodies, leading to a higher likelihood of children leading their own learning and requiring less adult facilitation or intervention. Helping caregivers feel comfortable with this can enable a more fulfilling experience with higher levels of interaction when they are present in the setting.

As well as the space being a safe, relaxing and comfortable place for young children to be in, the furniture, displays and resources should be designed, or organised, to encourage communication between adult and child, and between children, and to stimulate the imagination through spontaneous, open-ended play, exploration and discovery.

Having their eyes at a similar physical level means that parents and caregivers can share the same learning experience with their children. In an arts centre, having a sturdy step or a lightweight, folding stool can make all the difference for a child to be able to access the environment on the same level as the adult. Exploring or looking at an object together with the parent or carer enables deeper-level learning, conversation and relationship-building to be continued and extended in the home, making more sense for the child and the adult. Research shows that there is a high correlation between time spent exploring an object with verbal or physical interaction by caregivers and children's subsequent levels of recall (Piscitelli *et al.*, 2003).

Resources for creativity

The age range of birth to three encapsulates many different milestones depending on the experiences and environments each child is exposed to. No two toddlers will be engaged in the same way or for the same length of time. Therefore, the more open-ended resources can be, the easier it is for young children to take control of their own learning, at their own pace.

For this age range, resources should be carefully chosen to stimulate sensory learning experiences, especially enabling non-language-based communicators such as babies or children with obstacles to speech to express themselves just as easily, but also providing a level of challenge, physical or sensory, to keep fast problem-solvers engaged.

Tactile resources provide rich learning experiences for children's brains and bodies to be nurtured and connected. They help babies and toddlers tune in to the experience as kinaesthetic thinkers, where the sensory information they gain from handling objects and materials holds their attention for longer because it stimulates thoughts about the experience. As they take in information through their hands, it activates ideas and feelings in their minds (excitement, curiosity, anticipation, delight) that, in turn, are often expressed through their bodies. This connecting up of the physical and emotional parts of their brain and body with the subject matter helps children to make, store and recall important memories about the learning experience.

Interactive resources engage children's curiosity beyond the familiar, and provoke them to seek out new knowledge to build on their existing knowledge. Music and movement objects (such as silk scarves, brushes or feathers) provide opportunities for call-and-response with babies, helping adults affirm their attachment by imitating their babies' sounds and gestures. Drawing and mark-making helps toddlers relax and express themselves by way of enabling them to explore and regulate their emotions and feelings (Eisner, 2005). At the same time, it refines their observation skills, helps build connections through the process of making and storing symbols with new meanings and enables reflection and the outward expression of their experiences in their own language.

Fantasy resources, including role-play props and materials or costumes that are not predefined (limiting the imagination to a particular character or storyline), encourage young children to actively participate in their own story and their own worlds, rather than being passive participants in ours. Across the globe, pretend play is a strongly innate and natural phenomenon and these alternative worlds allow children to function at higher levels than normal, nurturing their executive function. As basic cognitive processes such as making choices, concentration and memory are triggered, higher-level executive functions will be activated to enable reasoning, planning, critical thinking skills and behaviour management, imagination, risk-taking, problem-solving and creativity (Bruce, 2005a).

Scholars from the Queensland Museums Collaborative, Piscatelli, Everett and Weier (Piscitelli *et al.*, 2003, p.37), suggest a series of provocations to consider before selecting which open-ended, intelligent materials and resources to use to enhance a creative experience, which reflect the conditions above. They ask educators to consider whether the chosen resources will encourage children to focus their attention and take a deeper interest; whether they present purposeful opportunities for empowerment and allow children to make choices, interact with peers and explore with their bodies at their own pace; whether it offers thoughtful starting points for adults to stimulate engagement and discussion; and whether it is appealing and fun to engage with.

All resources should have a universal design (i.e. be specifically inclusive for young children with physical, sensory or learning disabilities), making them especially inspiring for children who have to overcome more obstacles to creative engagement than usual.

Benefitting from local arts and cultural provision

Almost every town, city and village has a variety of cultural activities on offer that form the backbone of bringing the local community together. This ranges from local village fetes, sewing bees, choirs and crafts and book clubs though to larger arts or cultural festivals, arts centre performances, digital exhibitions, music events, games workshops or special events such as the UK's City of Culture, hosted by a different city each year.

In fact, a cultural event or centre is an ideal place to provide the levels of intellectual novelty and opportunities for social interaction that stimulate growth in the relationship between children and adults, whether they be parents or educators. For young children, they are fascinating places to visit with a wealth of sensory experiences to enrich their learning and support early years teaching.

Arts and cultural centres (such as museums, galleries, theatres, libraries, orchestras, arts centres, music and dance venues) play an important role in helping young children build knowledge and understanding about the world through social, familial and cultural experiences. This provision is most effective (Piscitelli *et al.*, 2003) when it is:

- child-centred – respectful opportunities for every child, no matter how young, to enjoy and benefit from cultural experiences

- developmentally considerate – understanding how young children learn and express themselves through all parts of their bodies and brains

- open-ended – offering a key to unlocking children's enormous bank of perspectives based on their own contexts and prior knowledge

- interactive – enabling co-learning to develop between adult and child

- play-based – engaging a child in the way they learn best, i.e. holistically, heuristically (learning through exploration) and through all the senses simultaneously

- empowering – giving children choices, opportunities for mastery and control of their own learning journeys, prioritising their agency throughout the visit.

To make visits welcoming and stress free for caregivers and educators, most cultural providers try to make these qualities visible throughout the design, programming, marketing, signage, language and staff interactions.

Early years professionals and families are enormously welcome in arts and cultural centres. Gone are the days when there was nowhere close by to park the car, cafes only had adult meals on the menu and three-year-old children were expected to walk calmly and quietly throughout the venue. Even in cultural centres where there aren't the latest facilities for bottle warming or buggy parks, staff are well trained in family-friendly practices and will welcome opportunities to help, guide and support adults with young children. The culture of arts centres towards children has changed so much for the better over the last decade, partly due to funding that has enabled educational practices and training to be better resourced, but mostly because many arts educators recognise the importance of supporting children's creativity from birth.

Arts and cultural providers with an education remit are generally cognisant as to why and how their service is relevant to young children, how children's bodies and brains move and work, and how they relate to the people and spaces around them through multiple modes. Nowadays, children are usually offered materials, resources and activities that help them experience and express themselves in relevant ways that may not have previously been associated with the purpose or content of a museum, for instance.

Cultural staff can be a fantastic resource for settings focusing on topics about the world in general or specific arts and cultural themes, knowing where best to guide children to in the venue and how to build on the interests and knowledge they might have. Cultural centres work hard to become effective communicators and relationship builders with families and educators because they understand that this can go a long way in supporting young children (and their carers) to have positive, exciting experiences. In short, children are welcome to be themselves in cultural venues.

The following aspects of partnerships between education and arts/ cultural organisations were highlighted in the NACCCE report (1999, pp.140–143) and offer starting points to ensure young children and families will have the best possible experience and opportunities for creative learning during their visits. They are also relevant for activities in the home, the setting and beyond.

Effective partnerships enable cultural and educational partners to:

- strengthen the setting's relationship with its community through sharing skills, expertise and resources

- raise the profile of the setting and the part it plays in the social, cultural and economic life within the community

- learn new skills and techniques for use in the setting

- deepen their understanding of children in different social and cultural situations

- develop their understanding of different disciplines and how they can interact with each other

- try out new teaching strategies

- deepen their understanding of, and practical experience in, the creative process, including imaginative thought, problem-solving, research, technical skills, editing, risk-taking, reflection, presentation, evaluation, critical thinking and dialogue

- experience working as part of a collaborative team

- build self-confidence and self-esteem in learning new skills, meeting new people, sharing ideas

- increase confidence and expertise in making judgements and evaluating experience

- new contexts

- reflect on their own work and methods in new contexts

- develop creative communication and teaching skills with children and adults

- find ideas for their own creative work through partnerships across settings and disciplines.

Working collaboratively with artists

It might seem like a luxury to invite an artist in to an early years setting when an educator can do all things creative with their children. But the brilliant thing about artists is that they can bring something unique and completely different that complements what educators are already doing, especially those who are experienced in early childhood practices. The best partnerships are ones that have clear expectations but are also open to surprising things happening as the adventure progresses. The worst ones are those with expectations that an artist is there simply to entertain or cover staff absence. So, it is important to acknowledge the authority and expertise of the educator, the artist, the child and the family in these partnerships from the start, and ensure that the voices of all have equal space to be heard. Each has something special to bring to the party that should be greater than the sum of its parts.

That's not to say that there aren't sometimes struggles and challenges along the way, as with any social group working together. Artists and educators may come from quite different philosophical perspectives; one might prefer a more structured, measuring-progress methodology and the other a more open-ended, go-with-the-flow approach. Tensions can arise from the apparent freedom the artist might have from curriculum and regulatory obligations, or the apparent obsession educators might have with planning and assessment for everything. But if relationships can be built around the tremendous advantages that both sides bring then these differences will be what make for a highly engaging project rather than 'more of the same'. Fundamentally, if the vision for a creative project is created together, regularly revisited and shared keenly, then any potential conflicts will be surmountable through good communications, reflection and preparation.

The vast majority of experience and research shows that children respond extremely well to artists' interventions. This is partly due to artists' ability to listen, tune in using sensitive, non-verbal methods and engage children very quickly, especially those who have a heightened sensory perception of the pleasure and agency of creative interactions. Through this *pedagogy of mutuality*, artists capture the imaginations of children in new and exciting ways that empower the mind of the child (Bruner, 1996).

It is also partly due to the training of artists making them particularly adept at observation skills that can complement those of educators from different perspectives. And it is partly because artists, by their very nature of being tuned in to their own creativity and having an openness to others' aesthetic senses, seem to be able to communicate on a par with young children through highly creative languages, and nurture aesthetic responses that may never before have been witnessed.

Artists can bring a wealth of advantages to the setting, including:

- distinctive art-form techniques and specialist approaches
- new ideas for activities and provocations
- different approaches to extend or scaffold a child's line of enquiry
- recognition of, and respect for, children's identities as artists
- ability to improvise or run with children's imaginary concepts
- creative approaches to team working
- introducing interesting materials that elicit a higher quality arts experience
- different perspectives on children's creative responses
- alternative insights to help see different opportunities and meanings
- modelling immersion in the arts without inhibitions
- raising levels of critical thinking through deep observation
- modelling language for the actions and techniques of different art forms
- fresh inspiration for the centrality of creative approaches to learning
- ability to stimulate more risky thinking outside the normal boundaries
- cultivating positive attitudes to in-depth arts practice
- more weight to help build a creative pedagogy or culture in the setting
- fresh approaches to inclusivity and integration of cultural contexts
- high levels of expectation regarding what children are capable of
- support in raising confidence of educators in being creative
- ability to tune in to children quickly through experience with non-verbal methods.

Recruiting artists for an education project

Cost is quoted as one of the most common reasons for not employing an artist. Yet, compared with the cost of most other education professionals, artists' fees are generally the lowest outgoing and often achieve just as high (and sustainable) outputs, where that is important.

Current guidelines advise between £200 and £400 per day (this can vary as artists may have their own daily rates depending on experience). Be clear what the artist fee covers – any other agreed costs (materials, travel, etc.) should be paid in addition to this fee. Project costs should always be negotiated in advance, ensuring that it is clear which costs the artist is liable for, and which the setting is liable for.[1]

To create a partnership that works for all, it is important to select each other carefully. The following questions are designed to help educators and artists think through the most important aspects for a successful recruitment process.

Geography

Where is the setting located (or where will the project take place) and how far out will you need to advertise for an artist, especially if you are in a rural area? Depending on the art form, national and local arts networks may have social media or newsletter channels through which artists can be invited to apply.

Stakeholders

Are any other settings or stakeholders involved, such as funders, professional services like speech and language therapists or caregivers who could be a valuable part of the partnership?

Timescales

Think about the timetable for the project. Potential milestones might include:

o   Deadline for artists expressing an interest/applying

o   When will you meet or interview the artist?

o   When will you select the artist?

o   When will you meet the selected artists to plan the project?

o   When do you want the project to happen?

o   How long do you expect the artist to work on the project?

---

1   Find more information on rates for artists at https://static.a-n.co.uk/wp-content/uploads/2018/01/Guidance_on_fees_and_day_rates_for_visual_artists_2018.pdf

o   How will the time be structured?

o   Are you allowing enough time for planning and evaluation?

o   Do any of the dates clash with other events?

Intended beneficiaries

Be clear who the artist will be working with. Specify:

o   age of the children and group size

o   any particular physical, health or learning needs

o   particular areas of interest/enquiry/learning to explore

o   anything you feel is relevant to describe the group dynamics

o   environmental opportunities or limitations to be aware of.

Overall aim or main enquiry question

Be clear what your vision is for the project. You should describe the overarching purpose of the project. For example: *To explore movement and music with 20 four- to five-year-old boys and find new ways of listening and communicating.* You may be keen to meet broad EYFS learning goals but it is worth focusing on the specific opportunities that a creative intervention could offer, such as creative approaches to non-verbal communication, learning new sensory languages in children with special educational needs, exploring family integration through drama, investigating new methods of making and managing noise, encouraging greater risk-taking, developing empathy through dance or other issues linked specifically to your children and staff.

Try and get input from all those involved with planning the project, so that everyone agrees from the start what direction you want the project to take.

State what changes, if any, you hope to provoke. Then you will be able to use your aim as a foundation for measuring your progress.

Key outcomes

Think about what outcomes you want to achieve in order to deliver the aim of the project, without becoming too obsessed with visible, tangible outcomes. Remember that lots of learning will take place in the mind and body and not necessarily be measurable through observation. Each outcome should have a single key result and contribute to achieving your aim.

Project budget

Use the following as a starting point for budgeting and always err on the realistic side about the amount of time a creative project might take to plan:

o planning and preparation time (artist)

o fees for workshops (artist)

o fees for staff reflection and debrief meetings (artist)

o fees for any additional staff continuing professional development (artist)

o materials and equipment

o transport (e.g. visits to a museum or gallery)

o sharing and celebration event

o evaluation

o documentation

o contingency.

Role of the artist

This is an opportunity to think about how the artist might work in partnership with your staff team, and this role may evolve as the project develops. Artists will have ideas as well, but if you have thought about this beforehand it will help them to know what your expectations of them are and how they might interact with the setting during the project.

o How much interaction would you expect the artist to have with staff?

o What can you do to help integrate them into the team, in terms of planning, observation, reflection, documentation and evaluation of the project?

o Might you want them to be involved in staff training on specific arts or creative approaches? Or would you want their role to be focused only on this project?

o How might you help them settle in once the project begins?

Desirable skills and knowledge areas for the artist

Think about the group the artist will work with and the objectives of the project, and identify what level of skills or experience they might need.

o   Are you looking for a specific arts skill like photography, singing or movement, or is it more important for them to be an all-round creative facilitator?

o   Do you want an artist with a specific sort of training such as Developmental Movement Play, Reggio Emilia, Kodály, or sign language?

o   Do they need to know your curriculum, understand early childhood development theory, or have knowledge of specific special educational needs or are you happy for staff to cover this knowledge?

o   What sorts of generic skills and approaches are you looking for, such as a good team worker, a self-motivator, listening and observational skills, ability to adapt approaches, openness to collaboration with staff and to listen to children's ideas?

Staff involved in project

Think about collaborative working in advance so that everyone knows what to expect.

o   What are the skill levels and experience of staff working with the artist?

o   What role will the educators/support staff/other adults have during the project?

o   Are parents, volunteers or other adults (not staff) going to be involved?

o   Can you provide materials and equipment to support the artist's role?

Reflection and renewed practice

Consider ways the artist can help support the learning needs of the target group and how the project team will reflect on the learning experience.

o   What is your longer-term strategy for building a legacy from the project?

o   How can the learning be transferred to other staff or families and embedded into daily practice?

o   Will you be documenting the creative process as part of the project?

o How will all voices be made visible, heard and felt during this process?

o What role will the artist have in documentation?

o Have you built in to the project plan enough time to reflect, share ideas, document observations and disseminate this documentation?

Next steps

Finalise regulatory checks and practicalities for managing the project.

o Where and how will the opportunity be advertised or shared?

o What information do we need from the artist, such as previous examples of project work, curriculum vitae, Disclosure and Barring Service (DBS) check or references from previous settings or employers?

o Who will be the main point of contact/supervisor for the artist?

o Who should be invited to the sharing event to celebrate staff and children's creativity and joy at the end of the project? When and how should invitations be issued?

Settings working with freelance artists should be aware that DBS checks are not always portable. A previous DBS check is not a substitute for your organisation's own checks, safeguards or responsible practice. It is the responsibility of the organisation employing an artist to ensure that the relevant DBS/safeguarding documentation is satisfactory and in place at the time the work is delivered, in line with your own safeguarding policies.[2]

---

2   Find out more at www.gov.uk/government/publications/dbs-update-service-employer-guide

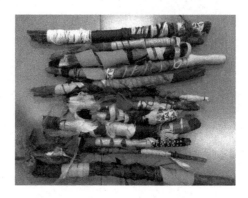

Creative documentation

In her attempt to shift the purpose of documentation away from assessment and towards relational understanding, Reggio Children founder Carla Rinaldi promotes a *pedagogy of listening*. In this mode, the educator makes a choice not to rely on their own preconceived knowledge in making a *reasonable* interpretation of children's intentions and thereby *assigning* their identities, but to help children search for meaning by asking the questions that drive us all: 'What? How? Why?' By actively listening to their many languages, educators open opportunities for children to create theories that Rinaldi considers 'the best expressions of being human' and the most important to 'influence the development of [their] identity' (Rinaldi, 2001, p.2).

This objective for making learning visible is encapsulated in the idea of creative documentation, extensively explored and promoted through the research of the Reggio Emilia settings, and further through the work of the Project Zero team at Harvard, among others. In the same way that creative pedagogies are not simply about curriculum provision or assessment, documentation is also about a way of thinking – a culture of research – based in enabling children's voices to be heard, their thinking to be seen, their cultures and identities to be revealed and their creativity to be sensed. The sophisticated forms of symbolic representation realised by children from Reggio Emilia are testament to this approach, where their theories are documented both by the educators and the children themselves through the integration and presentation of children's many creative languages.

Creative documentation is a way of creating, exploring, evaluating and gathering the stories of children's lived experience, as well as the world of their dreams and imaginations. It helps to give a more rounded and respectful glimpse into the life of each child based on who they are, not what they have attained against academic goals. These limited aspects of their learning are often selected to give a particular impression for parents, professionals and regulators which, arguably, does not represent the truth about the child's knowledge. Instead, the gathering and displaying of creative processes and products, aspects of thinking, knowing and not-knowing, acknowledges children's agency. In recognising the richness of knowledge, expertise and understanding owned by our children, this act of creative documentation effectively declares an equalising of power that removes the adult's privilege as 'expert'.

In their seminal publication on documenting children's research, *Making Learning Visible* (Rinaldi *et al.*, 2001), the Reggio Emilia team offer a number of insights and provocations to stimulate creative ideas for documentation and share the wonder of young children's minds. Their approach to documentation reveals 'the intimacy of daily contact and deep immersion in the life, rhythm, energy, and ecology of the subject of research' (Seidel in Rinaldi *et al.*, 2001, p.332). This highly creative approach, full of possibility and visible thinking, continues to inspire settings to use documentation differently on a number of levels, where previously they might have simply collected data for inspection or assessment processes. It aims to provide a visible memory of children's thinking to reflect on existing knowledge and serve as a starting point for new understandings, to help educators gain insights into children's learning processes as a tool for improvement, and to provide parents with an understanding of what goes on in the school setting to involve them more closely (Organisation for Economic Co-operation and Development, 2004). Because it is no longer about what it looks like but about the stories it tells, this opens up horizons for more purposeful methods of documentation, considering a whole range of visual and moving media as relevant as well as wall displays and folders, such as:

- learning journals exploring trajectories of ideas and thinking

- observation sheets to keep track of thinking and learning processes

- scrap books for memory recall of specific events and activities

- wall panels for longer-term projects or to show developmental paths

- photographic images of children's consultations

- film clips of children's creative expressions

- paintings depicting group stories

- stone and stick sculptures in gardens

- audio recordings of children's poems and stories.

As children represent their mental images to others, they represent them to themselves, developing a more conscious vision (interior listening). Thus, moving from one language to another, from one field of experience to another, and reflecting on these shifts and those of others, children modify and enrich their theories and conceptual maps. But this is true if, and only if, children have the opportunity to make these shifts in a group context and if they have the possibility to listen and be listened to, to express their differences and be receptive to the differences of others (Rinaldi, in Organisation for Economic Co-operation and Development, 2004).

This approach expands educators' views on the purposes of early education, turning documentation into a much more meaningful process at the heart of the early learning culture. In one setting I visited, children wanted to get to know their locality better and were encouraged to use charcoal-rubbing techniques to document the different shapes, patterns and designs in the built environment and architecture around them on their way to school. Their rubbings of drainage grates, manhole covers, railings, brick patterns, pavement textures, bark ripples and lots of other features were made into a large map that was then used by other children to 'spot' the features and understand the visual geography and ecology of their environment. The children saw their locality differently as a result; they took pride in it by getting to know its beauty and its idiosyncrasies as well as its history and connections to people (and their stories) around them.

For many children, their sense of confidence is improved by a deepened understanding of their natural and human geography. The process of documentation helps children convert their internal ideas and discoveries into external artefacts that are visible, not just to themselves but to others. Their interests become better known and understood in their own cultural context both by themselves and others in their lives.

In many settings, children take photographs of the environment to discuss what they do or do not like about it, which enables further thinking about alternative possibilities for supporting their interests and informs discussion on how the environment might be changed immediately or designed better in the future. By children documenting and reflecting on their learning, their ideas can be taken from one context and applied in another. Their ideas therefore become validated, valued and appreciated both by themselves and by others. Again, children's agency is recognised and empowered on many levels in this process.

Often, children's interests can seem unclear to us adults. It can be a puzzle to understand why a child chooses to behave in a certain way. In one setting, a teacher observed a child sitting engrossed by an old wall for long periods of time while the new play area nearby did not seem to attract him. As he was unable to share his ideas verbally at this point, the teacher was curious about what was compelling the little boy to spend so much time at this wall as part of his own play. The teacher decided to bring a selection of the boy's favourite drawing materials outside every day, and by looking at these drawings he discovered that the little boy was studying some beetles that lived in the hole in the wall at the edge of the play area. The boy documented not only the lives of these beetles but also the journey of his thinking (his 'thinking in action'), which revealed his deep fascination with the anatomy and movement behaviours of the beetle family.

A different teacher may have raised concerns about the child isolating himself by his fascination for the wall. This might have resulted in a very different approach that would have stopped this boy's creativity in its tracks and positioned him as having a problem rather than a unique, creative intelligence. Adults' perspectives on children (and their ensuing actions) can be critical to enabling or inhibiting children's creativity. Without innovative ways to document, we can often miss the small things that are so important to children, and our preconceptions of a situation can remain unchallenged.

This child's drawings opened up an extensive series of interactive conversations, through words and materials, enabling him to share his love of beetles (and now extensive knowledge of their lives) with his friends. This simple act helped reposition the child's significant knowledge as a reflexive ethnographer in a community of wider curiosity, enquiry, critical thought and appreciation.

> By means of documenting, the thinking of the documenter thus becomes material, that is, tangible and capable of being interpreted. The notes, the recordings, the slides and photographs represent fragments of a memory that seems thereby to become 'objective'. While each fragment is imbued with the subjectivity of the documenter, it is offered to the interpretive subjectivity of others in order to be known or re-known, created and recreated, also as a collective knowledge-building event. The result is knowledge that is bountiful and enriched by the contributions of many (Rinaldi *et al.*, 2001, p.148).

Chapter 11

Creative Pedagogies

The role of the creative teacher

Many educators would probably consider *effective* teaching to mean finding a balance between the formal transfer of skills and knowledge, and the provision of opportunities for children to experiment, question and create theories for themselves. This balance is often formed in an environment where the emphasis is on recognising and nurturing a child's capacities by finding the right conditions, resources, inspirations and expertise for learning to happen. But the balance is also shaped by a belief in a) a hierarchy of knowledge, where some areas of learning are considered more important than others, often with art and creativity at the bottom of that hierarchy, and b) a hierarchy of teaching methods where more formal instruction and (cognitive) knowledge transfer (based on privileging the experience of the expert) is positioned higher than scaffolding, co-construction or child-oriented, embodied methods of investigation, research and theory testing.

> Educators can model creativity by thinking divergently, solving problems, displaying flexibility and evaluating ideas. Discussing alternatives or thinking divergently when introducing a topic or project, demonstrates to children that creativity is something to be valued. (Leggett, 2017, p.851)

Finding a balance that works for children and educators within such a highly regulated environment in the early years is not easy. Many educators find themselves taking far more time to reflect on, plan and make decisions about their pedagogical position and classroom culture than is provided for in their job description. This is not just a case of how to meet the expectations of 'quality' in curriculum provision, teaching standards and learning outcomes. It is also about considering what 'knowledge and skills' means for each child, how they might engage deeply with each area of learning, and how such provision can be differentiated to ensure parity of esteem across content and methods, access to a range of opportunities, and support for additional needs. Pedagogy is so much more than what is written down in curriculum frameworks or guidance materials. It is fundamentally about the philosophical standpoint on which teaching and learning is based, what worldview of children and childhood is upheld, whether that actively positions all children equally and fairly in practice as well as policy, what theories of learning are considered important, whether educators' insight and learning are nourished, what content is prioritised (and why) and which teaching or learning methods are chosen to achieve this.

In addition, educators are frequently tackling invisible challenges. Many are coping with pressures from all sides to *produce* highly intelligent, socially 'well-adjusted' children (whatever that means). This is often against the tide of wider social and environmental forces. It is therefore no wonder that it can seem especially challenging to cultivate creativity within such a pressurised expectation of compliance. It can feel like too high a risk to take when the odds are already stacked against us. It may feel that we know where we are with targets and outcomes – we can observe them, measure them, describe them in a familiar language and defend them. We might agree that it doesn't give the whole picture of who a child is, or respond particularly well to their interests, modes of learning or potential trajectory, but resources are limited and at least it is a good enough start.

However, since the evidence set out in this book shows how creative environments enhance children's natural dispositions for learning and development, perhaps it is not such a difficult challenge to have a *creative* pedagogy as the starting point. A clear set of values, policy and practices that enrich the imagination will open up learning possibilities in every way. The more difficult challenge, it seems, is in knowing *how* to enhance children's own creative behaviours (what Craft (2002, p.148) refers to as 'teaching for creativity') if an educator has not at first learned how to teach creatively.

This is important because, while aspects of creative practice can be learned and matured within particular environments and time periods, the ability to be creative at any level, at any time, requires that 'the *habit* of being inclined to creative behaviour and the *quality of alertness, or sensitivity*, to opportunities of creative behaviour are just as important' (Craft, 2002, p.57, original italics). In addition, it is good to remember that creativity comes from a wide range of abilities, skills, sensations and aptitudes, rather than a single, special talent, much of which can be cultivated and practised on a daily basis in the early years setting.

Eisner describes the educator as someone who 'designs situations that build on what children value or know...situations that will, in turn, create an appetite to learn... Situations that contain tasks or materials that will engage children in meaningful learning, learning that they can apply and that connects with other aspects of the world' (Eisner, 2005, p.47).

Yet many early years educators struggle with how to teach the arts. According to Lindsay (2016), a number of educators interviewed for research at the University of Wollongong, Australia, acknowledged that they would not model the visual arts skills required for young children to know what to do, for fear of providing a standard that might negatively influence, limit or even damage the children's innate creativity. However, these same teachers recognised the importance of modelling in most other domains, and agreed with their curriculum policy statement that 'guidance and teaching by educators shape children's experiences of becoming' (Lindsay, 2016, p.5). The result of this fear was an almost complete dearth of arts or creative practice throughout the participant settings. This clearly contradicts Eisner's understanding of the role of the educator, as he asserts that, 'there are no complex tasks or forms of thinking whose mastery is best optimised by pedagogical neglect' (Eisner, 2005, p.46).

With some notable exceptions, educators are not, in general, arts specialists and training in the arts is not provided in any great detail for trainee teachers or practitioners. As a result, myths prevail about the nature of creativity, the ability for it to be taught and the challenges of mastering art techniques. Despite this, many educators have a positive belief about the value of the arts in young children's lives and would happily endorse using arts processes. Many passionately articulate the positive ways the arts can aid progression in the different areas of learning. However, this is often less passionately applied in practice due to lack of content knowledge, artistic skill or confidence, and pedagogical practices are sometimes ingrained with very traditional approaches to the arts, if they exist at all.

It seems to me that any educator who has a legal duty to fulfil certain aspects of a curriculum requiring the presentation of differentiated teaching techniques to a large classroom of children will discover that instilling a culture of creativity – or a creative pedagogy – at the heart of their teaching will be one of the most effective ways to achieve this. A creative pedagogy involves cultivating the habit of paying attention to the creative possibilities that Craft (2002) refers to. This happens not by trying to fulfil the learning outcomes identified within Expressive Arts and Design area of the EYFS, but by fostering imaginative approaches to:

- curriculum content (numeracy, social and emotional, physical, language and literacy, etc.)

- the physical environment, indoors and out

- the choice of, and access to, resources

- communications with parents and professionals

- the ways in which children's creativity is made visible through documentation and celebrated through music and movement performances

- the wider culture of the educational setting.

Above all, it is about paying attention to *who* and *how* children are and identifying each child's creative thought processes and practice. It is from this viewpoint that all the other important aspects of a child's education, which are listed above, will be seen as exciting processes and details on that child's learning journey, rather than just being the destination of that day's teaching. It is all about the intention and purpose behind our teaching and caring – why we do what we do. In fact, what we teach ought to be secondary to this.

Even now, some people believe that imagination and self-expression have no place in the more formal subjects where the purposes of education are taken *more seriously*. However, the evidence (and many educators' experience) strongly demonstrates that, by taking creativity seriously (as children do) and implementing a creative pedagogy across all domains, an educator can tap in to both the knowledge *and* the imaginations of children via many different modalities. A creative pedagogy provides a holistic, generative approach to ensuring that their engaged and enthusiastic response to learning works as well as, if not better than, traditional pedagogical approaches (Hardiman *et al.*, 2019). As Duffy illustrates:

> Creative teaching is an art; it involves practitioners in using their imagination to make learning more interesting, exciting and effective to ensure that all children want to become involved and are enthused about learning. Sadly, too many experiences offered to young children are dull, repetitive and far from creative, rather a way of occupying children and covering the walls; creating something does not necessarily indicate creativity. Creative teaching involves taking risks, leaving the security of structured lessons behind and learning from the children. (Duffy, 2010, p.23)

A creative environment gives freedom to adults to be confident to express their own creativity and to model experimenting with different techniques, as well as to scaffold, encourage and validate children's own ideas. Initially, educators, parents and caregivers may be concerned with the effectiveness of using a new approach, or feel they are not suitably qualified to create a process, activity or artwork that stands up to inspection by another adult. The fear of judgement is a very real inhibitor in teaching. However, evidence across many fields (e.g. health, education, social care, biology, neuroscience) shows that becoming immersed in the process of creativity helps to transfer focus away from worrying about the outcome and on to the enjoyment of creating. Of course, we should acknowledge that creativity can be fun! To do so is not to undervalue it or take it any less seriously, but to acknowledge the important place of humour and joy in young children's lives.

It can be hard work sometimes exploring possible solutions to a problem or trying to observe and scaffold children's thinking or to facilitate shared group learning. But the process of having ideas, experimenting, evaluating and expressing creatively should be enjoyable and interesting to the creator, whether adult or child.

So, whether introducing stories, collage, clay, photography, music, weaving, woodworking, singing or dancing, educators need not worry about what their creation might look like. After all, young children are unlikely to be at all bothered by this. If some music makes you want to move, let your body move. If a particular combination of colours, patterns and textures makes you want to explore painting in a certain way, then do it. Have a go, get immersed, and 'wallow' in the experience, as Bruce (2005a) put it. The quicker our adult inhibitions can be moved out of the way, the more intentional the modelling of creative techniques will be and the more expressive and confident children will become in their own creative processes.

> Free-flowing processes can be inhibited in many ways, one of which comes from giving people a fear of failure... In order to learn we need to be in a position in which we are open to receiving ideas, processes, sensations and

feelings – the gamut of human experience. We need to have been allowed to respond to these experiences in ways that aren't inhibited through being told that this or that response is wrong or insufficient. In these circumstances we will be creative in thought and action. We will advance in whichever field of human activity we can think of. (Michael Rosen in Duffy, 2010, p.10)

Many psychologists, including Rogers, Maslow, Runco (2014), Sternberg (1999) and Amabile (1996), have shown that, when we are deeply immersed in creative processes, the sense of being self-conscious is replaced by a sense of enjoyment and community. Just as Csikszentmihalyi (1997) described in *his state of flow*, when someone is so intently focused on the process or activity being undertaken, they lose themselves to the enjoyment and satisfaction of it and the experience of learning becomes its own reward. This state is very similar to the one we experience when we see our children deeply immersed in their play. It is a state where goals, objectives and external rewards fly out of the window as the excitement of the present moment becomes all that matters.

A state of flow is very important to foster in young children, as it allows them to reach a deeper level of thinking and learning. Relentless instructions, questions or talking for the sake of it constantly interrupt thought and effectively limit the continuity and depth of children's thinking to a superficial level that prevents deeper connections being made across knowledge domains (Amabile, 1996).

Eisner (2005) proposes that this slowing down and wallowing in the arts invites children to pay attention to the expressions of the world around them as well as their own imaginations so that they can craft an emotional or sensory response to this through the materials available to them. It is a conscious way of counteracting the efficiency that happens in practice where we:

> act upon the world with the least amount of energy that will satisfy the realisation of our purposes. We try to do things efficiently to avoid wasting time, effort and energy. What we do not typically seek are the expressive features or the emotional tone of what we pay attention to. The arts teach us how to secure the *feelingful* experience that slow perception makes possible...and how to develop the child's mind through this experience. (Eisner, 2005, p.34)

One way to pay attention to, and have an aptitude for, arts and creativity in the educational setting is to consider the different ways of actively facilitating deeper creative interactions, languages and thinking with (and between) children. Once these techniques are practised, modelled, facilitated and mentored with staff and children, educators become more attuned to the distinctions of creative thinking and practice between different children and the techniques become second nature and an inherent part of the setting's creative pedagogy.

Environments of enquiry

While in empirical science, facts are measured by objective, logical explanations, many aspects of the world, including creativity, obviously don't fit well into this. It is the ongoing dichotomy for education that values logic over wonder and continues to promulgate the idea that there is a single truth or one right answer for almost everything worth learning. The fall-out in teaching is enormous, with so many educators exhausted by trying to balance the drive of the curriculum towards learning facts with the reality of multiple truths that exist in children's experiences of life. Teaching facts and trying to help children learn them out of context can be hard work.

If, however, the starting point is concepts rather than facts then the channels for experimentation and explanation open wide. Several arts or creative-based approaches to learning work through concept- or project-based learning models for this reason, such as the Reggio Emilia approach, the Project Approach or Experiential Education. Rather than starting with the facts that need to be known, the approach starts by posing a challenge, asking a question or offering a provocation that might at first seem confusing, such as 'What is rain for?'

Children might offer immediate answers and some highly creative responses. But they may not yet have gathered all the knowledge required to know for sure. So following this brainstorm, the educator's first question has to be, What do we need to know to find out for sure? This effectively shifts the agency and centre of expertise to the children as researchers, who might begin to create a research list of all the facts they need to know about, such as rain, clouds, sky, ground, bucket, grass, flowers and so on. Older children may go straight to a deeper research method, asking more questions such as: Why does rain fall down? Where does it come from? What are clouds? Does it live in the sky? Why is it wet? Where does rain go when it falls? And so on.

The starting point is to identify the things we need to know in order to learn about and answer this question. Educators can provide relevant resources such as books, pictures, videos or tools for real experiments (to capture rain, for instance). Once children start to research these questions, the individual facts become much more meaningful within a context that is relevant and exciting to them. Therefore, facts become easier to memorise, analyse and apply in real-world terms.

It is a subtle shift in pedagogical strategy where the goal is not to impart knowledge from the adult expert but to facilitate learning by the child expert, who has all the tools to understand if the concepts are accessible and relevant. The goal is to support children to ask the right questions that will pull in the information they need to make sense of the problem. This might be described as *pull teaching* rather than *push teaching*. Research shows that, through this approach, factual knowledge is retained at a much deeper level partly because of its alignment with context and partly because of the methods used to re-centre children's agency in gathering that knowledge.

Enquiry-based learning is an art that becomes easier (and more exciting) with experience, knowing what questions to ask and when, what tools and resources to provide and when, how to help children to stay in their Zone of Proximal Development and avoid becoming frustrated with the level of challenge, how to scaffold children's best theorising and help them draw on previous knowledge, when to jump in to provoke new thinking and when to stand back and let them work things out. It helps children build strong critical thinking and enquiry skills, teaching them that there may be multiple answers to big questions, and it helps educators bring learning to life and cultivate children's creativity as their lightbulbs are turned on and they respond on a deeper level.

> By encouraging creativity and imagination, we are promoting children's ability to explore and comprehend their world and increasing their opportunities to make new connections and reach new understandings. (Duffy, 2006, p.9)

Active and intentional listening

Active listening, or active questioning as it is sometimes referred to, is exactly what it says on the tin – an intentional, conscious act that is the opposite of passive listening, the mode most people understand best by the term 'listening'. As scholar Barbara Piscitelli (2003) from the Queensland Museums Collaborative discusses, it is a way of encouraging looking closely, observing detail, seeing and hearing new perspectives and facilitating children's interpretations of experiences, objects, materials and ideas, rather than relying on adults' interpretations. It is simple really, we just need to get ourselves out of the way. When educators intervene it needs to be intentional, for a purpose that makes sense, where 'questions can be used to acquire a sense of children's existing knowledge in order to make subsequent learning more relevant and to challenge children's thinking' (Piscitelli *et al.*, 2003).

As an intentional teaching strategy, active listening is at the heart of becoming attuned to children's creativity. Through active listening, children's embodied behaviours, gestures and languages become active, not passive, and can be practised in a range of ways, depending on the intention of the learning situation. It involves non-directive, directive and scaffolding strategies to challenge and extend a child's knowledge, engagement and agency (Bruner, 1996). These strategies are no different from those used in daily teaching practice. But the act of intentional listening to children's creative modes of expression will tend to lean more towards non-directive and scaffolding methods, highlighting how more directive strategies lead to passive teaching and learning behaviours. Less directive, more facilitative, listening-based approaches will often generate more creative responses, unusual ideas, complex thinking and communications because they increase the agency and centrality of the child in that learning situation. Building on the work of the Queensland Museums Collaborative (Piscitelli *et al.*, 2003), the lists below identifies the extended creative languages (verbal and embodied) that might be used for active listening in a way that enhances children's creativity.

Non-directive

- ○ Close physical proximity
- ○ Listening
- ○ Acknowledging
- ○ Commenting

- Encouraging
- Praising
- Modelling
- Movement mirroring (non-verbal)
- Affirmative singing

Directive

- Demonstrating
- Instructing
- Directing
- Task analysis
- Reinforcing
- Musical call-and-response
- Copycat movement games
- Visual art or craft templates
- Pre-defined costumes

Scaffolding

- Facilitating
- Reflecting back/clarifying
- Coaching
- Focusing attention
- Providing information
- Explaining
- Reading
- Recalling
- Suggesting
- Imagining/hypothesising
- Prompting
- Challenging

- o   Co-constructing
- o   Role play/improvising
- o   Developmental movement play
- o   Story-building (e.g. 'Yes! And?' games)
- o   Guided group painting
- o   Multi-textured fabrics
- o   Musical conversations
- o   Photographic consultations

This kind of 'intentional' listening to children's ideas helps children's imagination, creativity and play to flourish, as well as stimulating the educator's role in 'providing provocations, suggesting ideas, seeking alternatives, finding possibilities, planning and encouraging children' (Leggett, 2017, p.851).

Possibility thinking

In a world where very young children have most things done for or to them, it is vital to find opportunities in the setting for them to practise the mastery of skills, ideas generation, problem-finding and problem-solving. By looking at the world in different ways and playing with different possibilities and alternative solutions, not only do children become more familiar with many alternative problem-solving approaches, but they also develop an aptitude for divergent thinking, which helps them to observe underlying patterns, connections, parallels and phenomena in the world around them (Runco *et al.*, 2014).

In reviewing various creative teaching strategies, Professor Anna Craft (2002) proposed an approach called *possibility thinking* that 'encompasses an attitude which refuses to be stumped by circumstances, but uses imagination, with intention, to find a way around the problem' (2002, p.111). Craft describes a creative resilience or resourcefulness that emerges from a child wondering 'what if...?' about something in their environment, and then having the courage, curiosity and encouragement to try out possible answers to that question. It is a spectrum of possibility thinking that engages questions from the conscious to the subconscious, from the verbal to the non-verbal, from the well formulated to those that are just an inkling of an idea. It is a state of mind and body that provides a solid starting point for learning and play across all domains and is what 'drives the capacity of individuals to find their way through life experiences with a creative attitude and approach, enabling them to make the most of situations, even those which appear to pose difficulties' (Craft, 2002, p.113).

In order to foster the art of creative thinking, Craft clarifies the need for educators to support and progress children's thinking along a continuum. A child's starting point might be 'What does this do...?' where they are focused on learning procedural or conceptual knowledge. It is easy to get stuck here, focusing on directive teaching strategies whereby the child is simply responding to instructions or, worse still, not engaged in problem-solving in the activity at all (i.e. the adult does it for them).

A more generative focus would involve shifting the child's thinking to 'What can I do (or be) with this...?', 'What might it become...?'. This involves a greater generation of thought and ideas, practices physical and cognitive skills in the manipulation of the object or idea, and ultimately strengthens the agency of the child in testing out their theories to gain knowledge, ownership and mastery of the situation. In some situations, their question will be more specifically, 'How can I get around this problem...?', which shows more progressive thinking from problem-finding to solution-finding, or from concrete concepts to abstract ideas.

The sorts of questions educators can model or scaffold to facilitate this kind of transition in possibility thinking include 'I wonder' questions, such as those developed for the *visible thinking* routines (Gardner, 1982) highlighted in the next section:

- I wonder what would happen if...?

- What would it be like if we did this instead...?

- Suppose that...

- What would change if...?

- Can you imagine how you could do it differently...?

All these questions are designed to shift the power for choice, decision-making and ultimate action to the child, and build a set of complex intelligences and aptitudes in both mind and body that also provide strong foundations for *being and becoming* in the world. As children discover their creative power, as it were, it can significantly increase confidence, self-esteem and fulfilment overall. And all of these rely on one core ingredient – creative thinking (in both adult and child). That is not to say that these questions should be continually verbalised or replace all other methods of constructive teaching, but they provide starting points, or points of connection and transition for children's learning, whether through verbal or non-verbal play, den-making, drawing, maths, literacy or baking.

Craft's research showed that, where educators created time and space for children to engage in rich possibilities, the resultant thinking unlocked children's interests and creativity at a much deeper level because it was active, relevant, empowering, motivating, engaged the whole child (body and mind), collaborative, reflective, memorable and enjoyable. It was also timeless insofar as possibility thinking creates ongoing dialogue about the endless, innovative possibilities that might occur (and need testing out and evaluating) as a result of this strategy. 'Our task, regarding creativity, is to help children climb their own mountains, as high as possible. No one can do more' (Loris Malaguzzi in Edwards, Gandini and Forman, 2012, p.77).

Visible thinking

Possibility thinking gained traction in the early 2000s at about the same time as a research project for creative teaching strategies in the classroom was being developed in the US called *visible thinking*.[1] Developed by the Project Zero team at Harvard University, visible thinking was designed to enrich curriculum content by fostering students' creative intelligences, informed by Howard Gardner's *multiple intelligences* (2011) research at the time and

---

1   See www.pz.harvard.edu/projects/visible-thinking

the research-based pedagogy emerging in Reggio Emilia (2001). Created to stimulate deeper understanding of content, greater motivation for learning, and positive attitudes towards opportunities for thinking, the visible thinking (VT) routines were founded on four 'thinking ideals' of understanding, truth, fairness and creativity. The routines are flexible enough to be incorporated into any learning environment, formal or informal, with simple strategies to help extend and scaffold thinking by making the thinking process visible to both students and teachers through speech, gesture and expression. Aimed mainly at primary- and secondary-age children, the routines are generally given a structure and a vocabulary in order to enable children to talk about their thinking, so they can cultivate both convergent as well as divergent thinking skills.

One example of a routine more suitable for early years is the *Thinking Keys* routine. This was developed by Stephanie Martin, kindergarten teacher at International School of Amsterdam, and helps children evaluate and reflect on their thinking. Taking a resource related to any area of EYFS content, the educator might invite children to explore the resource with the following questions:

- *Form:* What is it like?

- *Function:* How does it work?

- *Connection:* How is this like something I have seen before?

- *Reflection:* How do you know?

While seemingly simple, these questions give children a structure through which to foster critical thinking about the form, function, connectivity and potential of any concept or object. At the same time, the process challenges the children to use relevant vocabulary or physical/sensory exploration and extends both their descriptive and expressive skills.

Another VT routine that is not at all dissimilar to Craft's possibility thinking and suitable for very young children is *See, Think, Wonder.* This routine is designed to encourage close observation and thoughtful interpretation, stimulate curiosity and enquiry, and join up existing knowledge so that it becomes relevant and meaningful. It also helps build collaborative and creative thinking with a view to broadening children's perspectives by gaining insights into each other's imaginations. It is a great way to draw in children who are generally reluctant speakers by focusing on their own ideas and reinforcing the message that all children's thinking is valued.

- *See:* After choosing an object such as an artwork, image or artefact, children are asked to make an observation about it, or to describe what they actually see in the picture. This question can be repeated many times so that children extend their observations and realise the aim is not to achieve a single right answer.

- *Think:* Children are then asked why they think this is happening or what they think might be going on here. Again, repetition of this question, 'What else is going on here? Why do you think that?' helps to extend the depth and complexity of what children are thinking about in relation to the image or object.

- *Wonder:* Children are then asked what this makes them wonder about the object or about anything or anyone in the picture. This stage takes children into the realms of their imagination from an already deep thinking position, which is the best starting point for imaginative journeys to flourish. This step can lead into many other activities over a long period to extend the stories, journeys, fantasies, role plays and other possibilities that arise from this exercise.

In giving their responses, children can be encouraged to verbalise their thoughts individually in one sentence, as in, 'I see… I think… I wonder…' Or children can be asked to respond as a group to one question at a time, sharing their observations and thoughts in separate stages. For more confident children, a further question of 'How does that make you feel?' can also stimulate further thinking on a social or emotional level, helping them to articulate, express and better understand their feelings.

It can be challenging to ensure that children stick to one step at a time and do not rush on when their imaginations have already gone on ahead, but the art of breaking it down helps children articulate and hear their own thinking develop clearly. This approach enables them not only to have their thoughts and opinions heard (by themselves and others), but also to explore new views or possibilities triggered by the perspectives of others (Rinaldi *et al.*, 2001). At the same time, it can deepen educators' insights (and challenge any preconceptions) into their children's interests and help to identify any gaps in understanding that may need further support. For reluctant speakers or non-verbal communicators, the exercise can easily be adapted to use arts-based methods for communication, such as drawing, movement, music or clay play.

None of the questions requires a 'right' answer; they are simply prompts for the generation of ideas, evaluation and expression. They provide clear steps into creative thinking and discussion that help children practise evaluating their imaginative ideas and developing critical thinking and theorising, which will inform learning across all the domains. Crucially, these strategies also help educators learn how to 'improvise in the face of uncertainty' (Eisner, 2005, p.48) or harness the idea of *not knowing*. That is, trusting children to explore ideas and possible solutions that are meaningful for them, rather than reinforcing the traditional, deeply flawed ideology of the educator being the provider of all the answers.

> A commitment to developing children's human resources must begin from a recognition of how wide, rich and diverse these resources really are. (NACCCE, 1999, p.39)

From 'process and product' to 'play and stray'

As the traditional definitions of creativity have been based on what can be measured through observation, we often associate creativity with having arts skills or producing art products. For educators who feel they are not artistically competent, have never been trained in an arts skill or feel their skills would be judged negatively by others, the desire to 'have a go' is understandably subdued and their natural creativity can remain underdeveloped. The overwhelming concern is of being 'wrong' – something both children and adults report as being a major cause of stress in modern educational environments (Van der Kolk, 2015).

This lack of confidence in an educator's own creativity and their ability to build and recognise creativity in others presents a dichotomy in early years settings, where advocacy for the processes of learning is often outweighed by a preoccupation with documenting and assessing the products of children's actions in order to be able to provide evidence as to their progress. It is not an easy balance to strike as, inevitably, assessment regimes make the observation of behaviours towards certain outcomes a necessity. But how many times has this task been undertaken regardless of where the child is in their thinking, feeling and doing on that day? How many times have activities been set out with the sole purpose of capturing the right photos for the learning journal? As a result, how many opportunities for opening up a rich seam of creative thinking with each other might have been lost?

This apparent focus on 'process' is actually an obsession with the observable 'products' of learning. Photographing children pouring water between containers at the water table, dressing up in the role-play corner or stacking the pots and pans in the outdoor mud kitchen is one way of showing how they are applying what they have learned. And on the one hand, it is important to be able to discern levels of mastery in certain technical skills that can be seen in children's mark-making, number blocks and pottery creations in order to decide what level of challenge to offer in the next sessions.

On the other hand, while some processes of learning are visible, tangible and linear, I would maintain that many others are invisible, intangible and entangled, and only made known – or sensed – through a deep understanding of the child. This comes through attuned, shared play, collaborative making, active listening, spending time in relationship and being curious researchers together. It is this relationship that creates an inner awareness as to the young child's state of being, state of play, state of mind and state of creativity. It is a bond that unites what is seen with what is heard, felt, touched and sensed intuitively, and operates on a physical, chemical, biological, neurological and emotional level. Therefore, knowing when to come alongside and just be there with, and for, the child, and when to stand back and observe takes the whole body and mind, not just a decision based on timetables and task lists.

The following illustration by designer Tim Murray depicts the 'ideal' creative process that is so easy to become focused on in a bid to achieve specific outcomes, with the risk of missing the richness of the learning taking place.

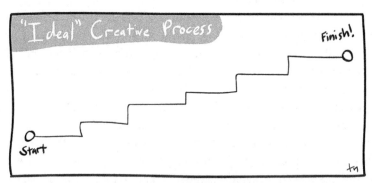

A linear process – predictable, incremental movements towards a known target.
(This version of the creative process is a myth.)

Figure 11.1: Ideal creative process
(illustration by Tim Murray @paperbackdesign, with kind permission)

Ideally, there should be no hierarchy or competition between teaching methods, where products trump processes, or vice versa. There are valid purposes for both in any learning environment, but my point is that there are alternative ways of practising and valuing products *and* processes without dressing one up as the other. Imagine how different early education might be if there were no paper-based assessments, and children's *progress* was defined by the intuition, the sense, the deeply held knowing of the educator and caregiver, of *who* and *how* the child is in themselves at any one time (as opposed to *what* they are doing).

I would like to hazard a guess that the focus of pedagogy would shift dramatically to *being present*, being *in the moment* with children rather than having to demonstrate their *having been*. I would argue that this is the difference between process (being) and product (having been), and this impacts on the arts and creative practices in terms of how we view what we are doing or making, and why. Thankfully, in England at least, the regulatory body, Ofsted, is committed to changing its assessment framework to try to reduce the time spent on unnecessary data collection and increase the amount and quality of intelligent interactions with children, based on sharing experiences rather than trying to 'deliver' a curriculum.

> Time will be their greatest ally. Giving oneself time to pause, to stop for a moment and reflect, often means giving quality to the learning that takes place and the relationships that are formed. (Rinaldi *et al.*, 2001, p.15)

It is important not to polarise the product versus process debate though. This is a false dichotomy as there is clearly room for both and, indeed, both are required in different proportions depending on whether we are learning with and from, or learning about, our children (Rinaldi *et al.*, 2001). The problem commonly experienced is that the values of freedom, expression, joy, imagination, improvisation, experimentation and so on are associated with the creative *process*, whereas the values underpinning skills progression, representation of ideas, refinement of crafting techniques, mastery, goal orientation, creating solutions to problems and creating beauty are associated with creating a *product*, and assigned a higher status as such.

No matter what regulatory framework is in place, we need to challenge the cultures and attitudes that reinforce the dominant idea (and associated value judgements) of the product being the main goal, or being more important in the learning process. If the educational setting has been particularly driven by assessments and targets in the past, changing this culture and people's mindsets might require space and time for educators to try things out, to play with creative resources again and again, without any specific product in mind. It can help to have a theme or provocation, if only for the sake of finding a starting point for the imagination. The result of such playfulness is that educators will begin to find a sense of familiarity and confidence, and an openness towards different materials and tools, and not feel bound by preconceived ideas of what something should look like or should become. Sometimes the process does lead to a product, which is fine, and at other times, the journey of exploration and discovery is actually all that is necessary.

Once educators begin to chart their position on this playful journey they see themselves making *progress*, not just by gaining a command of materials, tools and techniques, but also of ideas, imagination and possibility (Craft, 2013). They learn to flex their *imagination muscles*, ideas flow more easily, and the things that formerly limited creative thinking become less prevalent. This provides a bedrock of knowing how to access the same modes, methods and depths of thinking and doing with the children. It requires educators to practise being comfortable with the *values* of process, trusting the richness of their own imaginations once unleashed, playing with creative ideas and processes repeatedly and experiencing how generative and meaningful they become in themselves.

Combining this focus on listening to each other and ourselves, and listening with the materials, we become attuned to the deeper creativity within the body, mind and spirit, and aware of the things that were not immediately visible (Osgood, 2017). Working creatively with our methods, materials and approaches in a way that traditional teaching methods do not offer is an important contribution to a child's development and education. This is the attitude and culture of a creative pedagogy, dedicated to a more democratic exploring (listening to, asking questions of, trying on for size) the know-how and the know-why of ourselves and our children, where we become more connected by our differences. Becoming immersed in this practice is not always a known or comfortable space for educators. I wholly recommend educators give themselves permission to *play and stray* from familiar territory.

Dewey (1934) was progressive in his ideas to move education towards embracing playfulness as a valid form of learning. His manifesto for enquiry-based approaches to schooling (in *Experience and Education*, 1963) was highly creative in its recognition of children's innate desire to research the world and express their ideas about it, and has informed much creative education practice today. While he valued the creative process and product equally and understood the characteristics of both to connect emotions, ideas, freedom and expression, he nevertheless held that play 'is transformed into work' when the 'activity is subordinated to production of an objective result' (Dewey, 1934, p.291).

Sadly, this is a very real danger for children and staff where the overtly goal-oriented focus can lead to high levels of stress and a feeling of being uncreative. A creative pedagogy simply requires a commitment to intentionally open up children's ideas, scaffold their enquiries, consider and model techniques that could help extend these enquiries (which is where additional arts training can have most effect) and enable the child to achieve an expression of the idea that is important to them. In achieving higher levels of technical mastery, a child can be freer to experiment creatively with their products and processes, their materials and tools. These are simply the characteristics of a skilled educator who takes children's learning seriously.

As I have maintained throughout, with the right conditions and awareness, a sense of creativity is something everyone can possess and enjoy to the full, as expressed in the NACCCE report:

> Creativity is possible in all areas of human activity, including the arts, sciences, at work, at play and in all other areas of daily life. All people have creative abilities and we all have them differently. When individuals find their creative strengths, it can have an enormous impact on self-esteem and on overall achievement. (NACCCE, 1999, p.6)

To work towards a high level of artistic skill in a particular domain such as drawing or pottery does require discipline and commitment, just as with any skill – there is no way around this. That is not the path many educators wish to take but it should not preclude them from thinking, doing and being highly creative. In doing so, educators will challenge this artificial *product versus process* dualism and embrace the values inherent in both, as well as recognising the nuances. For instance, while beauty is considered by many as an ultimate mark of quality in a product (ignoring the enormous subjectivity of that belief which makes it untenable as a global standard), it is arguably more useful to explore the concept of beauty as an important but often intangible process of 'know-how' (process) rather than 'know-what' (product).

Lindsay (2016) explores how, in the Reggio Emilia designated space called the *atelier*, the idea was to integrate the artistic, creative and expressive languages of children as a valid way of building know-how, alongside the more conventional forms of know-what taught at school. It was a way of challenging the hierarchy of knowledge and teaching methods perpetuated through conventional schooling. Vea Vecchi (2010), an experienced atelierista (a designated teacher with an arts training) in the municipality of Reggio Emilia, describes the atelier as a thoughtful approach to teaching and learning. Vecchi describes how it was designed to 'illustrate the extraordinary, beautiful and intelligent things children knew how to do' by eliminating the 'widespread work circulating in early childhood services at the time, where mostly teachers' minds and hands were central and children had a marginal role, which led to the same stereotyped products for all' (in Lindsay, 2016, p.6).

I would argue that the concepts of product and process are deeply intertwined, ambiguous methods of meaning-making that involve building relationships between know-how and know-what and between adult and child creators. By paying attention to our materials or objects and exploring emerging meanings for ourselves, as well as observing any received meanings in the creations made by others, we encourage a sensitivity both to one's own and others' embodied gestures, choices and expressions, since 'listening is a sensitivity to everything that connects us to the others' (Rinaldi, 2001, p.4).

This raises implications for research-based educators in knowing how to establish a creative pedagogy, to truly move cultures previously driven by targets and products towards a playground of product-process thought action. It might require building an *environment of trustful silence* with practitioners who are used to language as a way of teaching and learning, and providing an assessment-free space to experiment, or play and stray, and discuss emerging meanings 'in the hope of reaching a future with generative possibilities for kaleidoscopic childhoods' (Osgood, 2017, p.10).

In his cartoon below, designer Tim Murray beautifully depicts the thoughts that occur to those of us who sometimes feel creatively challenged. Often, the hardest part of creativity comes just before the breakthrough occurs! But it is worth holding on for the precious times when we experience those magic moments with our children and colleagues.

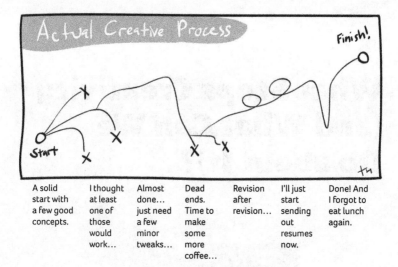

Figure 11.2: Actual creative process

(illustration by Tim Murray @paperbackdesign, with kind permission)

Chapter 12

What Stops Creativity (and What Can We Do about It)?

Eminent chemist, psychologist and creativity researcher Teresa Amabile (1996) considers the exploration of what obstructs creativity as one of the most powerful ways to finding your creative element. Amabile asserts that, depending on whether we love or hate the task in hand, it derives a desire either to immerse ourselves in it no matter what the challenges, or to find every reason to avoid it. The main question being, What motivational forces either empower or disempower creativity? Does motivation simply come from the enjoyment and satisfaction of being immersed in a purposeful activity, as Bruner (1996), Torrance (1963) and Bruce (2005a) identified? Is it about the innate drive to fulfil our potential, as Carl Rogers (1954) and Csikszentmihalyi (1997) believed was possible with the right conditions in place? Is it, as Koestler believed, more to do with having a freedom from control in order 'to achieve the unconscious, playful forms of thought that produced creative insights' (Sternberg, 1999, p.298)?

Amabile (in Sternberg, 1999) asserts that there are two types of motivation: intrinsic, which is conducive to creativity, and extrinsic, which is detrimental to it (although there are some positive impacts). Intrinsic motivation is one that comes from an internal desire to engage in an activity for its own sake because it is enjoyable, interesting, challenging and satisfying. Extrinsic motivation is not so much driven by a desire for fulfilment but by an ambition to meet an externally designated goal, such as an expected outcome, regulation, requirement or reward, like wages. Extrinsic motivation is only rewarded by the external recognition or valuing of the task being completed (i.e. any personal sense of fulfilment is dependent on others or on the social or cultural environment). It is now thought that there are strong links between creativity, purpose, wellbeing and intrinsic motivation.

Since I argue throughout the book that creativity is a fundamental human characteristic, an essence that is felt, heard, seen and sensed on many levels through the mind, body and spirit, it stands to reason that teaching for creativity should be focused on encouraging intrinsic motivation. However, since many professionals in both early education and the arts struggle with the many obstacles to arts or creative practice, it remains true to say that we still live in a world that drives us towards greater productivity using external motivations. In this book, I have collated ideas and thinking towards a much more intrinsic approach to valuing young children's creativity. Yet this is no doubt one of the greatest tensions in education, where educators who are committed to nurturing children's innate characteristics may not actually experience this model for themselves, and still have to fulfil external obligations anyway.

> Young people's creative abilities are most likely to be developed in an atmosphere in which the teacher's creative abilities are properly engaged. To put it another way, teachers cannot develop the creative abilities of their pupils if their own creative abilities are suppressed. (NACCCE, 1999, p.103)

According to research over the last two decades (Runco *et al.*, 2014; Sternberg, 1999; NACCCE, 1999; Prentice, 2000; Churchill Dower, 2008; Churchill Dower and Sandbrook, 2013, 2018) little has changed in terms of the identified obstacles to creativity in early years. This final chapter focuses on identifying what these obstacles or challenges are to nurturing creativity in the early years along with some ideas gained through 30 years of practice as to what alternative approaches might be possible for practitioners. In doing so, I sum up what are the main problems facing professionals and caregivers in trying to cultivate creativity in the 21st century.

EXPERIENCE, SKILLS AND KNOWLEDGE - PROBLEMS

o *Universal worksheet/toolkit-led approaches replacing educators' professional intuition about nurturing their children's creativity.* This reinforces the message that the arts can only be taught as a specific set of activities (sometimes measured through skills such as cutting, pasting, tying and folding, which are more technical/ physical than imaginative activities), and that achievement in these activities will determine how *creative* a child is.

o *Lack of personal opportunities for arts or creative experiences (e.g. going to the theatre, making pottery, crafting, singing in a choir or playing an instrument).* This makes it hard to discern what well-crafted, creative experiences look and feel like. It can lead to an over-reliance in the classroom on recreating existing stories, imitating famous paintings, completing templates, worksheets or other teacher-led toolkits.

o *Lack of arts and cultural theory (as it applies to young children) underpinning educational practices, which could lead to a deeper understanding of why, and how, different arts approaches can work.* This often results in a 'revolving smorgasbord of entertaining arts activities...with narrow or pre-determined outcomes' (Lindsay, 2016, p.10) being used repeatedly, rather than educators being able to develop a deeper, creative pedagogy.

o *The overt focus on simple, goal-oriented ideas in many early education publications, resources catalogues and in social media.* This distracts practitioners away from the realisation that they are very capable of developing arts-based skills themselves, as are their children. Approaches based in action research, rich in reflection and personalised enquiry, are great starting points if the sector's media outlets would reflect a more dominant focus towards this.

o *Lack of creative confidence, fear of failure or disbelief in one's own creativity as legitimate.* This is perpetuated by the target-driven climate, which reinforces the message of 'beautiful' creative products being the measure of 'good' creative skills and knowledge. Pressure also comes from the wider climate of social media, which perpetuates idealistic notions of what 'effective' professionals should be achieving.

CURRICULUM/ASSESSMENT/PEDAGOGIC CULTURE – PROBLEMS

o *Lack of clarity in curriculum frameworks as to how to interpret creativity in practice (in the EYFS it is only mentioned in the 'creating and thinking critically' Characteristic of Effective Learning), combined with the lack of arts references.* This makes it an almost invisible area of learning and downgrades its importance in a child's early education.

o *The language of the curriculum and support guidance encouraging misconceptions about 'creativity' being about a way of producing things, and setting this in opposition to 'playful processes', which are described more clearly as ways to encourage early learning and development.* This binary representation is disingenuous to the complex and integral relationship between play and creativity, process and product. It reinforces faulty conceptions about what creativity is and what it can do and reduces its possibilities as a teaching tool.

o *A culture of initiative-overload.* Many initiatives are designed to focus on national 'problem' areas such as numeracy or literacy, rather than on being locally fit for purpose or considering an integrated, pedagogical approach through creative teaching and learning to address all areas of learning.

o *Lack of external training or professional development for educators and practitioners in arts or creative practices that will provide both knowledge and nourishment.* There is also a lack of internal space and time in settings to *play and stray* from familiar practices, which would enable learners to access and trust the richness of their own imaginations and become comfortable with the values of process.

o *A target-driven climate with observations and assessments becoming increasingly reductive and an intense focus on the gaps in a child's knowledge and skills – their know-what rather than their know-how or know-why.* There is a dominant focus on data gathering to build assessment evidence, often to the detriment of time spent researching the world and learning together.

o *A disproportionate focus on literacy and numeracy at a younger age to the exclusion of creative and relevant thinking processes, despite the plethora of expertise on young children's multiple modes and methods of learning and development during this period.*

○ *Progressive or inhibitive influence of leadership.* Managers and heads who value, believe in and understand the power and agency of children's artistic and creative domains, and its (tried and tested) positive impacts across all areas of learning, will very often find a way to develop a pedagogy and culture of creativity in their setting, seeing many possibilities in their available resources and partnerships. Conversely, where this leadership buy-in does not exist, arts and cultural processes and products are unlikely to flourish beyond what is required to fulfil curriculum or assessment regimes, and the creative skills of both educators and children will remain dormant or, worse, inhibited.

FUNDING AND RESOURCES - PROBLEMS

○ *Lack of funding for projects with artists or creative organisations or trips to galleries, museums, libraries and theatres to experience arts and culture outside the setting.*

○ *Lack of funding to prioritise arts and cultural skills training or attend creative teaching/creative leadership courses (for instance) as part of ongoing professional development, and to buy in cover where required for this to happen.*

EXPERIENCE, SKILLS AND KNOWLEDGE - POSSIBILITIES

○ Invest in creative or arts training and professional development opportunities to build both skills and confidence as well as an arts-specific language that helps describe what is happening during periods of creative learning. This can happen by attending training at local arts and cultural centres, universities or colleges offering arts-based courses, joining arts and early years networks (where ideas and challenges can be shared, and *beautiful product* fears or pressures to perform can be relieved in a supportive community), or establishing an arts-based action research group to focus on particular projects within or between settings.

○ Sign up for newsletters[1] and read the latest research or case studies in arts, cultural and creative practice for young children in order to develop a broader appreciation of arts and creative processes. This builds confidence to trust young children's ability to develop

---

1   For example, https://earlyarts.co.uk/ebulletin-signup

their own ideas and artistry, and helps to resist the urge to fall back on adult-defined activities or artistic outputs. Combining this with arts-skills training also helps raise confidence in art-form mastery, encouraging a *have-a-go* culture in the setting, and increasing ideas for starting points to unleash the imagination.

o   Set aside space and time to practise the processes of creativity – thinking, making, exploring, discovering, improvising and reflecting. Identify a few meaningful provocations that might stimulate diverse responses using different materials, tools and techniques (this could be an image, a story, an emotion, a memory, an object), and have a go. Do it regularly, even if only for ten minutes at the start of each staff meeting, to see what emerges. Resist any quality judgements and embrace a *play and stray* culture to help develop a familiarity with pushing your ideas outside the normal boundaries, and becoming comfortable with the unknown.

o   Throw out any predefined templates for creative activities such as drawing and painting, sewing and sculpting kits, unless they provide good starting points or provocations for more complex thinking. Audit and reconsider all resources used as a time-saver, especially if they do not stimulate a child's full potential of ideas or choices and limit the focus to copying skills or colouring and cutting out someone else's design. There is a place for these in terms of developing fine motor skills, of course, but creativity will only be nurtured if it also involves imaginative stimulus.

o   In the same way, providing predetermined (ready-made) costumes for role play may be counter-productive by limiting children's imaginations to the dispositions or characteristics (sometimes derogatory) already associated with that costume. Rather, offer materials, textiles, hats, props, wigs, masks, shoes and accessories that open up the possibilities of who, what, where or how children could be. Be prepared for not knowing, or needing to know, who, what or how children are during these periods. As long as they are safe, this is their time to make sense of the world in languages that may not make any sense to adults. Our gift is to preserve the space and offer them that freedom without judgement or pressure to progress.

o   Make time to visit children's arts festivals, local theatre, music or dance events, museums, galleries and libraries and become more immersed in arts and cultural experiences personally and professionally. The more you see and hear, the more refined your filters will become as to what rocks your boat and inspires you to respond creatively, and the more confident you will become in creating these environments within your setting. Do not be afraid to try things out – arts and cultural experiences can be different, unusual, surprising and interesting, but above all, they can also be a lot of fun.

CURRICULUM/ASSESSMENT/PEDAGOGIC CULTURE – POSSIBILITIES

o Invest time in exploring links between creative behaviours and areas of learning across the curriculum, then plan thoughtful activities that take children into their creative 'ZPD' (see Chapter 7).

o Observe, sense and recognise repeated patterns of creative behaviours, aptitudes and responses to certain provocations, and develop a creative pedagogy for the setting that will both excite and challenge your children, using this to provide the optimal conditions for creative behaviours to flourish in both children and educators.

o Heads and managers may not be aware of the local cultural and creative training opportunities available with the arts, cultural and education spheres. If you are a passionate creative educator, help connect them to those networks, or ask creative heads from other settings to invite yours to an appropriate event. Recommend research or resources, such as those identified through this book, to ensure your leadership team have the benefits of children's creativity on their radar. The most effective changes are often inspired from within settings, not from top-down directives.

o A culture of creativity means giving yourself permission to explore your own creativity! Do not be put off by the terms imagination, arts, creativity, make-believe or fantasy play. Viewed from an educator's perspective, these are simply processes of learning with different techniques, skills, environments and outcomes. They are valid forms of caring and educating that ultimately have a real and tangible impact on young children's learning, and that adults should enjoy as much as they do.

FUNDING AND RESOURCES – POSSIBILITIES

o Where lack of funding prevents visits to arts centres or libraries, arrange for local arts and cultural professionals to visit the setting and bring some meaningful creative treasures/stories/musical instruments/scratch theatre performances or rehearsal ideas/ costumes or props with them that might invite the children to think differently. Many will be happy to do so as part of their family development programme.

o Where live arts experiences are not available, feast on the case studies of inspiring settings implementing arts and creative pedagogies in daily practice, such as Earlyarts,[2] Take Art,[3] The Carousel Project,[4] Arts and Health Ireland,[5] Cultural Learning Alliance,[6] Sound Connections,[7] Museum of London,[8] Creativity Portal.[9]

o Where budget cuts have curtailed arts or cultural projects, the visibility of children's creativity, processes of thinking and impacts on learning remains a shining example to all through documentation. Consider publishing your own case studies on your setting's website to draw attention to the impact of creativity with parents and partner organisations and raise the profile of your creative approaches to teaching and learning.

o Provide creative play postcards featuring your own projects and highlighting links to children's learning to hand out to parents and caregivers as an introduction to conversations about creative play. This will encourage them to consider creativity a legitimate part of their child's development, and offer tangible ideas that they

2 https://earlyarts.co.uk/inspiring-case-studies
3 https://takeart.org/early-years/case-studies
4 www.thecarouselproject.org.uk
5 www.artsandhealth.ie/case-studies
6 https://culturallearningalliance.org.uk/practice
7 www.sound-connections.org.uk/work-area/early-years
8 www.museumoflondon.org.uk/supporting-london-museums/information-services/ early-years-toolkit
9 http://creativityportal.org.uk/?q=&r=,early-learning-and-childcare&c=,case-studies

can continue in the home. Earlyarts postcards are available as a starting point.[10]

o Almost all art forms can be explored without needing a huge budget. But this is not to say that materials should be of poor quality. It is important to try and acquire the highest quality resources. For instance, poor quality pastels, paints and brushes produce a dullened version of colours and lines and can be less inspiring to play with. Cheaply made musical instruments will not produce the quality or richness of tone that more carefully crafted instruments will, again resulting a less passionate response in children. But many well-made instruments and materials can be picked up secondhand, plus there are many ways to engage children in the process of making percussion instruments such as drums, shakers, blocks and cymbals out of recycled materials that make a range of unusual and very satisfying sounds.

o Indeed, there are many ways of accessing high-quality arts resources on a budget if a little investment of time can be put into scouring secondhand shops, scrap stores, car boot sales or auction websites, especially for role-play props and accessories. Pound shops and supermarkets are also great sources of cheaper, mass-produced resources that are still conducive to a creative imagination, such as long rolls of paper, feathers, silk scarves, ribbons, buttons, sequins, wool or string, flour for playdough, soft materials, pegs, foil, sandpaper, paint rollers, coffee machine filter papers, cotton reels, containers and tools for applying patterns and shapes such as baking or sugar-craft tools. Of course, many natural materials are free, including sticks, feathers, flowers, pebbles, shells, seeds, stones, sand, driftwood and foliage – provided they are not removed inappropriately from their natural environment.

o The best resources are often found in people. Creativity can be sparked by inviting an inspiring child, teacher, parent, business person, politician, sports person, author, artist, scientist, nurse or soldier to speak on their creative activity, values and choices. They can help us imagine ourselves in situations we have not yet experienced but that might add meaning to our own lives, beyond anything we have experienced before. In this increasingly over-stimulating world around us, it is often the actions of another person that will trigger these creative possibilities in ourselves. And it is often in collaboration with others, experiencing their ideas and filters on life, that we take our creativity to a new level that might not have been possible on our own.

---

10 https://earlyarts.co.uk/shop-teaching-packs/creative-family-postcards

○ Space and time are two of the most precious resources a child will need to play with, and reflect on, their creativity. Do everything possible to make that space and time available, both indoors and out.

Creativity is not solely about the new, it also involves opening ourselves out to ideas, influences and resources that are all around us, that we cannot control totally, yet that can be harnessed to making our lives richer and more sustainable. (Landry and Bianchini, 1995, p.21)

The reason why most people go into early education or arts education is because they care for young children. They find them fascinating, challenging, funny, caring and inspiring. The current climate is raising the temperature in early years environments, brains and bodies to perform, prove, produce and persevere, which, on the whole, is not a great deal of fun. Neither does it appear to be making a huge deal of difference to the achievement of children in terms of their security, happiness, attainment or overall wellbeing. But it is in danger of overtaking the purposes of education and masking why we wanted to work, play and be with children in the first place.

Creative environments, however, can bring out the best in children and us because they nourish and are nourished by our internal drive for community, expression, understanding, love and curiosity. Creativity is an embodiment of our innate humanity, our agency and power, the essence of who each of us is now and can be in the future. It provides all we need for communication, confidence, expression, community, cognitive and somatic development, happiness and wellbeing, and it does so without the need for performance-related measures, if we are brave enough.

There are greater things at work than we can influence in our lifetime, and time is painfully short for important issues to be addressed such as climate change, health and wellbeing. But none of us is without the opportunity to be creative if we want to. So I urge you not to hesitate. Please prioritise the nurturing of your creativity and open up your children's worlds to all that is possible within them and around them. And enjoy the adventure wherever you can.

Philosophy Glossary

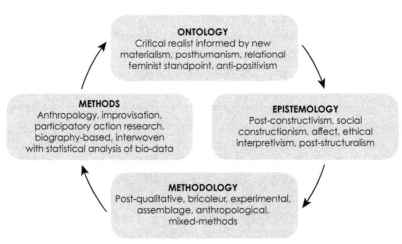

Figure I.1: *Theoretical and methodological underpinnings of the concepts in this book*

This glossary explains the author's philosophical and methodological underpinnings as depicted in Figure I.1. in the Introduction of this book.

Critical realism

Emerging from the work of Roy Bhaskar in the late 1900s, this builds on the concept of realism, which is the halfway house between empiricism (where things are only believed to exist if they can be experienced, seen and measured, such as the forces of gravity) and idealism (where things can exist as an *essence* or a sense in our conscious minds, even if they are not seen or able to be measured in material form, such as a set of ideals on how the world should be, or the indescribable sense of transcendence in a piece of music).

Realists believe in 'an actually existing world that is independent of our perceptions of it' (Williams, 2016, p.190) (i.e. things we cannot necessarily see or understand still exist whether we believe in them or not). Plus, even though everything cannot be known completely, what cannot be seen (such as what goes on in our minds) can still be measured (with a degree of subjectivity). So cause and effect *can* be evidenced on the acceptance that causes are often complex, not binary or linear, and sometimes emerge over time when certain dispositions are triggered by certain conditions. Therefore, we may not always identify the causes of what those causes actually are, especially if they involve an unseen force or essence such as creativity.

Critical realism takes this one step further towards what one of its founders, Bhaskar (2008), calls a 'depth ontology'. This effectively explains how our experiences of the world arise from the relationship between the underlying conditions for things to happen and the causal powers in the world – both of which are evolving and changing over time and space. Critical realists also hold that there are some effects that cannot help but happen regardless of the conditions (this is called *natural necessity*), which has evolved from positivist theories on the laws of natural science, but this can contradict beliefs in the subtle social and cultural effects on the world, and the acknowledgment that reality can be complex. Ultimately, critical realism embraces the relative truths of any statistical measurement – it stacks up against relative standards, but accepts that there is no one right way of measuring social constructs such as class, ethnicity, cultural identities and creativity, because there is no single 'norm' baseline from which to measure. Hence the need to be 'critical'.

New materialism

This is a relatively new philosophical field that attempts to bridge several disciplines, including the natural, human and social sciences. It aims to identify what (and why) life and knowledge are, as part of the wider natural, social, cultural, political, spiritual and even transcendental contexts. It tries to move beyond the limitations of social constructionism (where knowledge is created, known and embedded through social interaction) and cultural theory, which defines the metaphysical concepts of being and knowing, agency and structure, objects and subjects primarily through language, and break open the realms of understanding beyond the somatic (body-centred) or material knowledge of the world. In early education practice, it is about exploring the relations between materials, objects and people without being limited by language, but expanding our concepts of what things mean through the ways they intra-act with each other through body, materiality, spirit and essence (Barad, 2007).

For instance, the concept of intelligent materials in the Reggio Emilia approach was designed to provoke deeper thinking both for practitioners considering the purpose or potential of the materials available for play-learning and for children to access different modes of expression that came naturally to them. Open-ended materials that were carefully chosen for potential connections to children's interests or schemas, or as provocations for new thinking, might be more likely to stimulate a child's imagination and enhance their complexity of thought and action. For instance, instead of simply building a scrap sculpture to use up some empty boxes, intelligent materials (or loose parts) are carefully chosen and positioned to inspire different ways they might be transformed, connected, constructed, deconstructed or repurposed based on a child's lines of enquiry.

Traditionally, we would see the practitioner or child as having the power – or agency – in their choices and subsequent responses, and the materials just being, well, fairly static materials! Through a new materialistic lens, one might question why you are drawn to a particular material, as if *it* has chosen *you*. What is the attraction, force or essence of a material – its power or agency – that makes you want to interact with it? This may, of course, be based on a complex number of variables, such as interest, familiarity, novelty, aesthetic beauty, social conditioning, openness to the unknown, willingness to take risks, recommendation by a trusted person and so forth. Some of those factors *belong* to the person, some *belong* to the material.

New materialism considers the more-than-human element of the relationship as much as the human element, and attempts to recognise the *voices* of the materials at work, as much as the people, in order to reduce any privileging of human knowledge in explaining what is going on, as if humans are in complete control of the situation. This theoretical perspective has been largely influenced by quantum physicist Karen Barad (2007), whose idea of agency is 'not a human "capacity to act"…but as a relational performance enacted intra-actively within an entangled assemblage of material and embodied human' (Chappell *et al.*, 2019, p.299), which is in constant change in response to those relationships. Barad explains that 'to be entangled is not simply to be intertwined with another, as in the joining of separate entities, but to lack an independent, self-contained existence' (2007, p.ix). This means that neither humans nor materials or any other thing in existence has agency in isolation, without being in relation to each other, which makes a lot of sense when you think about it. From birth, we bring a genetic and cultural history, then a social history full of intra-actions (even at a biological or molecular level) with the humans and non-humans around us – the environment – that shape who we are. We are not independent of those, and neither are the non-human elements in the world (including nature, animals, materials, objects etc.). Without each other, we simply would not exist.

Posthumanism

This is also an emergent field, departing from the belief of humanism (where human qualities, moralities and rights are considered universal, self-determined through rationality and without any transcendental or supernatural origin). Instead, posthumanism acknowledges our sometimes irreconcilable differences, the fact that individuals do not all develop at the same rate against expected 'norms' (which empiricists would say, if not met, somehow identifies us as deficient or abnormal), and that those 'norms' – other people's truths – do not reflect our own story, or our whole truth. It does not accept dominant ideologies which serve to dehumanise people by (for instance) assuming children are less capable beings than adults with no agency or purpose of their own or that the end goal of childhood is to be a 'better' adult according to a limited set of economic, cultural and social standards. Rather, posthumanism acknowledges people's multiple identities, cultures, heritages, social, political and complex lives at any age and holds those respectfully in equal measure for who they are now, in the present moment (Murris, 2016).

Contrary to developmental theory, posthumanism holds that there is not one version (or series of stages) of childhood that all children should aspire to, and focuses on decentring the human away from being measured against someone else's universal or generalised hierarchy of definitions that are detached from a person's own truth. Neither is childhood or adulthood made up only of material things or behaviours that can necessarily be seen and understood and are influenced only by nature or nurture/culture. Rather, people have agency, essence, intention and purpose expressed through an entangled mass of influences. These might include their genetic and cultural heritage, their social and cultural situations, their dreams, possibilities, potential and ideas, and their relationships with many other people – even materials, concepts, spiritualty and essences beyond what can be identified or articulated, often referred to as their *more-than-human* elements. This means challenging the purposes of education systems that acknowledge only a tiny part of what is it to be human and even then, measure it through blinkered hierarchies of inequality and of relationship only to fixed concepts of what is real. A posthuman view asks that we go beyond our current definitions of education or the arts as only being valid while being useful for something. As an essential human essence, the arts have an important place in children's experiences of being and this surely has to reignite discussions as to what this means, and how we meaningfully embrace the arts, in education. As education scholar Gert Biesta points out, 'Rather than asking what education *produces*, we should be asking what education *means*. And rather than asking what education *makes*, we should be asking what education *makes possible*' (Naughton *et al.*, 2017, p.13, author's italics). We could perhaps ask the same of the arts.

Each individual child is a conglomeration of every physical and psychological influence and therefore cannot be defined by his or her past; their social and cultural *matter* is always in flux. A posthuman child is situated in the middle of all this, not defined by their past or someone else's idea of their future, but in the immediacy of who they are now in relation to the world round them (Murris, 2016; Rautio, 2013).

Relational (social) feminism

Building on the work of Mary Wollstonecraft in the 18th century and the suffrage movement in the 19th century, second-wave feminism began to emerge through the work of Betty Friedan in the 1960s. Friedan focused attention on the oppressive roles of women in industrialised society through her work on *The Feminine Mystique* (1963). In its essence, second-wave feminism is about removing the obstacles to female participation in the advancement of science and ensuring that the widest possible reservoir of insight, understanding, cultures and talent is informing our worldviews. The narrow, westernised, privileged standpoints, mostly written by white, western-educated males that have dominated science for many centuries were predicated upon an untested (and therefore, ironically, unscientific) assumption that women were somehow incapable of major scientific achievement. Significant female thinkers overcame unproven prejudices and obstacles based purely on gender, and challenged 'the ruling self-image of science by their distinctive visions and ways of working' (Benton and Craib, 2011, p.63). This challenge symbolised the failings of empirical science as an objective project, classifying anything that did not fit the dominant ideology (in terms of race, gender, age, dis-ability, economic and social status) as 'other' to their 'norm', deficient or defective in some way, and promoted as such in the eyes of the world.

As such, the feminism mantle has also been taken up as a framework for egalitarian-based thinking for many men and women in order to halt marginalisation and oppression due to culture, class, colour, ability, faith, biological and gender identities, and has shared some Marxist principles in relation to challenging the conditions and causes of exploitation and oppression. My own prefix of 'relational' feminism highlights a disassociation from the binary thinking that pervaded the early industrial capitalism, that pitted male and female as equal but opposite, with 'femininity, emotion and subjectivity being opposed to masculine objectivity and rationality', referred to as the *separation of the spheres* (Benton and Craib, 2011, p.65). My philosophy moves instead towards a more ambiguous idea of complementary roles, identities, societies, languages and psychologies, not bound or divided by gender, race or class, but by our interdependence and relationships as much as our particularity and differences. It is an ideology that seeks reclamation of 'science as a human project instead of a masculine project, and the renunciation of the division of emotional and intellectual labour that maintains science as a male preserve' (Keller, 1985, p.178). Keller's appreciation of psychologist Ernest Schachtel's concept of 'world-openness' as being a scientific observation of the world in the service of a love 'which wants to affirm others in their total and unique being' illustrates relational feminism beautifully (Keller, 1985, p.119). It repositions it as a pluralistic, interactive, dynamic (rather than mechanical, law-based) science of reciprocity and provides a key to the essence of creativity, which is discussed throughout this book.

Anti-positivism

Positivism was first set out by Auguste Comte in 1830. It is a theory of knowledge – how we know what we know – and began as a way of understanding the observed phenomena in the natural world through scientific methods of explanation, which all sounds perfectly logical. However, it works on the basis of deduction – a theory or hypothesis is made about the way something works, then through the process of observation of certain casual events (or recurring patterns of experience), the evidence and argument are built up to support that theory. The theory is proved wrong if the observations do not provide irrefutable proof, and encourages attempts to try to find an alternative theory that explains the evidence. The flaw in the logic is that not all variables can be accounted for in seeking the necessary evidence, nor can constant changes in the natural, physical and social worlds and the effect these have on the subject be easily recognised or measured.

Therefore, it can never cover all possibilities in stating its 'proof', meaning that positivist laws once again do not explain the whole story. Positivism believes in *value freedom*, meaning anything that is unobservable (or unmeasurable using empirical scientific methods), such as our minds, intuition, morality, aesthetics, beliefs or values, is considered unworthy of scientific validity, and thus there are lots of fundamental gaps in the knowledge base of positivism (Williams, 2016).

The goal of positivism is to produce irrefutable statements of fact about all known causal connections (based on the uniform and regular laws of nature), which can then be generalised to predict and explain all events and behaviours that happen in the social world, without accounting for consciousness, purposefulness, innate dispositions or the unpredictability of human behaviour. Quantitative analysis of data and variables to produce empirical research enables these law-like statements of universality to reign supreme at the top of the hierarchy of science over any kind of more complex reasoning as to why things happen in the way that they do, the assumption being that the replicable patterns and numbers behind the theories (which are always hard to dispute) tell the whole story. There is certainly a place for well-executed empirical research but it is only part of the picture and needs to be combined with other mixed methods and worldviews to find a sense of truth, and express it in more than just numbers and language.

Positivism also fails to account for its methodological subjectivity both in the choice of what to measure and in the interpretation of data, which is all measured against prior knowledge that is inevitably value-laden. Claims that positivism is objective are deeply flawed, and yet this approach still drives dominant ideas of what constitutes the scientific basis of education, society and culture. Empirical science – using the natural sciences as the model to explain the social sciences – is considered by positivist scientists (and many policy makers) as the highest and most reliable form of knowledge and is used to create structures and policies intended to control or regulate the behaviour of individuals or groups in society, and to resolve conflict according to the dominant expertise (Benton and Craib, 2011). The limitations of this methodology have caused damage over the centuries to our understanding of who (and why) people are, how things work, and how we know what we know, and is the reason why I am actively anti-positivist in my language, research and reasoning. Having said this, while I cannot endorse its epistemological values as such, I acknowledge the polymathic intelligence of several positivist philosophers and scientists, and without their early work we may never have had a departure point from which to progress.

Constructivism

Begun by Dewey (1934), Piaget (1973) and Bruner (1990), this is a way of understanding how we make meaning by constructing and reconstructing our own realities in relation to our own experience of objects (i.e. independent of the social constructs around us). This is especially true for babies growing in-utero and discovering the evolving natural and unnatural orders of things for themselves. Then, in the early years, children demonstrate their unique views on the world, which are 'extremely coherent and robust' with an integrity and logic that is suited to their situation, contrary to the worldview that sees them as 'incomplete adults' (Ackermann, 2001, p.3). In this sense, knowledge is not simply received from others, memorised and regurgitated, but is a unique experience gathered through interactions with the world, objects and people, and shaped through children's own preferences, interests, ideas and dispositions, some of which may be socially influenced, some of which may be genetically or culturally inherited, but all of which are a unique reality for that child, formed as the child grows. Constructivism focuses on the internalisation of knowledge creation and ensuing actions, forming and informed by our internal compass – our individual, personal and private identities.

Social constructionism

Articulated by Vygotsky (in Vygotsky and Cole, 1978), this extends constructivism to acknowledge the context of knowledge creation. Whereas constructivism states that knowledge is believed to be uniquely created from scratch as we discover ourselves and the world around us, social constructionism emphasises the role of social interaction and experience that has gone before (by many generations, back to the beginning of time) and, while we may create new ideas to explain our worlds, 'those subjective understandings can only be understood in their social context' (Williams, 2016, p.204). Constructivism builds on the theory behind idealism that the individual can have ideas, or a sense of mind, and that a person's worldview is made up of these and others' ideas, entirely subjective (contrasting with realism which maintains that there is a still an objective reality that exists in nature apart from the subjective reality in our minds). However, social constructionism takes this further to argue that everything we know is influenced – or constructed – through our relationships and experiences with the environment around us, including the social world that came before us. This means that we are socially (environmentally, culturally, economically, politically) situated through our expression, communication, relations and interactions – our public identities (Ackermann, 2001). Even in-utero, our genetic make-up, knowledge and experiences have a direct causal relationship to our parents' (and their parents', and their parents'...) genetic heritage, ways of life, values, social, health and cultural choices within this. Meaning for children is made through the construction of ideas with the educators, caregivers, friends and animals around them, and all those who have gone before and imprinted their social worldview on what things actually are and mean.

This epistemological stance triggered what came to be known as the 'science wars', which posited the ultimate chicken and egg question – what came first, the world and all its matter (followed by human consciousness and social constructs), or human thought which then gave the physical world an existence, a language, an identity? Answers on a postcard, please! Of course, this is almost impossible to answer as it is dependent on our faiths, value systems, cultures and heritage, the limitations of our scientific mechanisms for dating the natural world, and the fact that 'we simply cannot know [scientifically] whether there is a reality beyond our social constructs as they are all we can know' (Ackermann, 2001, p.206).

Ethical interpretivism

The epistemology of interpretivism arose through the work of Max Weber in the late 1800s followed by Boaz and Durkheim in the late 1900s in response to an increasing concern that the objective for causal explanation in natural science was incommensurate with social science. It complements the ideas of social constructionism that 'knowledge is essentially *situated* and thus should not be detached from the situations in which it was first constructed and actualised' (Ackermann, 2001, p.5). Empirical science aims to establish an unequivocal cause and effect that reveals a single truth of the matter, as if objects and their relationship to other objects around them have a linear relationship and a single meaning. However, interpretivism allows us to see the relationships of objects in context, which means they may have different meanings or truths in other contexts. It also recognises the agency of other objects, materials or beings, which is their intention and purpose to move in a certain direction that may not be predictable in the way that natural science experiments might be. Therefore, the goal of being able to replicate an experiment anywhere and achieve exactly the same results to confirm a theory (such as gravity) is not applicable to social science where the conditions, situations and relationships create dynamic and unpredictable patterns of behaviour. So, casual explanations in the social world have to make sense within an adequate interpretation of meaning and truth.

Interpretivism also builds on the epistemology of idealism – that 'there is nothing we can know except that which we know through our minds' (Williams, 2016, p.111), and some people even hold that everything that exists is merely a perception, or an interpretation of the truth. However, most interpretivists do not go that far and still accept some causal explanations of the world with the caveat that, beyond natural science, these require further interpretation in order to explain social reality. This, then, accounts for how people can attribute different meanings, or causes, to the same behaviour, or how many different behaviours can be motivated by the same cause, which gives alternative ways of knowing the same phenomena in the social world.

This web of meanings is considered valid if we accept its fallibility, that is, that our interpretation is itself subject to individual psychological assumptions as to cause and may appear to misrepresent what has happened. This apparent misrepresentation may still be valid in understanding what has occurred and is the essence of social reality...there are no fixed truths. Ethical interpretivists, however, will attempt to remove any privileged knowledge by abandoning their own minds, judgements and interpretations in order to capture and make visible, as accurately and authentically as possible, the minds and meanings of those they are researching – they try to be systematically objective.

Post-structuralism

Structuralism is focused on language as a force that shapes and determines our social and cultural, singular or plural identities, on the basis that language existed before social beings did and so we have very little influence on changing its core structures and impacts. The structure of language (referred to as the *sign*) can be broken into its corresponding parts of *the signifier* – the marks on paper or the sound made by the voice – and *the signified* – the concept or idea being expressed by such marks or sounds (Benton and Craib, 2011). More positivist philosophers have attempted to create a theoretical structure around this that strictly defines the signifiers and signified (i.e. determines what we mean when we write this or say that), and promotes this as the only available truth or reality. This structure is sometimes hijacked for political and social objectives to promote or deconstruct specific identities for the 'good of society', such as the subtle images that associate young men wearing casual hoodies with 'threatening' overtones or the language of pity and suffering that surrounds young children, defining them as only physically vulnerable and emotionally dependent, instead of viewing their capacity for strong, independent thinking and emotional resilience. This can become political oppression at best and social engineering at worst.

But beginning in the mid-20th century, progressive theorists such as Derrida, Foucault, Deleuze, Guattari, Habermas and Butler introduced the concept of post-structuralism, moving away from this rigid, rational structure of linguistic signs towards an understanding of the more complex languages of our subconscious, which signify non-rational meanings as well as rational ones. It incorporates the structures of ideas and the relationships between knowledge, power and freedom (or oppression), emphasising the fluidity and multiplicity of identity that can be reflected in more thoughtful, purposeful linguistic structures. Post-structuralism challenges the ways in which traditional western canons have defined different categories or *types* of people in terms of binary opposites, as somehow deviant, abnormal, unreasonable or mad by interpretation of their behaviours against traditional linguistic structures. The underlying concern is that, despite our free choice, societies will self-police using biased judgements that have been established for centuries in language structures, as we are subordinated to the linguistic structures taught in our early years, which we believe to be rational thinking. Even when we look for thoughtful, more meaningful ways of expression and communication, we are limited by the speech (and associated signifiers) available to us. As Crotty points out, 'we have a need to define and classify' – especially people – which results in displacing our real experiences of them so that 'rather than concepts pointing us towards realities, realities are relegated to being mere exemplifications of concepts' (Crotty, 1998, p.81) (i.e. the more we categorise, the more we generalise).

Post-structuralism introduces the concept of *deconstruction* to tackle this, which 'involves a constant questioning and dismantling of implicit or explicit notions of presence (i.e. the firm and finite meaning of a word)' (Benton and Craib, 2011, p.167). Just as the philosophy of phenomenology asks us to critically call into question what is taken for granted (Crotty, 1998), post-structuralism invites us to broaden our consciousness of the many different, sometimes ambiguous, meanings of any single word within other cultures and from other perspectives. It asks us to recognise the ability of language to empower or disempower identities, to centralise or decentralise dominant worldviews, to unite or divide communities. It attempts to break down homogenous, universal definitions of reality that apply to all cultures and places and accept fragmented difference instead of unified identity. In this way, post-structuralism attempts to honour and make visible the cultural and social differences in humanity that make up people's subjective truths or worldviews.

Affect

Developed by psychologist Silvan Tomkins in the 1960s, on the surface this theory seems to incorporate the study of emotional states, feelings, intensities, memories and senses and the impact (or *affect*) they have on the mind. But, going deeper, affect clearly explores not just states of mind or psychology but also the physical (visible and invisible, somatic and neural) impacts on the body – how and why emotions are embodied, and what, literally, moves us (Wetherell, 2012). This opens up a world of questions about how internal and external forces motivate or change us, how we are disrupted or disturbed, inspired and influenced, empowered or disempowered. It leads us towards a highly complex set of processes or mechanisms by which to understand what affects us, and how.

This is particularly useful as a frame of reference to help us move away from disembodied texts, languages or curricula that view children's learning and development as divorced from their humanity, vitality or emotional make-up. Without considering affect, teaching, observation and assessment risk missing swathes of embodied impression and expression that a child might access by way of their meaning-making that is a valid and important part of their knowing and being. It is a way of 'introducing the physical [the visceral], the emotional and the sensual' back into learning (Wetherell, 2012, p.9). For children who have low levels of verbal or written language skills or are unable to communicate effectively because of physical or emotional challenges, tuning in to their individual emotions evident in their bodies (*embodied affect*) may be the only way of observing their needs and progress.

Through the frame of affective practice, 'attention is thrown onto becoming, potential and the virtual in preference to the already formed objects that are the usual fare of social science (institutions, identities, economies, social classes, etc.)' (Wetherell, 2012, p.3) which has huge relevance for studying aspects of children's creativity.

Across the Early Years Foundation Stage curriculum and especially in the Expressive Arts and Design area of learning, children are taught and judged according to their crafted skills and disembodied knowledge. Dance and movement are judged by the scientific elements of space, speed and height, and music is judged by the mathematical elements of pattern, rhythm and sequence, highlighting how 'the affective in the arts has been removed. One could say that affect and to be affected would have interfered too much with the assessment process' (Naughton *et al.*, 2017, p.3). The result is that there is little room for knowing children's imagination, creativity or affect, and little incentive towards creative teaching, creative environments or creative cultures. Since the deeply innate properties of creativity are in our heritage, our bloodlines, our bodies and minds, as is discussed further in this book, this creates a deep sense of dissatisfaction, an ever-present internal struggle for expression, for those of us still intensely connected to our creative drive, as most children are.

Bricoleur

A methodology arising from the French word, *bricolage*, meaning do-it-yourself, the *bricoleur* is a term first coined by anthropologist Claude Lévi-Strauss to describe the repurposing of materials at hand to make something new. It is often used to describe a particularly inclusive methodology incorporating elements of different epistemologies, approaches and methods that recognise plurality and fluidity rather than a single truth or identity in researching the world. The researcher, like a film maker or a jazz improviser, assembles several images or stanzas into a montage of perspectives using several different research methods that bring 'psychological and emotional unity to an interpretive experience' (Denzin and Lincoln, 2013, p.9).

The bricoleur approach is ideal for interdisciplinary research as it can combine a multitude of methods or tools, from ethnographic observation or anthropological immersion to reflective practice, interviews, surveys, case studies, psychoanalysis, visual or physical expression, virtual or digital presentation, participatory arts-based methods, action research, biography-based and experimental empirical methods using quantitative analysis. In doing so, this methodological strategy is able to bring a variety of 'angles of vision' to create a richness in the complexity and a depth of vision in a simultaneous 'display of multiple, refracted realities' that is sensitive to the social, cultural and multiple identities of those being researched (Denzin and Lincoln, 2013, p.10).

A bricoleur approach that considers the 'many interpretive paradigms that can be brought to any particular problem' (Denzin and Lincoln, 2013, p.10) helps us challenge the status quo in what constitutes valid and valued knowledge and enables richer *understanding*. This is a beautifully simple, yet deeply complex, troubled, misunderstood and even traumatic concept. Understanding is a perfect aspiration towards truth (or, at least, an acknowledgment of the many truths that exist across heterogeneous communities). Yet understanding is fraught with so many obstacles that it, in itself, needs constantly re-observing, re-evaluating, re-evidencing and re-imagining.

About the Author

While I am trained in the arts and am not a practising teacher (though I have taught in early years, secondary and further education), I am passionate about how we tune in to children, and what the purposes of education might be. Once upon a time I trained in all the aspects of theatre because I had an insatiable thirst for it that came from deep within and could not be quenched. Finding and honing a language of expression helped me make a bit more sense of life and what I might have to offer, and I am still drinking at that wellspring. Now I have various identities as a parent, an arts educator, a musician and singer, a storyteller, a researcher, a business woman, a trainer and a social entrepreneur, with a penchant for design and dance. The crazier side of me loves anything to do with mountains – biking, running, climbing or flying – even spending a short period flying with the British Paragliding Team. I aim to bring this vitality into Earlyarts, which I founded in 2002 and which now runs training, research, publishing and consultancy in the UK and the Middle East. Earlyarts is dedicated to learning and sharing knowledge about the innate creative powers of our youngest children and, as such, enjoys the virtual company of over 25,000 arts, cultural and early education professionals through its networks. I have advised governments, written for national newspapers, authored books and won awards. But none of this makes any difference unless our children are cherished for who they are, not who the world wants them to be.

Appendix

Early Years Infrastructure, England, 2018

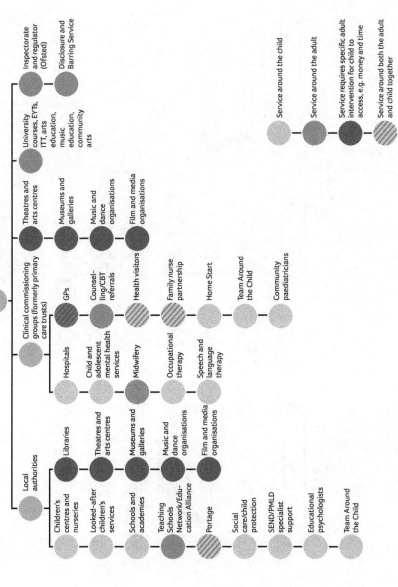

Government funded

Local authorities

Children's centres and nurseries

Libraries

Looked-after children's services

Theatres and arts centres

Schools and academies

Museums and galleries

Teaching Schools Network/Education Alliance

Music and dance organisations

Portage

Film and media organisations

Social care/child protection

SEND/PMLD specialist support

Educational psychologists

Team Around the Child

Clinical commissioning groups (formerly primary care trusts)

Hospitals

GPs

Child and adolescent mental health services

Counselling/CBT referrals

Midwifery

Health visitors

Occupational therapy

Family nurse partnership

Speech and language therapy

Home Start

Team Around the Child

Community paediatricians

Theatres and arts centres

Museums and galleries

Music and dance organisations

Film and media organisations

University courses, EYTs, ITT, arts education, music education, community arts

Inspectorate and regulator (Ofsted)

Disclosure and Barring Service

Service around the child

Service around the adult

Service requires specific adult intervention for child to access, e.g. money and time

Service around both the adult and child together

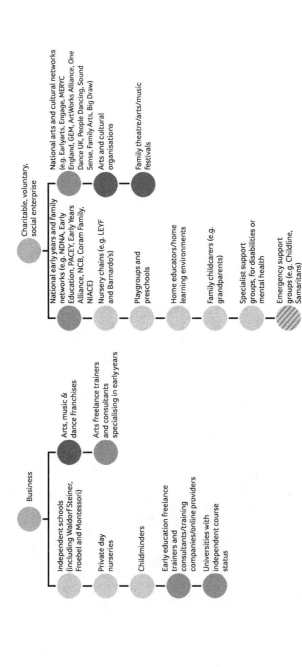

Business

Independent schools (including Waldorf Steiner, Froebel and Montessori)

Private day nurseries

Childminders

Early education freelance trainers and consultants/training companies/online providers

Universities with independent course status

Arts, music & dance franchises

Arts freelance trainers and consultants specialising in early years

Charitable, voluntary, social enterprise

National early years and family networks (e.g. NDNA, Early Education, PACEY, Early Years Alliance, NCB, Coram Family, NIACE)

Nursery chains (e.g. LEYF and Barnardo's)

Playgroups and preschools

Home educators/home learning environments

Family childcarers (e.g. grandparents)

Specialist support groups, for disabilities or mental health

Emergency support groups (e.g. Childline, Samaritans)

National arts and cultural networks (e.g. Earlyarts, Engage, MERYC England, GEM, ArtWorks Alliance, One Dance UK, People Dancing, Sound Sense, Family Arts, Big Draw)

Arts and cultural organisations

Family theatre/arts/music festivals

References

Ackermann, E. (2001) 'Piaget's Constructivism, Papert's Constructionism: What's the difference?' [Online] Accessed on 01.11.18 at: http://learning.media.mit.edu/content/publications/EA.Piaget%20_%20Papert.pdf.

Ackermann, E. (2004) 'Constructing Knowledge and Transforming the World.' In M. Tokoro and L. Steels (eds) *A Learning Zone of One's Own; Sharing Representations and Flow in Collaborative Learning Environments*. Vol. 20, pp15–37. Amsterdam, Berlin, Oxford, Tokyo, Washington DC: IOS Press.

Ackermann, E., Gauntlett, D., Whitebread, D., Weckstrom, C. and Wolbers, T. (2010) 'The future of play. Defining the role and value of play in the 21st century.' [Online] Accessed on 03.03.19 at: http://outdoorplayandlearning.org.uk/wp-content/uploads/2016/07/future_of_play_report.pdf.

Adobe (2012) 'State of Create Study. Global benchmark study on attitudes and beliefs about creativity at work, school and home.' [Online] Accessed on 31.08.18 at: www.adobe.com/aboutadobe/pressroom/pdfs/Adobe_State_of_Create_Global_Benchmark_Study.pdf.

Amabile, T.M. (1996) *Creativity in Context: Update to the Social Psychology of Creativity*. Boulder, CO; Oxford: Westview Press.

An, R. and Bonetti, S. (2017) 'Developing the early years workforce: What does the evidence tell us?' *Early Years Development – Policy Analysis*. [Online] Accessed on 28.12.18 at: https://epi.org.uk/publications-and-research/analysis-developing-early-years-workforce-evidence-tell-us.

Athey, C. (2007) 'Continuity between Schemas and Concepts.' In C. Athey, *Extending Thought in Young Children: A Parent-Teacher Partnership*, second edition, p.174. London: SAGE Publications.

Bamford, A. (2006) *The Wow Factor: Global Research Compendium on the Impact of the Arts in Education*. Waxmann Verlag.

Barad, K.M. (2007) *Meeting the Universe Halfway: Quantum Physics and the Entanglement of Matter and Meaning*. Durham, NC; Chesham: Duke University Press.

Benton, T. and Craib, I. (2011) *Philosophy of Social Science: The Philosophical Foundations of Social Thought*, second edition. Basingstoke: Palgrave Macmillan.

Bergen, D. and Modir Rousta, M. (2019) Developing Creativity and Humor: The Role of the Playful Mind.' In S.R. Luria, J. Baer and J.C. Kaufman (eds) *Creativity and Humor*, pp.61–81. San Diego, CA: Academic Press.

Bergen, D. and Woodin, M. (2017) *Brain Research and Childhood Education: Implications for Educators, Parents, and Society.* New York, NY: Routledge.

Berrol, C.F. (2006) 'Neuroscience meets dance/movement therapy: Mirror neurons, the therapeutic process and empathy.' *The Arts in Psychotherapy*, 33(4) 302–315.

Bhaskar, R. (2008) *A Realist Theory of Science* (revised edition). London; New York, NY: Routledge.

Bowlby, J. (1969) *Attachment and Loss.* London: Hogarth Press.

Boyatzis, R.E. and Hazy, J.K. (2015) 'Emotional contagion and proto-organizing in human interaction dynamics.' *Frontiers in Psychology*, 6, 806. [Online] JUN. Accessed at: https://doaj.org/article/8fb961e5467943428c3a8855ce0d9627 and https://doi.org/10.3389/fpsyg.2015.00806.

Bradbury, A., Jarvis, P., Nutbrown, C., Roberts-Holmes, G., Stewart, N. and Whitebread, D. (2018) 'Baseline assessment: Why it doesn't add up.' [Online] Accessed on 15.11.18 at: www.morethanascore.org.uk/wp-content/uploads/2018/09/Baseline_Assesment_It_Doesnt_Add_Up.pdf.

Brėdikytė, M. (2011) 'The Zones of Proximal Development in Children's Play.' Doctoral thesis. University of Oulu, Finland.

Brown, E.D. and Sax, K.L. (2013) 'Arts enrichment and preschool emotions for low-income children at risk.' *Early Childhood Research Quarterly*, 28(2) 337–346.

Brown, S. and Vaughan, C. (2009) *Play: How It Shapes the Brain, Opens the Imagination and Invigorates the Soul.* New York, NY: Penguin Group.

Bruce, T. (2005a) 'Play, the Universe and Everything!' In J. Moyles (ed.) *The Excellence of Play*, second edition, pp.256–267. Maidenhead: Open University Press.

Bruce, T. (2005b) *Early Childhood Education,* third edition. London: Hodder Education.

Bruner, J.S., Ross, G. and Wood, D. (1976) 'The role of tutoring in problem solving.' *Journal of Child Psychology and Psychiatry and Allied Disciplines*, 17(2) 89.

Bruner, J.S. (1990) *Acts of Meaning.* London; Cambridge, MA: Harvard University Press.

Bruner, J.S. (1996) *The Culture of Education.* London; Cambridge, MA: Harvard University Press.

Buckingham, D. and Jones, K. (2001) 'New Labour's cultural turn: Some tensions in contemporary educational and cultural policy.' *Journal of Education Policy*, 16(1) 1, 14.

Catterall, J.S. (2012) *The Arts and Achievement in At-Risk Youth: Findings from Four Longitudinal Studies. Research Report #55.* Report. Washington, DC: National Endowment for the Arts.

Chappell, K., Hetherington, L., Keene, H.R., Wren, H. *et al.* (2019) 'Dialogue and materiality/embodiment in science|arts creative pedagogy: Their role and manifestation.' *Thinking Skills and Creativity*, 31, 296–322.

Churchill Dower, R. (2008) 'Fostering Creative Learning for 3–5 Year Olds in Four International Settings.' In A. Craft, T. Cremin and P. Burnard (eds) *Creative Learning 3–11 and How We Document It.* Stoke on Trent: Trentham Books.

Churchill Dower, R. and Sandbrook, B. (2013) 'Supporting the growth of early childhood arts practice in Ireland – An international view.' In *Early Childhood Arts – Three Perspectives*, pp.43–106. Dublin: Young People, Children, and Education (YPCE) department, The Arts Council Ireland.

Churchill Dower, R. and Sandbrook, B. (2018) 'Early years arts and culture: Current practice and options for future development.' pp.1–58. [Online] Accessed on 01.11.18 at: www.artscouncil.org.uk/publication/early-years-arts-and-culture.

Cizek, F. (1921) *The Child as Artist: Some Conversations with Professor Cizek.* Knightsbridge, England: Children's Art Exhibition Fund.

Clapham, M.M. (2011) 'Testing/Measurement/Assessment.' In M. Runco, *Encyclopedia of Creativity,* second edition, pp.458–464. London: Elsevier.

Clark, J., Griffiths, C. and Taylor, H. (2003) 'Feeding the mind: Valuing the arts in the development of young children.' [Online] Accessed at: http://dm16174grt2cj.cloudfront.net/Downloads_Research/Feeding_the_Mind.pdf.

Connell, G. and McCarthy, C. (2014) *A Moving Child is a Learning Child: How the Body Teaches the Brain to Think (Birth to Age 7).* Minneapolis, MN: Free Spirit Publishing.

Craft, A. (2002) *Creativity and Early Years Education: A Lifewide Foundation.* London: Continuum.

Craft, A. (2013) 'Childhood, possibility thinking and wise, humanising educational futures.' *International Journal of Educational Research,* 61, 126–134.

Crotty, M. (1998) *The Foundations of Social Research: Meaning and Perspective in the Research Process.* London: SAGE Publications.

Csikszentmihalyi, M. (1997) *Creativity: Flow and the Psychology of Discovery and Invention.* New York, NY: HarperPerennial.

Cultural Learning Alliance (2012) 'ImagiNation – Key Research Findings: The case for cultural learning.' [Online] Accessed on 03.03.19 at: https://culturallearningalliance.org.uk/wp-content/uploads/2017/08/CLA-key-findings-2017.pdf.

Cultural Learning Alliance (2018) 'Evidence on English Baccalaureate.' [Online] Accessed on 28.12.18 at: http://culturallearningalliance.org.uk/evidence.

Dahlberg, G., Moss, P. and NetLibrary, I. (2005) *Ethics and Politics in Early Childhood Education.* London; New York, NY: Routledge Falmer.

Daly, A. and O'Connor, A. (2016) *Understanding Physical Development in the Early Years: Linking Bodies and Minds.* Abingdon, Oxfordshire; New York, NY: Routledge.

David, T., Goouch, K., Powell, S. and Abbott, L. (2003) *Young Brains.* Nottingham, Queen's Printer: Primary National Strategy. The Early Years Foundation Stage team.

Davies, B. (2014) *Listening to Children: Being and Becoming.* London; New York, NY: Routledge.

Deguara, J. and Nutbrown, C. (2018) 'Signs, symbols and schemas: Understanding meaning in a child's drawings.' *International Journal of Early Years Education,* 26(1) 4.

Deleuze, G. (2004) *Foucault.* Paris: Éditions de Minuit.

Denzin, N.K. (1992) *Symbolic Interactionism and Cultural Studies: The Politics of Interpretation.* Oxford: Wiley-Blackwell.

Denzin, N. K. and Lincoln, Y. S. (2013) *The Landscape of Qualitative Research,* fourth edition. Los Angeles, CA: SAGE Publications.

Denzin, N.K., Lincoln, Y.S. and Giardina, M.D. (2006) 'Disciplining qualitative research.' *International Journal of Qualitative Studies in Education,* 19(6) 769–782.

Department for Digital, Culture, Media & Sport (2018) 'DCMS Sectors Economic Estimates 2016: Business Demographics.' [Online] Accessed on 18.02.19 at: www.gov.uk/government/statistics/dcms-sectors-economic-estimates-2016-business-demographics.

Department for Education (2012) 'Early Years Foundation Stage statutory framework (EYFS).' [Online] Accessed on 03.03.19 at: www.gov.uk/government/publications/early-years-foundation-stage-framework--2

Department for Education (2018) *Childcare and Early Years Provision: Parents' Survey, 2017–2018.* Colchester, Essex: UK Data Archive: Department for Education.

Department for Education (2018) *Survey of Childcare and Early Years Providers: Main Summary, England, 2018.* London: Department for Education.

Dewey, J. (1934) *Art as Experience.* London: Allen and Unwin.

Dewey, J. (1963) *Experience and Education.* New York, NY: Collier Macmillan.

Diamond, M. and Hopson, J. (1998) *Magic Trees of the Mind: How to Nurture Your Child's Intelligence, Creativity, and Healthy Emotions from Birth through Adolescence.* New York, NY: Penguin Putnam.

Dissanayake, E. (2017) 'Ethology, interpersonal neurobiology, and play: Insights into the evolutionary origin of the arts.' *American Journal of Play,* 9(2) 143.

Duffy, B. (2006) *Supporting Creativity and Imagination in the Early Years,* second edition. Maidenhead; New York, NY: Open University Press.

Duffy, B. (2010) *Born Creative.* London: Demos.

Early Education (2012) 'Development Matters in the Early Years Foundation Stage (EYFS) – Non-statutory guidance material to support practitioners in implementing the statutory requirements of the EYFS.' [Online] Accessed on 03.03.19 at: www.early-education.org.uk/development-matters.

Edwards, C.P., Gandini, L. and Forman, G.E. (2012) *The Hundred Languages of Children: the Reggio Emilia Experience in Transformation,* third edition. Oxford; Santa Barbara, CA: Praeger.

Eisner, E.W. (2005) *The Arts and the Creation of Mind.* New Haven, CT; London: Yale University Press.

Fink, A., Benedek, M., Grabner, R.H., Staudt, B. and Neubauer, A.C. (2007) 'Creativity meets neuroscience: Experimental tasks for the neuroscientific study of creative thinking.' *Methods,* 42(1) 68–76.

Finke, R.A., Ward, T.B. and Smith, S.M. (1992) *Creative Cognition: Theory, Research, and Applications.* London; Cambridge, MA: MIT Press.

Finlay, L. (2002) 'Negotiating the swamp: The opportunity and challenge of reflexivity in research practice.' *Qualitative Research,* 2(2) 209–230.

Finnegan, J. (2016) 'Lighting up young brains – How parents, carers and nurseries support children's brain development in the first five years.' [Online] Accessed on 04.03.19 at: www.savethechildren.org.uk/content/dam/global/reports/education-and-child-protection/lighting-up-young-brains.pdf.

Friedan, B. (1963) *The Feminine Mystique*. New York, NY: W.W. Norton & Company.

Fritz, T.H., Ciupek, M., Kirkland, A., Ihme, K. *et al.* (2014) 'Enhanced response to music in pregnancy.' *Psychophysiology*, 51(9) 905–911.

Gardner, H. (1982) *Art, Mind, and Brain: A Cognitive Approach to Creativity*. New York, NY: Basic Books.

Gardner, H. (2011) *Frames of Mind: The Theory of Multiple Intelligences*. New York, NY: Basic Books.

Gerhardt, S. (2004) *Why Love Matters: How Affection Shapes a Baby's Brain*. Hove; New York, NY: Brunner-Routledge.

Grace, J. (2017) *Sensory-Being for Sensory Beings: Creating Entrancing Sensory Experiences*. London: Routledge.

Grosz, E. (2008) *Chaos, Territory, Art: Deleuze and the Framing of the Earth*. New York, NY: Columbia University Press.

Halliday, J. (2017) 'How to improve the school results: Not extra maths but music, loads of it.' *The Guardian*. [Online] Accessed on 08.07.2019 at: www.theguardian.com/education/2017/oct/03/school-results-music-bradford.

Hardiman, M.M., JohnBull, R.M., Carran, D.T. and Shelton, A. (2019) 'The effects of arts-integrated instruction on memory for science content.' *Trends in Neuroscience and Education*, 14, 25–32.

Heath, S.B. and Wolf, S. (2005) 'Focus in creative learning: Drawing on art for language development.' *Literacy*, 39(1) 38–45.

Hebert, T.P., Cramond, B., Speirs Neumeister, K.L., Millar, G., Silvian, A.F. (2002) *E. Paul Torrance: His Life, Accomplishments, and Legacy*. Report. Storrs, CT: National Research Center on the Gifted and Talented, University of Connecticut.

Hesmondhalgh, D., Oakley, K., Lee, D. and Nisbett, M. (2015) *Culture, Economy and Politics: The Case of New Labour*. Basingstoke; New York, NY: Palgrave Macmillan.

Hogue, R.J. (2015) 'Developing an appreciative understanding of epistemologies in educational research – One blogger's journey.' [Online] Accessed on 01.11.18 at: www.researchgate.net/publication/275834166_Developing_an_Appreciative_Understanding_of_Epistemologies_in_Educational_Research_-_One_Blogger's_Journey.

Hughes, P. (2010) 'Paradigms, Methods and Knowledge.' In G. MacNaughton, S.A. Rolfe and I. Siraj-Blatchford (eds) *Doing Early Childhood Research: International Perspectives on Theory and Practice*, second edition, pp.35–62. Maidenhead: McGraw-Hill Education.

International Development Committee (2017) *DFID's work on education: Leaving no one behind? First Report of Session 2017–19*. House of Commons, London: International Development Committee.

Isaak, N.J. and Just, M.A. (1995) 'Constraints on Thinking in Insight and Invention.' In R.J. Sternberg and J.E. Davidson (eds) *The Nature of Insight*. Cambridge, MA: MIT Press.

Kaufmann, G. (2003) 'What to measure? A new look at the concept of creativity.' *Scandinavian Journal of Educational Research*, 47(3) 235–251.

Keller, E.F. (1985) *Reflections on Gender and Science*. New Haven, CT: Yale University Press.

Kelly, Y., Sacker, A., Del Bono, E., Francesconi, M. and Marmot, M. (2011) 'Child of the new century – What role for the home learning environment and parenting in reducing the socioeconomic gradient in child development? Findings from the Millennium Cohort Study.' *Archives of Disease in Childhood*, 96(9) 832–837.

Kolb, A.Y. and Kolb, D.A. (2010) 'Learning to play, playing to learn: A case study of a ludic learning space.' *Journal of Organizational Change Management*, 23(1) 26–50.

Kronfeldner, M.E. (2009) 'Creativity naturalized.' *The Philosophical Quarterly (1950–)*, 59(237) 577–592.

LaingBuisson. (2017) *Children's Nurseries UK Market Report 2017*. London: LaingBuisson.

Lakoff, G. and Johnson, M. (1999) *Philosophy in the Flesh: The Embodied Mind and Its Challenge to Western Thought*. New York, NY: Basic Books.

Landry, C. and Bianchini, F. (1995) *The Creative City*. London: Demos.

Lawson, V. (2007) 'Geographies of care and responsibility.' *Annals of the Association of American Geographers*, 97(1) 1–11.

Leggett, N. (2017) 'Early childhood creativity: Challenging educators in their role to intentionally develop creative thinking in children.' *Early Childhood Education Journal*, 45(6) 845–853.

Levitin, D.J. (2012) 'What does it mean to be musical?' *Neuron*, 73(4) 633–637.

Lindsay, G. (2016) 'Do visual art experiences in early childhood settings foster educative growth or stagnation?' *International Art in Early Childhood Research Journal*, 5(1) 1–14.

Longino, H.E. (1990) *Science as Social Knowledge: Values and Objectivity in Scientific Inquiry*. Princeton, NJ; Oxford: Princeton University Press.

Lonie, D. (2010) 'Early years evidence review: Assessing the outcomes of early years music making.' [Online] Accessed on 11.11.18 at: https://network.youthmusic.org.uk/sites/default/files/uploads/research/Early_years_evidence_review_2010.pdf.

Lowenfeld, V. and Brittain, W.L. (1987) *Creative and Mental Growth*, eighth edition. London; New York, NY: Macmillan.

MacLure, M. (2006) 'The bone in the throat: Some uncertain thoughts on baroque method.' *International Journal of Qualitative Studies in Education*, 19(6) 729–745.

Malloch, S. and Trevarthen, C. (2018) 'The human nature of music.' *Frontiers in Psychology*, 9, 1680.

Mandell, N. (1988) 'The least-adult role in studying children.' *Journal of Contemporary Ethnography*, 16(4) 433–467.

McArdle, F. (2016) '"Art education" in the early years: Learning about, through and with art.' *Art in Early Childhood: Research Journal*. 2016: No. 5. [Online] Accessed on 03.03.19 at: http://artinearlychildhood.org/journals/2016/ARTEC_2016_Research_Journal_1_Article_3_McArdle.pdf.

Mukherji, P. and Albon, D. (2018) *Research Methods in Early Childhood: An Introductory Guide,* third edition. Los Angeles, CA: SAGE Publications.

Muñiz, E.I., Silver, E.J. and Stein, R.E.K. (2014) 'Family routines and social-emotional school readiness among preschool-age children.' *Journal of Developmental and Behavioral Pediatrics,* 35(2) 93–99.

Murris, K. (2016) *The Posthuman Child: Educational Transformation through Philosophy With Picturebooks.* London: Routledge.

National Advisory Committee on Creative and Cultural Education (NACCCE) (1999) *All Our Futures: Creativity, Culture and Education.* London: Department for Education and Employment.

Nan, Y., Liu, L., Geiser, E., Shu, H. *et al.* (2018) 'Piano training enhances the neural processing of pitch and improves speech perception in Mandarin-speaking children.' *Proceedings of the National Academy of Sciences of the United States of America,* 115(28) E6630–E6639.

Naughton, C., Biesta, G. and Cole, D. (2017) *Art, Artists and Pedagogy: Philosophy and the Arts in Education,* first edition. Milton: Routledge.

National Scientific Council on the Developing Child (2007) 'The timing and quality of early experiences combine to shape brain architecture.' Working Paper 5. [Online] Accessed on 04.03.19 at: https://developingchild.harvard.edu/resources/the-timing-and-quality-of-early-experiences-combine-to-shape-brain-architecture.

Nietzsche, F.W. (1990) *Twilight of the Idols and The Anti-Christ.* London: Penguin.

Nutbrown, C. (2011) *Threads of Thinking: Schemas and Young Children's Learning,* fourth edition. London; Los Angeles, CA: SAGE Publications.

O'Byrne, W.I., Stone, R. and White, M. (2018) 'Digital storytelling in early childhood: Student illustrations shaping social interactions.' *Frontiers in Psychology,* 9, 1800.

O'Gorman, K.D. and MacIntosh, R. (2015) *Research Methods for Business & Management: A Guide to Writing your Dissertation,* second edition. Oxford: Goodfellow Publishers.

Ogden, P. (2018) 'Play, Creativity, and Movement Vocabulary.' In T. Marks-Tarlow, D.J. Siegel and M. Solomon (eds) *Play and Creativity in Psychotherapy,* pp.92–109. New York, NY: W.W. Norton & Company.

Organisation for Economic Co-operation and Development (2004) 'Starting strong: Curricula and pedagogies in early childhood education and care – Five Curriculum Outlines.' [Online] Accessed at: www.oecd.org/education/school/31672150.pdf.

Osgood, J. (2017) 'Opening Pandora's Box: Postmodernist Perspectives of Childhood.' In S. Powell and K. Smith (eds) *An Introduction to Early Childhood Studies,* fourth edition. London: Sage Publications.

Page, J. (2018) 'Characterising the principles of professional love in early childhood care and education.' *International Journal of Early Years Education,* 26(2) 125–141.

Paley, V.G. (1990) *The Boy Who Would be a Helicopter.* London; Cambridge, MA: Harvard University Press.

Panksepp, J. (2005) 'Beyond a joke: From animal laughter to human joy?' *Science,* 308(5718) 62–63.

Panksepp, J. (2018) 'Play and the Construction of Creativity, Cleverness and Reversal of ADHD in Our Social Brains.' In T. Marks-Tarlow, D.J. Siegel and M. Solomon (eds) *Play and Creativity in Psychotherapy*, pp. 242–270. New York, NY: W.W. Norton & Company.

Piaget, J. (1973) *To Understand is to Invent: The Future of Education*. New York, NY: Grossman.

Piscitelli, B., Everett, M. and Weier, K. (2003) *Enhancing Young Children's Museum Experiences: A Manual for Museum Staff*. Report: Queensland University of Technology (QUT) Museums Collaborative.

Popper, K. and Notturno, M.A. (1996) *Knowledge and the Body-Mind Problem: In Defence of Interaction*. London: Routledge.

Porges, S.W. (2007) 'The polyvagal perspective.' *Biological Psychology*, 74(2) 116–143.

Prentice, R. (2000) 'Creativity: A reaffirmation of its place in early childhood education.' *Curriculum Journal*, 11(2) 145–158.

Rautio, P. (2013) 'Children who carry stones in their pockets: On autotelic material practices in everyday life.' *Children's Geographies*, 11(4) 394–408.

Reggio Children (2001) 'RECHILD – Reggio Children Newsletter.' *RECHILD*, (5) 10. [Online] Accessed on 24.02.19 at: www.reggiochildren.it/wp-content/uploads/2011/08/rechild05_100ling.pdf.

Richards, R. (2007) *Everyday Creativity and New Views of Human Nature: Psychological, Social, and Spiritual Perspectives*. Washington, DC: American Psychological Association.

Rinaldi, C. (2001) 'The relationship between documentation and assessment.' *Innovations in Early Education: The International Reggio Exchange*. [Online] Accessed on 15.11.18 at: www.reggioalliance.org/downloads/relationship:rinaldi.pdf.

Rinaldi, C., Giudici, C. and Krechevsky, M.E. *et al.* (2001) *Making Learning Visible: Children as Individual and Group Learners*. Reggio Emilia, Italy: Reggio Children and Project Zero.

Robinson, K. (2001) 'Mind the gap: The creative conundrum.' *Critical Quarterly*, 43, 41.

Robinson, K. (2006) 'Ted Talks.' *Do Schools Kill Creativity?* www.ted.com/talks/ken_robinson_says_schools_kill_creativity.

Robinson, K. (2010) *The Element*. London: Penguin.

Robinson, K. (2012) 'Nurturing compassion in people who make a difference.' Earlyarts UnConference 2012. [Online] Accessed on 05.06.2019 at: https://vimeo.com/53456183.

Rogers, C.R. (1954) 'Toward a theory of creativity.' *ETC: A Review of General Semantics*, 11(4) 249–260.

Rogoff, B. (2003) *The Cultural Nature of Human Development*. New York, NY: Oxford University Press.

Royal Conservatory (2014) 'An overview of current neuroscience research: The benefits of music education.' [Online] Accessed on 02.12.18 at: http://files.rc.mu/Examinations/2018/Files/Mar21/Benefits-Music-Education/Benefits-of-Music-Education.html.

Runco, M.A. (2003) 'Education for creative potential.' *Scandinavian Journal of Educational Research*, 47(3) 317–324.

Runco, M.A. (2016) 'Commentary: Overview of developmental perspectives on creativity and the realization of potential.' *New Directions for Child and Adolescent Development*, 2016(151) 97–109.

Runco, M.A. (2014) *Creativity: Theories and Themes: Research, Development, and Practice,* second edition. San Diego, CA: Academic Press.

Russ, S.W. (2016) 'Pretend play: Antecedent of adult creativity.' *New Directions for Child and Adolescent Development*, 2016(151) 21–32.

Sand, G. and Ledos de Beaufort, R. (1886) *Letters of George Sand.* Vol. 3. London: Ward and Downey.

Schore, A. (2000) 'Attachment and the regulation of the right brain.' *Attachment & Human Development*, 2(1) 23–47.

Schore, A. (2017) 'Playing on the right side of the brain: An interview with Allan N. Schore.' *American Journal of Play*, 9(2) 105.

Schore, A. and Marks-Tarlow, T. (2018) 'How love opens creativity, play and the arts through early right-brain development.' In T. Marks-Tarlow, D.J. Siegel and M. Solomon (eds) *Play and Creativity in Psychotherapy.* New York, NY: W.W. Norton & Company.

Siegel, H. (2006) 'Epistemological diversity and education research: Much ado about nothing much?' *Educational Researcher*, 35(2) 3–12.

Sousa, D.A. (2006) 'How the arts develop the young brain.' [Online] Accessed on 17.12.18 at: www.aasa.org/SchoolAdministratorArticle.aspx?id=7378.

Sternberg, R.J. (1999) *Handbook of Creativity.* New York, NY: Cambridge University Press.

Thomas, M. (2015) 'Children have different learning styles.' [Online] Accessed on 27.12.18 at: www.educationalneuroscience.org.uk/resources/neuromyth-or-neurofact/children-have-different-learning-styles.

Torrance, E.P. (1963) *Education and the Creative Potential.* London; Minneapolis, MN: University of Minnesota Press.

Torrance, E.P. (2004) 'Preschool Creativity.' In B.A. Bracken (ed.) *The Psychoeducational Assessment of Preschool Children,* third edition. Mahwah, NJ: Taylor and Francis.

Treffinger, D.J., Young, G.C., Selby, E.C. and Shepardson, C. (2002) *Assessing Creativity: A Guide for Educators. Research Monograph Series.* Storrs, CT: National Research Center on the Gifted and Talented, University of Connecticut.

Trevarthen, C. (2002) 'Origins of Musical Identity: Evidence from Infancy for Musical Social Awareness.' In R.A.R. MacDonald, D.J. Hargreaves and D. Miell (eds) *Musical Identities*, pp.21–38. New York, NY: Oxford University Press.

Van der Kolk, B.A. (2015) *The Body Keeps the Score: Mind, Brain and Body in the Transformation of Trauma.* London: Penguin.

Vecchi, V. (2010) *Art and Creativity in Reggio Emilia: Exploring the Role and Potential of Ateliers in Early Childhood Education.* Abingdon, Oxfordshire: Routledge.

Viereck, G. S. (1929) 'What life means to Einstein: An interview.' *Saturday Evening Post.* 1929 October 26 edition.

Vygotsky, L.S. and Cole, M. (1978) *Mind in Society: The Development of Higher Psychological Processes*. London; Cambridge, MA: Harvard University Press.

Vygotsky, L.S. (2004) 'Imagination and creativity in childhood.' *Journal of Russian and East European Psychology*, 42(1) 7–97.

Vygotsky, L.S., Veresov, N. and Barrs, M. (1933) 'Play and its role in the mental development of the child.' *International Research in Early Childhood Education*, 7(2) 3–25.

Wetherell, M. (2012) *Affect and Emotion: A New Social Science Understanding*. Los Angeles, CA: SAGE Publications.

White, R., Lord, P. and Sharp, C. (2015) *Headteachers' Perspectives on the In Harmony Programme*. [Online] Accessed on 08.07.19 at: www.nfer.ac.uk/headteachers-perspectives-on-the-in-harmony-programme.

Williams, M. (2016) *Key Concepts in the Philosophy of Social Research*. Los Angeles, CA: SAGE Publications.

Winkler, I., Háden, G.P., Ladinig, O., Sziller, I., Honing, H. and Purves, D. (2009) 'Newborn infants detect the beat in music.' *Proceedings of the National Academy of Sciences of the United States of America*, 106(7) 2468–2471.

Witkin, R.W. (1974) *The Intelligence of Feeling*. Portsmouth, NH: Heinemann Educational Publishers.

World Economic Forum (2017) *Global Human Capital Report 2017*. World Economic Forum.

Wright, S. (2010) *Understanding Creativity in Early Childhood: Meaning-Making and Children's Drawings*. London; Los Angeles, CA: SAGE Publications.

Young, S. (2003) *Music with the Under-Fours*. London: Routledge Falmer.

Subject Index

genetic heritage 13, 16, 24, 47, 53, 91,
133–4, 237, 242
grandparents 78
grant aid 72–4
Guardian, The 170
Guattari, Félix 244
Guilford, J. P. 95

Habermas, Jürgen 244
Harvard University 155, 198, 214
hormones 33, 120, 123
human rights 68
right to arts and culture? 70–1
Hythe Community School 86

Idrees, Naveed 170
imagination 33–4, 115–16
links between imagination, play and
emotion 42–9
impact of creativity 50
challenge of valuing creativity 62–3
demonstrating cause and effect 50–2
ethical assessment methods for children's
creativity 59–62
methodological challenges for creativity
research 56–9
reflective questions 64
validating creativity research 52–6
In Harmony 167
inkblot tests 93, 97
innovation 33, 65, 103
intelligence 26, 91
interactive resources 187
International School of Amsterdam 215
interpretivism 54–5, 59
ethical interpretivism 242–3
Ireson, Nancy 179

Johns Hopkins University, Maryland 126
Jones, Gill 84–5

Kant, Immanuel 36–7, 54
kinaesthetics 97, 105, 115, 138, 143, 167,
185, 186
Kirkpatrick, Edwin A. 93

Kodály music method 167, 170
Koestler, Arthur 224

Labour Government 67, 77–8, 88, 89
language development 9, 30, 37, 40, 41, 46
music 166–7
LEGO Foundation 66
Lévi-Strauss, Claude 246
Levitin, Daniel 47
libraries 41, 72–3
listening 51, 99, 104, 162, 198
active and intentional listening 210–12
digital listening 176
listening to stories 136
reciprocity of listening 146–7
literacy 40, 66
London Early Years Foundation (LEYF) 72
Lowenfeld, Viktor 152

Malaguzzi, Loris 146, 148, 214
mark-making 41, 149–57
Martin, Stephanie 215
Marxism 68, 239
Maslow, Abraham 207
materials 94, 140
malleable and modelling materials 143–9
mathematics 40
McKee, David 139
memory 40, 41, 46
mental health 42
modelling 15
malleable and modelling materials 143–9
Modigliani, Amedeo 178–9
Montessori settings 75
Montessori, Maria 119
Moriyama, Kaiji 179
motivation 224–5
motor skills 41, 93, 142, 133, 146, 153, 156,
161
movement 160–1
movement and dance 158–64
movement companies 74
Moving Smart 158
Moyles, Janet 89
Mr Benn 138–9
Murray, Tim 218, 222–3

Author Index